Analytical Techniques in
Occupational Health Chemistry

Analytical Techniques in Occupational Health Chemistry

Donald D. Dollberg, EDITOR

National Institute for Occupational Safety and Health

Allen W. Verstuyft, EDITOR

Chevron Research Company

Based on a symposium

sponsored by the Division of

Chemical Health and Safety

at the 176th Meeting of the

American Chemical Society,

Miami Beach, Florida,

September 13–14, 1978.

ACS SYMPOSIUM SERIES **120**

AMERICAN CHEMICAL SOCIETY
WASHINGTON, D. C.   1980

Library of Congress CIP Data

Analytical techniques in occupational health chemistry.
  (ACS symposium series; 120 ISSN 0097–6156)

  Includes bibliographies and index.

  1. Industrial toxicology—Technique—Congresses. 2.
Instrumental analysis—Congresses. 3. Air—Pollution
Measurement—Congresses. 4. Work environment—
Congresses.
  I. Dollberg, Donald D., 1944–   . II. Verstuyft,
Allen W., 1948–   . III. American Chemical Society.
Division of Chemical Health and Safety. IV. Series:
American Chemical Society. ACS symposium series;
120. [DNLM: 1. Chemistry, Analytical—Instrumenta-
tion—Congresses. 2. Air pollution—Analysis—Con-
gresses. 3. Occupational medicine—Congresses. WA-
450 A532 1978]

RA1229.A5   615.9′02   79–28460
ISBN 0–8412–0539–6   ACSMC8 120 1-318 1980

SD
7/28/80
JW

ACS Symposium Series

M. Joan Comstock, *Series Editor*

FOREWORD

The ACS SYMPOSIUM SERIES was founded in 1974 to provide a medium for publishing symposia quickly in book form. The format of the Series parallels that of the continuing ADVANCES IN CHEMISTRY SERIES except that in order to save time the papers are not typeset but are reproduced as they are submitted by the authors in camera-ready form. Papers are reviewed under the supervision of the Editors with the assistance of the Series Advisory Board and are selected to maintain the integrity of the symposia; however, verbatim reproductions of previously published papers are not accepted. Both reviews and reports of research are acceptable since symposia may embrace both types of presentation.

CONTENTS

PREFACE

Chemists are proud of the contributions that the chemical profession has made to mankind. Knowledge of the structure of matter and the nature of chemical change has contributed goods and services for the public welfare. Unfortunately, the development of these goods and services has produced a number of occupational diseases that have adversely affected the health of the worker.

The chemical profession and the federal government have attempted to minimize worker exposure to compounds or reactions that result in an acute or chronic biological response. The American Chemical Society has sponsored several symposia during the past few years in which chemists have discussed potentially hazardous compounds. However, to assess the extent of hazardous exposure in the workplace, new demands have been made on analytical chemistry. The analytical chemist has responded by producing and developing new methodologies and instrumentation that permit the detection and monitoring of extremely low level concentrations of hazardous substances.

The purpose of this symposium was to bring together chemists actively working in the occupational health/industrial hygiene field to review the state of the art of analytical techniques and discuss research on sampling and identification of potentially toxic compounds in the workplace.

The National Institute for Occupational Safety and Health (NIOSH), the Occupational Safety and Health Administration (OSHA), research institutes, and academic and industrial laboratories have contributed to developing analytical methods, many of which are discussed in this book. We hope that this discussion will provide a helpful review for active practitioners of industrial hygiene chemistry and will be a source book for those entering the field.

We would like to acknowledge the contributions of the authors, the reviewers who have generously contributed their time, and our colleagues who have made suggestions on the content of this symposium.

National Institute for Occupational   D. D. DOLLBERG
Safety and Health
Cincinnati, Ohio

Chevron Research Company   A. W. VERSTUYFT
Richmond, California

October 5, 1979

Generation of Test Atmospheres of Toxic Substances for Evaluation of Air Sampling Methods

C. CLARINE ANDERSON, ELLEN C. GUNDERSON, and DALE M. COULSON
SRI International, Menlo Park, CA 94025

BRUCE GOODWIN and KENNETH T. MENZIES
Arthur D. Little, Inc., Cambridge, MA 02140

The need for measuring worker exposure to various toxic materials in the workplace atmosphere demands that appropriate tested methods be available for determining the exposure levels. A critical part of the protocol for testing methods is the preparation of test atmospheres of these toxic materials. For many types of samples, it is frequently sufficient to test analytical procedures on spiked samples, but this is strictly not true for measurements of industrial hygiene samples. For instance, adsorption of compounds onto a sorbent such as charcoal or silica gel may be weaker when the material is deposited from solution than when it is adsorbed as a vapor from a moving air stream. Storage stability is also frequently affected by the method of deposition onto the collecting medium. Material may adhere to the sampling tube or filter cassette during sampling. High humidity effects cannot be adequately tested on spiked samples. Another important area of interest is the collection of materials that may be present in both particulate and vapor phases at the concentration levels of interest. Frequently, vapor pressure data are not available, and a determination of whether vapor/particulate mixtures must be measured can be made only by preparing and sampling test atmospheres.

The preparation of synthetic atmospheres for nonreactive gases and vapors is relatively straightforward, but the preparation of fumes, aerosols, and particulates is considerably more difficult. For purposes of industrial hygiene sampling, a polydisperse aerosol containing respirable-size particles is required.

This paper describes some of the techniques used to generate synthetic atmospheres of toxic materials. The work was part of a study supported by the National Institute for Occupational Safety and Health to develop and validate methods for sampling and analysis of various materials found in the workplace atmosphere and was a joint effort of SRI International and Arthur D. Little, Inc. Emphasis was placed on reproducible and reliable generation techniques that could be used for a wide variety of compounds. Unique methods were devised for certain difficult materials. Over 230 compounds were studied, including gases, vapors, fumes, and

aerosols. The air concentrations ranged from 0.05 to 15 mg/m^3 for
particulates and from 0.05 to 2000 ppm for gases and vapors. We
describe below a special dilution system, which has been used to
produce several concentration levels simultaneously, and a number
of source generators, which supply a high concentration level for
dilution.

Dilution System

Figure 1 diagrams a serial dilution system designed by C. E.
Lapple of SRI International. It produces dynamically generated
test concentrations at three levels, each at a predetermined ratio
to the adjacent one. The important components of the system are
the primary chamber, which supplies a high concentration of test
air, a mixing and dilution channel, and three sampling chambers,
from which samples are drawn. All dilution and exhaust streams are
metered through critical flow orifices. A filtered compressed air
supply provides the dilution air. A vacuum pump is used for the
exhaust streams.

To start generation, the output from a source generator is
introduced into the primary chamber. Sufficient dilution air,
which may be humidified, is added to this output to reduce the concentration to the highest desired level, shown in Figure 1 as C_1.
A portion of this purposely contaminated air is drawn into the mixing channel. Excess contaminated air passes out of the primary
chamber into a disposal system. As the air moves down the mixing
channel, a fraction is drawn through the first chamber at specified
volumetric flow rate, Q_1. The concentration in this first chamber
is unchanged.

Clean filtered air is next metered into the channel at a rate
Q_a, causing the first dilution to a concentration C_2. A portion of
this air is then pulled through the second chamber. The next stage
of dilution is achieved by adding a second amount of air at a rate
Q_b to the channel. Part of this air, now at the lowest concentration, is used to supply the third chamber. The remaining air from
the channel is removed by the last meter at a rate Q_E.

The general relationship for the dilution ratio from chamber
to chamber is

$$\frac{C_2}{C_1} = 1 - \frac{Q_a}{Q_2 + Q_E}$$

where C_1 and C_2 refer to the concentrations in adjacent chambers;
Q_a, Q_2, and Q_E represent volumetric flow rates. The flow patterns
are shown in Figure 2.

In practice, the ratios and flow rates through the chambers
are chosen according to sampling needs, and the exhaust rate is
determined by solving the equation for Q_E. This expression is
somewhat more complicated for more than a two-stage dilution, but
can easily be set up and worked out. The system in use for the

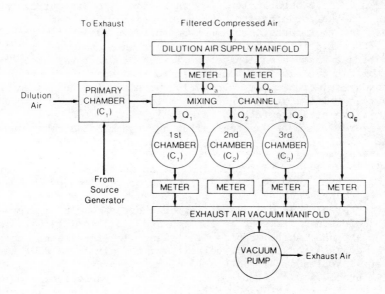

Figure 1. Schematic of three-stage dilution system; Q = volumetric flow rate and C = concentration.

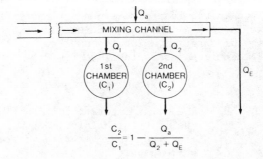

$$\frac{C_2}{C_1} = 1 - \frac{Q_a}{Q_2 + Q_E}$$

Figure 2. Calculation of dilution ratios; C_1 = concentration in first chamber, C_2 = concentration in second chamber, and Q = volumetric flow rate.

methods validation study operates with all flow rates equal to each other, so the dilution ratio is one-half.

Figure 3 shows the exhaust air disposal system. Several safety features have been built into its design. To prevent contamination of the surrounding atmosphere, excess air from the primary chamber and the exhaust streams from the dilution system are filtered, then fed into a combustion chamber where they are burned. The entire system is maintained at 1 inch of water vacuum to prevent toxic materials from escaping into the laboratory. A compressed air ejector causes a negative pressure in the system. A pressure-sensitive alarm connected to the primary chamber sounds an alert if the pressure returns to normal.

Figure 4 shows the actual dilution system. The tower at left is the primary chamber. Its large volume is important for use with aerosols because even at high air flow rates the velocity is low, which allows time for solvent evaporation when wet aerosol droplets are introduced. Low velocity also helps prevent impaction of particles with the chamber walls.

The three cone-shaped sampling chambers shown in Figure 4 have a 1-inch internal diameter at the top and a 6-inch internal diameter at the base where samples are taken. The increasing area creates gradual reduction of velocity as the air flows down the chamber. Samples are withdrawn from the cylindrical section. Its base is provided with fittings for use with a variety of samplers. All three of the test chambers may be monitored with either a total hydrocarbon analyzer or a gas chromatograph fitted with a gas sampling loop.

Source Generators

Source generators are used to supply the initial high concentration of analyte in the test air. In addition to using some commercially available generators, we developed several generators specifically for this program. The types of materials generated and the general techniques used are listed below.

Gases	Dilution of compressed gas
Vapors	Dewpoint saturation, then dilution Delivery with infusion pump In situ production from a precursor compound
Aerosols and aerosol/vapor mixtures	Atomization/spray drying Condensation of heated vapor
Metal oxide fumes	Thermal degradation of organic precursor compound after atomization

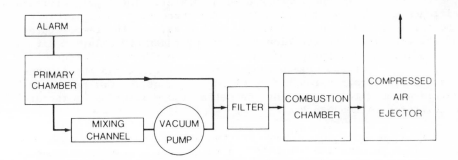

Figure 3.   Exhaust air disposal system

Figure 4.   Three-stage dilution system

Vapor Generator. Figure 5 shows a simple vapor generator used
for materials with accurately known vapor pressures. The three-
necked flask containing the chemical is placed in a controlled temperature bath. Nitrogen is bubbled through the heated liquid and
passes out through the thermostated condenser. The vapor-saturated
nitrogen is then diluted with air. The concentration of vapor in
the air is calculated using the vapor pressure at the temperature
of the condenser and the flow rates of nitrogen and dilution air.

A special adaptation was used for mercury vapor. Mercury-
coated Monel screens were placed in both the flask and the condenser; a concentration range of 0.05 to 0.2 mg of mercury per cubic
meter was used for evaluating the method for collection of mercury
on silvered Chromosorb P.

In Situ Generator. Very reactive substances such as stibine
must often be generated in situ. A method for preparing stibine,
reported by Gunn et al. [J. Phys. Chem., 64, 1334 (1960)], was
modified to permit continuous generation at a controlled rate.
The experimental apparatus is shown in Figure 6. A concentrated basic solution of potassium antimony tartrate containing
sodium borohydride is used. A sufficient amount of tartaric acid
is added to prevent hydrolysis and precipitation of the resulting
antimony compound. The solution is delivered with a syringe drive
under the surface of a solution of 4 N sulfuric acid, and stibine
is produced in the acidic medium. The net reation in the flask is

$$3BH_4^- + 4H_3SbO_3 + 3H^+ \rightarrow 3H_3BO_3 + 3H_2O + 4SbH_3 \uparrow$$

Nitrogen sweeps the gaseous reaction products out of the flask into
the dilution/sampling system.

Although the reaction is not quantitative, it was found that
reproducible concentrations of stibine could be generated, even at
different syringe drive delivery rates.

Aerosol Generator. The atomizer shown in Figure 7 was designed to produce aerosols of certain organic materials that are
soluble only in easily vaporized solvents such as isopropanol or
toluene. Difficulties were encountered when using other nebulizers
because of continual concentration of the solution resulting from
evaporation of the solvent, making it impossible to predict or control the test air concentration and the particle size.

In Figure 7, the base section has been enlarged for clarity.
A solution of the analyte is gravity fed at a controlled rate into
a small chamber at the base. Four small orifices connect the chamber to an annular opening surrounding a small nozzle. Compressed
air forced through the nozzle atomizes the solution. Large droplets impacting on the top and sides of the cylinder are collected
in a trough at the cylinder base and drain out into a collection
reservoir. Remaining aerosol droplets pass through a cyclone;
those less than 3 μm in diameter emerge from the cyclone into the

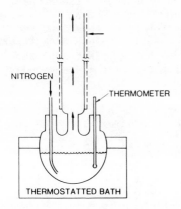

NITROGEN

THERMOMETER

THERMOSTATTED BATH

Figure 5. Vapor saturator

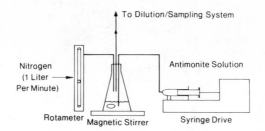

To Dilution/Sampling System

Nitrogen
(1 Liter
Per Minute)

Antimonite Solution

Rotameter   Magnetic Stirrer

Syringe Drive

Figure 6. Stibine generator

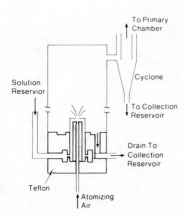

To Primary
Chamber

Cyclone

Solution
Reservior

To Collection
Reservoir

Drain To
Collection
Reservoir

Teflon

Atomizing
Air

Figure 7. Atomizer for aerosol generation

primary chamber of the dilution system. Larger particles are
separated out by the cyclone and drain to the collection flask.

With this gravity-flow system, the concentration of atomizing
solution is unchanged during the course of the generation, and
reproducible results are obtained. A solution volume of 3 liters
allows continuous generation for up to 4 hours. This aspirator has
been used with many compounds, including the pesticides methoxy-
chlor and 2,4-D.

Generator for Aerosol-Vapor Mixtures. Although aspiration and
spray drying is a convenient method for producing aerosols, it introduces a large volume of solvent into the test air and is not
appropriate for evaluating solid sorbents. The device shown in
Figure 8 was developed for preparing mixtures of aerosol and vapor.

The glass cylinder is enclosed in an aluminum block. The compound is placed on the lower glass frit, and the total block is
heated. Nitrogen gas is bubbled through the material to carry vapor out of the first section, where it is diluted with heated nitrogen. The mixture continues out of the second section and is
mixed with air. If the vapor pressure of the material is exceeded,
particle formation takes place upon dilution. Vapor may also be
present in the final mixture, depending on the air concentration.
This two-stage dilution is used because it was found that material
condensed on the glass when cool air was added directly to the vapor-saturated nitrogen, and reproducible results could not be
obtained.

The diameters of particles are expected to be less than 2 μm,
since a rapid quenching takes place.

Laskin-Type Nozzle Generator. A third type of atomizer, the
Laskin-type nozzle generator, is used to create test atmospheres of
particulate or aerosol and vapor mixtures. A pure liquid or melt
is used, and no solvent is necessary. Again, this is important for
evaluating filter and solid sorbent combination sampling trains.

With the Laskin-type nozzle shown in Figure 9, a high velocity
air jet issues directly into a liquid and entrains a filament of
the liquid into droplets, which are carried to the surface and out.
The nozzle is constructed of Teflon. A small orifice is drilled at
right angles to the axis of the air feed line. A liquid feed hole
is centered above the air orifice and longitudinal to the nozzle.

Figure 10 shows the nozzle in place in the liquid. As air
under pressure is applied to the atomizer nozzle, a high velocity
air stream emerges from the orifice. The bulk liquid is aspirated
through the liquid feed line hole, and the liquid column near the
region of the jet is atomized.

This nozzle has been used to generate polydispersed aerosols
of various organic liquids as the bulk phase. Particles in the
size range of submicrometers to 20 μm were obtained. The concentration varied by less than 10% over several hours as long as the
air pressure was well regulated.

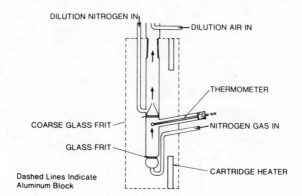

Figure 8. Glass generator for particulate/vapor test atmospheres

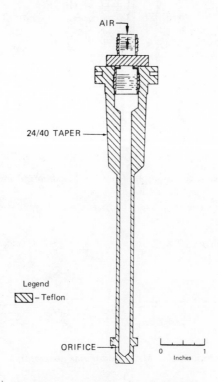

Figure 9. Laskin-type nozzle generator

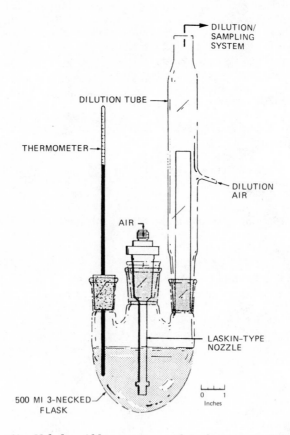

Figure 10. Nebulizer/dilution system with Laskin-type nozzle in place

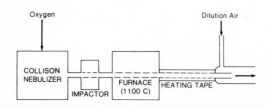

Figure 11. Metal oxide fume generator

Metal Oxide Fume Generator. Figure 11 shows a metal oxide
fume generator that has been used for such materials as magnesium
and copper oxides.

A Collison nebulizer is used to atomize an aqueous solution of
an organic salt of the metal, such as the oxalate or acetate. Oxygen is used as the atomizing gas. After passing through an impac-
tor, where large particles are removed, the oxygen stream is fed
into a 1-inch i.d. quartz tube heated to 1100°C, where the compound
is thermally decomposed. The residence time of aerosol particles
in the heated tube is sufficient to allow decomposition and oxidation of the organic material. The metal oxide is then mixed with
an appropriate amount of dry air to provide the final concentration.

Particles obtained by this method may have diameters less than
1 μm.

Summary

We have developed and used a number of generation techniques
for producing test atmospheres for the evaluation of methods of
collection of ambient air samples. These methods are applicable to
many compounds and, with modification, can be extended to cover
most materials. In principle, several compounds may be generated
simultaneously with these techniques. Testing over an appropriate
concentration range is easily accomplished using the dilution system we have designed.

This work was supported by the Measurements Research Branch of
the National Institute for Occupational Safety and Health.

RECEIVED October 17, 1979.

Applications of Optical Microscopy in Analysis of Asbestos and Quartz

WILLARD C. DIXON

U.S. Department of Labor, Occupational Safety and Health Administration,
390 Wakara Way, Salt Lake City, UT 84108

Optical Microscopy is a powerful tool in industrial hygiene for the analysis of asbestos, quartz or other substances. Electron microscopy and specialized techniques in optical microscopy such as ultraviolet, infrared, and fluorescence, although important, will not be considered in this paper.

Applications of visible light such as the use of polarized light, birefringence, retardation, angles of extinction, dispersion staining, and phase contrast will be explained, discussed and related primarily to asbestos with some discussion of quartz.

It will be assumed that the reader is familiar with the phase contrast method for the analysis of asbestos. If not, the equipment and procedures for the phase contrast analysis of asbestos have been described by the United States Public Health Service (1), National Institute for Occupational Safety and Health (2), (3), and by professional societies (4).

Index of refraction (n) is the ratio between the velocity of light in a vacuum and the velocity of light in a mineral or other substance.

The Asbestos Standard

Guidance on the minerals and fibers to be counted under the OSHA Asbestos Standard may be obtained by reference to the Federal Register.

The Federal Register (5) specifies that:
(a) 1. Asbestos includes chrysotile, amosite, crocidolite, tremolite, anthophyllite and actinolite.
2. "Asbestos fibers" means asbestos fibers longer than 5 micrometers.
(b) 1. Effective July 1, 1976, the eight hour time weighted average air borne concentration of asbestos fibers to which any employee may be exposed shall not exceed two fibers longer than 5 micrometers per cubic centimeter of air.

Phase Contrast Analysis

An employee's exposure to asbestos is evaluated by collection of asbestos fibers on a cellulose ester membrane filter. A Gellman G N-4 (6), millipore AA (7) or other cellulose ester membrane which clarifies well in the mounting medium is commonly used.

Samples are counted by phase contrast microscopy at 400-450X magnification using a 4 mm objective (8).

Phase contrast is a type of interference contrast, and is a useful technique for enhancing contrast. This enables the microscopist to see fine fibers that might not be seen otherwise. Phase contrast permits analysis of asbestos by morphology and by increased visibility of internal structure. Vegetable fiber, for example, will be more readily recognised since small differences in n is made more apparent.

Phase contrast is often adequate for an accurate analysis of asbestos, especially if it is not necessary to determine the variety of asbestos present, or if interference from other fibers is not a problem. An experienced analyst is not likely to confuse chrysotile with other fibers 'ii most cases.

An identification based solely on morphology in situations where the analyst is inexperienced or interference is severe may have positive errors if fiberglass, plant fibers or other fibers are counted as asbestos or negative error if an attempt is made to exclude such fibers without other optical tests.

Other Information

The NIOSH method for the analysis of asbestos (9) states that "The method is intended to give an index of employee exposure to airborne asbestos fibers of specified dimensional characteristics. It is not meant to count all asbestos fibers in all size ranges or to differentiate asbestos from other fibrous particulates".

The NIOSH method (10) also states, however, "In an atmosphere known to contain asbestos, all particulates with a length to diameter ratio of 3 to 1 or greater, and a length greater than 5 micrometers should in the absence of other information, be considered to be asbestos fibers and counted as such" (emphasis added).

Counting all fibers is an approach that gives greater protection to employees. However, economic and enforcement considerations may require that proof of the kind of fibers counted be made. In those circumstances where there is reasonable cause to believe other fibers are present as an interference, it is desirable to know how "other information" can be obtained.

This implies first of all a partnership between the industrial hygienist and the microscopist. The industrial higienist, when possible, should ascertain whether asbestos is being used or a source exists by taking bulk samples to be analyzed at the laboratory. Sometimes this information can be obtained from product labels or careful inquiry.

By carefully sharpening his sense of observation, the industrial hygienist can learn to recognize fibrous asbestos and non asbestos materials. For example, fiberglass held close to the ear in an envelope and pressed will give audible crinkling sounds. Caution, some old fiberglass insulation samples will contain two or three percent asbestos which will be detected only by microscopic examination.

Fiberglass placed in a mortar and ground with a pestle grinds rapidly and easily. Asbestos resists grinding in most cases, requiring cooling to liquid nitrogen temperatures for easy grinding.

Plant fibers burn easily if they haven't been chemically fireproofed. Note, however, that mineral fibers will glow when heated in the flame of a match. Do not confuse the red incandescence with combustion. Watch to see if the fibrous mass burns when the match is removed.

Fiberglass will often melt in the flame of an alcohol lamp and form round globules. Tweezers are useful for this test. If a combustion test is to be carried out, make sure that it is conducted in a safe area.

The industrial hygienist should have a stock of accurately labelled bulk materials for reference in order to know which kinds contain asbestos and which contain fiberglass, plastic, or other nonasbestos fibers. With commercial laboratories charging between $25.00 and $75.00 for a bulk analysis for asbestos, it can be wasteful to request an analysis of a material that should have been recognized as definitely asbestos free or asbestos containing. Of course, if there is any doubt whatever, an analysis should be performed since the consequences of failure to recognize asbestos can be serious to the safety and health of exposed employees.

When an air sample is taken, the industrial hygienist can aid the microscopist by referencing the sample number of the bulk samples to corresponding air samples. If the industrial hygienist has reason to believe asbestos is not present, he may request analysis of the bulk samples first. If asbestos is not found, the air samples may not need analysis, or possibly the analysis could be carried out on a statistical sampling basis with results on the first samples analyzed to be taken as a guide to whether further sampling is needed.

In many cases the microscopist will be able to conduct an analysis without a bulk sample for reference by removing fibers from the membrane for further testing. If the membrane has insufficient fibers for other tests, the microscopist should have the option of discontinuing an analysis until a bulk sample of suspect fibers or fiber containing material has been supplied for X-ray diffraction, or supplemental microscopic tests.

Polarized Light

Light vibrates in all directions perpendicular to its direction of propagation. If light is polarized by a prism, polarizing filter or in some other manner, the vibration is restricted to one plane. If a second polarizer is placed in such a position that only light vibrating at right angles to the first polarizer can be transmitted, the polars are said to be crossed. The use of single polars and crossed polars gives significant information about the mineral or crystal being studied.

It is desirable to be able to view fibers in various orientations in order to determine their reaction with polarized light. This test can be performed by rotating the polarizer and the ana lyzer simultaneously. It is much more convenient to have a rotating mechanical stage, however. Such a stage can freely move the particle through complete horizontal revolutions (360°). The stage must be centerable in order that the particle can maintain a uniform distance from the center and not swing out of view upon rotation of the stage. Stage controls are also required for left right or front back slide manipulation. If angles of extinction are to be measured, the stage must have degree markings at the edge. With some microscope makes this will add about $500.00 to the cost since the stage with degree markings must have a different microscope stand for mounting as well. If the stage doesn't have markings at the edge for precise measurement of angles of extinction, the fact that there is an angle of extinction can still be noted.

Phase contrast microscopy is compatible with the use of polarized light. If the initial microscope is a stripped down model to reduce expense, investigate whether it can be upgraded as needed. Make sure that polarized light can be added later, that a standard stage can be replaced with a rotating stage, that retardation plates can be used later, and if photography will ever be done, consider purchase of a trinocular head while deferring purchase of the camera and focusing accessories until the need arises at a later date.

If extensive work will be done with polarized light and retardataion plates, it is a time saver to be able to add and remove polars or plates rapidly.

The objectives must be designed for phase contrast and contain a phase ring. Common objective sizes are 40X, 43X and 45X. The objective must be 40 to 45X and have a numerical aperture between 0.65 and 0.75. The higher the numerical aperture, the better the resolution. Some objectives will have the numerical aperture marked on the side of the objective.

The condenser must be designed for phase contrast. A different objective magnification often requires a different condenser setting. Condenser turrets are often used for this purpose. If work will be performed at various magnifications, be sure that rotating the turret doesn't require the condenser to be recentered. The loss of time in this situation can be serious when it is desirable to work at various magnifications. The numerical aperture of the condenser must equal or exceed the numerical aperture of the objective.

Phase contrast requires Koehler illumination. Early publi-

cations of USPHS (11) describe a method of obtaining Koehler illumination with an external light source. The method of establishing Koehler illumination is also described in Appendix 1 of the
Joint AIHA-ACGIH Asbestos Procedure (12). It is more convenient
to purchase a microscope with built in Koehler illumination. The
use of crossed polars and retardation plates reduces the intensity
of light greatly. If this type of work is done, a high intensity
light source should be used to compensate for the light loss. A
12V 100W halogen source (13) produces a very intense white light.

10X widefield or Huygenian eyepieces are used, one of which
must be a focusing eye piece to hold the reticle. High eyepoint
widefield eyepieces are more comfortable, especially if glasses
are worn. The reticle defines the field to be counted. A Patterson Globe and Circle reticle defines a field which is twice the
area defined by a Porton reticle. The larger field accumulates
counts faster and is sometimes preferred for this reason since
this may save time or improve statistics when the fiber concentration is low.

Mineral Standards

The mention of commercial materials, equipment or processes
does not constitute an endorsement by the U.S. Government or any
of its agencies or employees.

Information about commercial sources of asbestos can be obtained from the Asbestos Information Association (AIA) (14), or
"Asbestos" (15), a magazine devoted to the asbestos industry.
Ward Scientific Company (16) sells mineral specimens including asbestos. The National Institute of Environmental Health Sciences,
(NIEHS) (17) supplies asbestos materials that have been characterized. Union Internationale Contre Cancer (UICC) asbestos materials, often used in cancer research, are obtainable in laboratory
quantity from Walter C. McCrone Associates, Inc. (18).

Deer, Howie and Zussman (19) give physical and optical constants for amphibole minerals in Vol. two, Rock Forming Minerals,
(chain silicates), and for Serpentine minerals (chrysotile) in volume three (sheet silicates). X-ray diffraction data is obtainable
from the Powder Diffraction file, Inorganic (20). This data can
be used for a double check of asbestos standards.

A pure quartz standard is best obtained by grinding a clear
quartz crystal. The quartz crystal can be identified by its characteristic form and interfacial angles according to Stenos law
(21). Quartz crystals can be obtained from Ward Scientific (22),
or other reputable supplier of mineral specimens. Data on silica
minerals is given by Frondell (23).

Mineral Systems

There are six mineral systems: Isometric, Hexagonal, Tetragonal, Orthorhombic, Monoclinic, and Triclinic. The Trigonal

system can be considered as a seventh system or a subsystem of the
Hexagonal system. The six mineral systems can be grouped into two
categories for convenience. One category includes all isometric
minerals. In this group of minerals, light will travel with the
same velocity in any direction. Substances which have a single n
are spoken of as being isotropic. Cubes are sometimes seen in
this group of minerals which includes table salt. Minerals of the
isometric system are referrable to three axes of equal atomic
spacing that make right angles with each other. Amorphous substances such as glass are also isotropic, having a single n, but
are not includable with any crystalline mineral system.

If a mineral or substance has more than one n, it is optically anisotropic. Light travels with a different velocity if vibrating in a different plane. All minerals except those in the isometric system are anisotropic. Anisotropic minerals exhibit
double refraction with polarized light. The light will be split
into two components vibrating at right angles. The rays will
each travel with a different velocity; that is, each component
will have a different n. The component having the high n will be
the slow ray and the component having the low n will be the fast
ray.

Minerals of the tetragonal system are referrable to three
crystallographic axes that make right angles with each other. The
two horizontal axes a_1 and a_2 have equal atomic spacing but the
vertical axis c has an atomic spacing that is not equal to a_1 or
a_2.

Minerals of the hexagonal system, such as quartz, are referrable to four crystallographic axes. Three axes, a_1, a_2 and a_3
lie in a horizontal plane and have equal atomic spacing with angles of $120°$ between the positive ends. The fourth axis, c, is
vertical and at right angles to the plane of a_1, a_2, and a_3 with
a different atomic spacing.

Polarized light having a vibration direction parallel to the
plane of a_1 and a_2 in minerals of the tetragonal system or parallel to the plane of a_1, a_2 and a_3 in minerals of the hexagonal system will be spoken of as the ordinary ray. This n is omega.

Polarized light having a vibration direction parallel to the
direction of the c axis of tetragonal or hexagonal minerals is spoken of as the extraordinary ray. This n is epsilon.

If optical examination shows two n's, the two indices will be
omega and epsilon or e', and the mineral belongs to either the
hexagonal or the tetragonal system. Caution: In some minerals,
one n may be so close to another n that it may be falsely assumed
that there are only two n's. Minerals of the tetragonal or hexagonal systems are uniaxial.

The method of determining n will be described later. If a
uniaxial mineral, i.e., a mineral having a unique c axis and omega
or epsilon as n is examined, the crystal can have one of three
orientations.

1. It may show omega in all directions. In order for this

to happen, the optical axis of the microscope must be
parallel to the c axis of the tetragonal or hexagonal
mineral.
2. It may show omega in one direction and epsilon at right
angles to omega. In order for this to happen, the mineral must be oriented with the c axis in the horizontal
position.
3. It may show omega in one direction and an index intermediate between omega and epsilon called ε' at right
angles to omega. In order for this to happen, the
mineral must be oriented with the c axis between the
horizontal and vertical position.

Examination of possibilities 1 to 3 shows that in every case,
omega will be seen in some orientation. In other orientations,
epsilon may be seen or various indices intermediate between epsilon and omega will be seen. This indicates that omega is the index most often seen in an uniaxial mineral whose particles are in
strictly random orientations. This gives the microscopist a method by which it can be determined which index is omega and which
index is epsilon when examining an unknown mineral. If it is then
determined that epsilon is a higher n than omega, the mineral is
optically positive. If quartz is used for illustration, omega =
1.544, epsilon = 1.553, quartz is therefore optically positive.
If epsilon is less than omega, the mineral is optically negative.
If the index of the mounting medium is selected to match the omega
index of the mineral and the mineral is examined with one polar,
in all positions in which the omega vibration direction of the
mineral matches the vibration direction of the polarizer, the mineral will disappear. If inclusions are present, the inclusions
will be seen but the edges of the particle will not be distinct.
After a 90° rotation, epsilon or some index intermediate between
epsilon and omega will be seen, depending upon the orientation of
the c axis, and the mineral particle will become more visible. If
birefringence, (n_2-n_1) is small, the change on rotation will be
less striking. If birefringence is high, 90° rotation will cause
the contrast to increase dramatically.

Biaxial Minerals

Crystals of the orthorhombic, monoclinic and triclinic systems are biaxial, i.e., possess two optic axis directions, each of
which is similar to the optic axis in uniaxial crystals. Biaxial
minerals have three indices of refraction, alpha being the lowest,
beta intermediate and gamma the highest. Minerals of the orthorhombic system have three crystallographic axes of unequal atomic
spacing that make angles of 90° with each other. Anthophyllite
is an orthorhombic mineral. Minerals of the monoclinic system are
referred to three axes of unequal atomic spacing. When properly
oriented, the (a) axis is inclined downward toward the front, (b)
axis is horizontal left to right and (c) axis is vertical. Asbes-

tos amphibole minerals except anthophyllite belong to the monoclinic system. Minerals of the triclinic system are referred to
three crystallographic axis of unequal atomic spacing that make
oblique angles with each other. Wollastonite, a triclinic mineral, is sometimes confused with asbestos. Hurlbut (24) gives an
introductory description of mineral systems.

Minerals having preferred directions of cleavage will not necessarily randomly lay in all possible orientations. If the orientation is random, the following four orientations may occur with
biaxial crystals:

1. A single index beta will be seen as the stage is
   rotated.
2. Any two of the three principle indexes are seen
   to be at right angles to each other. Rotation of
   the stage 90° brings the second index into view.
3. One principal index is seen and an index intermediate between alpha or gamma is seen in other directions.
4. Intermediate indices are seen in all directions.

Examination of the four possibilities in biaxial minerals indicates that there is no possibility of seeing the same index in
all particles of the mineral in some position of rotation of the
stage. A uniaxial mineral will always show omega in some position
of rotation.

If, however, a large number of biaxial mineral particles are
examined, the lowest and the highest index seen will be recognized
to be alpha and gamma respectively. Because of preferred orientation of fibrous asbestos minerals, alpha and gamma are more readily observed. Even though an inexpensive rotating stage can be
moved only in a horizontal plane, particles can sometimes be
oriented in a better direction for seeing n of the particle
by rolling the particle. (See section on fiber rolling.)

Interference figures are useful in determining the orientation of a mineral particle and whether the mineral is uniaxial or
biaxial, provided the particle is large enough to produce useful
interference figures. A consideration of interference figures and
interaxial angles is beyond the scope of this discussion.

If beta is close to alpha, i.e., (gamma-beta) > (beta-alpha),
the crystal is positive. If beta is close to gamma, i.e. (gamma-
beta) < (beta-alpha), the crystal is negative.

The main point of reference to the mineral systems in this
paper is that the internal symmetry which produces crystal forms
also makes possible optical tests which are useful in mineral i-
dentification. Polarized light is used in making these optical
tests.

Angles of Extinction

If a crystalline material is examined with the polars crossed
on a microscope having a rotating stage, it is noted that the par-

ticle has a position in which it becomes dark or possibly invisi-
ble. In this position, the particle is "at extinction". With rotation, it is noted that there are four such angles of extinction
and that they are 90° apart. It is also noted that there are four
positions of maximum brightness and that a position of maximum
brightness is 45° from a position of extinction. If the alignment
of a fiber which is at extinction is not parallel to the vibration
direction of a polarizer or an analyzer, the fiber will be at an
oblique angle to the polarizer or analyzer and it has inclined
extinction. If the boundaries of a long cleavage fragment edge
lie at an oblique angle to the plane of vibration of crossed
polars, the fragment has inclined extinction. If, as in the case
of a calcite particle, the vibration direction of the polars bi-
sects the angle between two faces, the particle has symmetrical
extinction.

Monoclinic minerals have an inclined angle of extinction.
Orthorhombic minerals have parallel extinction. Chrysotile can be
monoclinic or orthorhombic depending upon whether it is the ortho
or clino variety . The b axis of the clino variety is so close to
90° (93°), (25) that the fibers will appear to have parallel extinction unless this is carefully measured. Anthophyllite, an
orthorhombic mineral, has parallel extinction; that is, the angle
of extinction is zero degrees. All amphibole asbestos minerals
except anthophyllite are monoclinic. Although wollastonite is a
triclinic mineral, its extinction is parallel, or nearly parallel.
The angle of extinction of some asbestos minerals is shown in
table I (26, 27).

Table I

Mineral	Angle of Extinction
Anthophyllite	0°
Tremolite	15 - 20°
Actinolite	10 - 15°
Crocidolite	80 - 90°
Chrysotile	0°

McGraw Hill Book Company

If a mineral is known to be either anthophyllite or tremolite
by dispersion staining tests, the angle of extinction can then be
used to distinguish between the two. Caution: It is possible for
a mineral which usually has inclined extinction to have a few fibers with parallel or close to parallel extinction, depending upon
orientation. These fibers can be rolled into a position of maximum extinction. (See section on rolling fibers.)

Measurement of the angle of extinction can be performed as
follows: Line up the cross hairs (if the eyepiece does not have
a cross hair, it is possible to use the lines of a Patterson Globe
and Circle Reticle or a porton Reticle) with a natrolite particle
or fibers of an anthophyllite asbestos standard which is at extinc-

tion when the polars are crossed. The fiber should be parallel
to the cross hair and displaced slightly to the side so as to be
visible in brightfield. Tape the eyepiece so that it is immobi-
lized in this position. Check the alignment with several other
fibers to be sure that it is exact. Line up an unknown fiber with
the same cross hair line. Take a reading of the position of the
stage. With the polars crossed, move the fiber by rotation to its
position of maximum extinction. Take a reading of the position of
the stage again. Repeat the measurement to be sure that it is accurate. If the difference between the two readings is close to
zero, the fiber has parallel or nearly parallel extinction.

In making measurement of angles of extinction, measure the
highest angle of extinction obtainable by rotating the fiber a-
round its long axis, or look for those fibers in a randomly oriented group that show maximum extinction angles.

A binocular microscope which is adjustable for various interpupillary distances should always be used on the same interpupillary setting as was used for alignment of the cross hairs for zero
extinction, if the field rotates as interpupillary distance is adjusted.

Determination of the position of maximum extinction of some
dark fibers may be difficult. The fibers may appear to be dark
over a wide range of rotation of the stage. In such cases, it may
be possible to locate the position of maximum brightness. If the
position of maximum brightness is 45^0 from the cross hair, the
angle of extinction is zero.

Birefringence

If a mineral or crystal has more than one index of refraction,
interference colors can be produced between crossed polars. The
interference color seen will be a function of the difference between the two indexes of refraction and the thickness of the particle. This is expressed as:

$$\text{birefringence} = n_2-n_1 = \frac{\text{retardation}}{1000 \times \text{thickness}},$$

in which n_2 is the high index of refraction, n_1 is the low index
of refraction and in which retardation is the path difference between the fast and slow components as a result of the thickness of
the particle and the index of refraction of light. Retardation is
expressed as λ the wavelength of the missing color which produces the complementary color seen. The factor of 1000 is used to
convert thickness, usually measured in micrometers into nanometers.
If angstroms are preferred, use a factor of 10,000.

If the birefringence is low as in asbestos minerals, or if
the particle is thin, the color seen will be a low order white or
gray. A retardation plate or compensator added to the optical
path can add or subtract retardation. Whether retardation is
added or subtracted depends upon whether the slow ray of the com-

pensator is parallel or perpendicular to the vibration direction
of the slow ray in the particle.

   If the slow ray of the compensator is parallel to the slow
ray of the particle, the retardation of the compensator will be
added to the retardation of the particle and a higher order retardation color will result. If the slow ray of the compensator is
perpendicular to the slow ray of the particle, subtraction of retardation will occur and a lower order retardation color will result. With asbestos minerals, or other minerals having low birefringence, the two colors seen will be first order yellow with
the slow ray of the asbestos perpendicular to the slow ray of the
compensator and second order blue with the slow ray of the asbestos parallel to the slow ray of the compensator if the compensator has 550 nm of retardation, i.e. first order red.

   It should be noted that when rotation of the stage shows
first order yellow and second order blue, the second order blue
is the direction showing the vibration direction of the high index of refraction since in this position, the slow rays are parallel. The first order yellow would then indicate the vibration
direction of the low index of refraction.

   This principle of compensation enables the microscopist to
measure the thickness of a particle if the birefringence is known
or to measure the biregringence of a particle if the thickness
is known. The birefringence of a particle is useful for particle
identification by consulting tables of optical constants.

   Michel-Levy color charts (28, 29) relate birefringence, retardation color and particle thickness in graphical form.

   The birefringence of selected minerals is shown by Table II
(30).

Table II

Mineral	n_2-n_1
Crocidolite	0.004
Chrysotile	0.011 to 0.014
Anthophyllite	0.016 to 0.025
Tremolite-actinolite	0.022 to 0.027
Amosite	0.025 to 0.027
Gypsum	0.009
Anhydrite	0.044
Talc	0.030 to 0.050
Wollastonite	0.014
Quartz	0.009

McGraw Hill Book Company

Cleavage

   A mineral has cleavage if it breaks along definite plane surfaces. When a mineral breaks along a plane of structural weakness it exhibits parting. If a mineral breaks without cleavage or parting surfaces, it is fractured. A microscopist should

use every available clue in the analysis of particulates. Cleavage, parting or fracture characteristics may often be used to distinguish between particles which are otherwise similar. Wollastonite will give long fibers similar to tremolite or anthophyllite. However, wollastonite will have enough particles showing fracturing or feathering to a thin edge or curving slightly between parting planes to recognize that wollastonite is present. This will lead to other optical or chemical tests to confirm the presence of wollastonite. Quartz will have a characteristic conchoidal cleavage. Powdered glass particles will have the same cleavage. For this reason, a supplementary test such as polarized light will be necessary to determine whether there is a possible interference. Morphology is important and should always be carefully observed.

Phase Contrast and Polarized Light

The use of a single polar is compatible with phase contrast microscopy. Crossed polars produce a dark field in which fine fibers will not be seen. If a compensator such as a first order red plate is also used, most of the fine fibers will be seen provided the light source (31) is sufficiently intense. The microscope should be equipped for rapidly switching modes between phase contrast and phase contrast with retardation plates and crossed polars.

Phase contrast microscopy uses the principle of light interference. It is possible for fibers to appear dark or bright depending upon the thickness of the fiber bundle. If the fiber bundle appears bright when viewed with phase contrast, it will likely be bright with polarized light and give visible colors when retardation plates are used. Small fibers may not give a reaction with polarized light bright enough for useful optical tests. In such a case, examine the larger bundles having a similar morphology, if present. If chrysotile is present, the wavy character of the bundles and fibers or the way fibers spread from the bundles may be sufficient for identifiction. If this is not sufficient and dispersion staining also fails, electron microscopy will identify the fine fibers. A much larger number of fibers will be seen if electron microscopy is used.

Use of the Rotating Stage

The optical behavior of asbestos fibers viewed with crossed polars has been described. Crystalline fibers have positions of extinction 90° apart. The fact that crystalline fibers have retardation has also been mentioned. With crossed polars and a first order red plate in place, asbestos fibers will go from yellow to extinction to blue, back to yellow, etc., upon rotation of the stage. If the fiber bends, this is equivalent to a rotation of the stage and the color will change. If the fiber

is straight, only one color will be seen and this will depend
upon the orientation of the stage. If the asbestos bundle is
very large, several orders of color will be seen even without
a compensator. This is because of the birefringence and thickness of the particle as previously discussed.

If the fibers are talc, more than one order of retardation
colors will be seen on small bundles. This shading of retardation color can be a clue that a fiber thought to be asbestos is
actually something else.

Plant fibers will show cells of color with the first order
red compensator. The complicated color pattern reveals the complicated internal structure of the plant fiber and shows it to be
a non mineral fiber. Occasionally, plant fibers show a single
color when examined with crossed polars and first order red
plate. In such cases, close observation of morphology or dispersion staining can be used to make a distinction.

Removal of Fibers From the Membrane

If fibers remain unidentified after examination by phase contrast, polarized light, compensators, or measurement of angle
of extinction, the fibers can be removed from the membrane for
dispersion stain analysis by ashing, particle picking, or dissolving the membrane.

Removal of fibers has the disadvantage that the count of fibers is difficult to relate to a known area and therfore to the
concentration of fibers in air. However, it is possible to mark
the position of fibers on the membrane and remove selected
fibers for further analysis. This particle picking technique
is described in "The Particle Atlas" (32).

When asbestos is in a mixture with other fibers, it is possible to bracket the asbestos concentration by determining the percent of asbestos fibers in the mixture removed from the membrane
and applying this percentage to the total fiber count on the membrane.

Ashing a cellulose ester membrane in a muffle furnace is difficult due to the tendency of the membrane to flash when it is
heated. Low temperature ashing is a solution to this problem,
expecially if operated at a slow rate, but low temperature ashing
equipment will not be available in every laboratory. A cellulose
ester membrane can be ashed by folding the membrane, sample side
in, moistening with alcohol, then igniting the alcohol with a
small flame.

Instead of ashing, it is possible to dissolve the membrane in
acetone and separate fibers and particles by centrifuging, followed by removal of excess acetone. (Caution: acetone has a low
flash point. Use only as much acetone as needed and ground large
containers before pouring.) After the third treatment, an aliquot
can then be placed on a slide and after evaporation of the acetone, the particles can be blended into a medium with n selected

for identification of the particles present.
A quick and simple separation procedure is to place one drop
of medium of the same n on each of three slides, then cut a small
segment of the membrane and hold it with fine tipped tweezers.
Dip the membrane sample side down successively into each drop of
medium. After placing a cover slip over the medium, the slides
are ready for study.

Dispersion Staining

Dispersion staining is a convenient technique for determining
the identity of fibers and particles. Dispersion staining is
taught by McCrone Research Institute (33).
Identification of asbestos by microscopical dispersion staining has been described by Julian (34) and the technique is described in "The Particle Atlas" (35).
Zeiss and many other phase contrast microscopes produce the
equivalent of a central stop dispersion stain by using a phase 2
16X phase contrast objective with the phase 3 condenser ring in
place. Leitz manufactures a phase contrast microscope which produces central stop dispersion colors at 400X by using the number
5 condenser ring position. If the microscopes in use at other
labs do not produce a central stop dispersion stain in this way,
a "dispersion stainer" is available (36). The color resolution
(not the particle resolution) of a McCrone dispersion stainer is
a little better than that obtained from mismatching phase rings.
For dispersion staining analysis, it is necessary to have
quality high dispersion liquids. One source is R. P. Cargille
Laboratories, Inc. (37).

Analysis of Bulk Samples for Asbestos

A bulk sample is a gross sample of material such as a piece
of plaster or a rafter sample or other material which can be analyzed to determine whether there is a potential source of some
toxic substance such as asbestos or quartz. Bulk samples are
given a preliminary examination with a reflected light stereomicroscope for the presence of fibers. Fibers can be isolated from
the matrix at this time for identification by optical methods, X-
ray diffraction or electron microscopy, or further analysis can be
performed after pulverizing fibers in the matrix. If the material
to be examined is very hard, cut the material in a vise with a
hack saw and catch the cuttings on a plastic film. Asbestos fibers can be more readily identified if separated before fine
grinding if they are to be identified by morphology or polarized
light. Fine fibers may be candidates for X-ray diffraction or
electron microscopy.
Particles immersed in mounting media may be examined by transmitted light with a stereomicroscope before examination by phase
contrast. The advantage of stereomicroscopy is that visualizing

fibers in three dimensions gives additional visual cues for identification and estimation of percentage. For example, chrysotile
is often wavy and plant fibers may curl or curve at the edge in a
manner which is distinct. If masses of fibers are present, stereomicroscopy will enable one to see the underlayers more readily.
The range of the stereomicroscope from about 6X to 50X enables one
to obtain an overview of the entire sample (usually about 22mm^2).
Areas of special interest can be designated for a closer look at
higher magnification up to 400X by phase contrast and polarized
light. The entire slide should be examined at 400X. The preliminary scan will ensure that areas of special interest are not
missed. A small glass chip can temporarily mark an area of special interest.

Slides are prepared by blending a fraction of a milligram of
sample adhering to a paperclip or other clean disposable item
into a drop of mounting medium on a slide and covering with a
number 1½ cover slip. Dipping the paperclip into the drop of
mounting medium on the slide will make the particles adhere when
the sample is touched. The particles should be spread in a thin
even layer.

Two slides should be prepared, one with asbestos mounting medium (1:1 dimethyl phthalate and diethyl oxylate) or some nonvola-
tile transparent medium having an n which will give good contrast.
The n of the medium on the second slide will be close to that of
particles or fibers to be identified by dispersion staining. Slide
one will be used for quantitative analysis, slide two for qualitative analysis. Fine fibers may disappear when n of particles and
medium match. If asbestos concentration is micro-visually estimated, the analysis can be improved by having a second analyst confirm the first estimate. Comparison is made after both analysts
have written down their estimated percentage. If there is a spread,
both can take a second look, a third analyst can be consulted, or
other analysis can be performed such as X-ray diffraction. A
visual estimate is useful as a qualitative result giving guidance
in determining whether a potential source of air-borne asbestos
exists. The sensitivity will be better than X-ray diffraction
since microscopic analysis can detect parts per million of asbestos. If asbestos concentration is above 2%, X-ray diffraction can
give a more accurate determination of mineral concentration but
fiber concentration can only be determined by examination of morphology. Microscopy also permits determination of asbestos at the
worksite if the field analyst is properly trained.

The percent by number of asbestos in talc samples is determined by particle counting. If a scan of two slides shows no fibers present, there is no need for a particle count.

Asbestos System of Analysis

This paper will not discuss counting rules for asbestos. The
phase contrast method is fully described by NIOSH (38). It is

understood that all references to asbestos fibers will be to asbestos fibers greater than five micrometers in length. Asbestos
will often be easily identified on the basis of morphology and a
knowledge that there is a source of asbestos.

Step I. Examine the fibers with crossed polars. If the
fibers disappear with crossed polars, the following possibilities apply:

A. The fibers are asbestos fibers or other fine
mineral fibers but are so fine that any reaction
with polarized light is not visible to the eye.

Look for bundles having similar morphology but
large enough to react with polarized light as
an indicator that asbestos may be present. If
crysotile is present, much of it may be expected to be too fine to polarize light. If crocidolite is present, the birefringence is only
0.004, the bundles will have to be larger than
other asbestos minerals before the fibers will
be visible with crossed polars. Crocidolite
is also darker than other asbestos minerals
because of its natural blue absorbance color.

B. The fibers are fiberglass.

Bundles will be absent. Branching fibers are
unlikely. If branching occurs, the separation
point will be clearly defined. Fibers will
probably be thick compared to asbestos. All
fibers, including thick fibers, will show no
reaction with polarized light. Breaks in
fibers may resemble a break in a glass rod
with a chip on one side.

C. The fibers are fine fibrils, portions of plant
fibers which are too fine to be identified by polarized light.

Fine plant fibrils will not be present unless plant
fibers are present. Look for presence of plant
fibers as an indicator. Plant fibers will usually
be easy to identify by their morphology and internal structure. If plant fibers are present, fibrils small enough to have no reaction with polarized light will still be rare.

D. The fibers are diatomaceous earth or sponge
spicules.

If diatomaceous earth is present, honeycomb structures and diatoms or other marine organism fragments
will be seen in bright field. Examine the slide in
brightfield and note that the fibers appear very
white or a white granular appearance may be present.
Examination at higher magnification is helpful. It
is possible to use a 65X objective without having to
go to oil immersion. If diatomaceous earth is present, analyze a bulk sample by X-ray diffraction. If
the material has been calcined, it is likely to have
been converted to cristobalite.

E. Perlite veins are present.

Perlite is an expanded volcanic glass. It is thin
and diaphanous except where interconnections of
glassy bubbles give the impression of veins. If
the veins are separated from the glassy film, they
may loosely resemble chrysotile asbestos. The separation is seldom complete. Close observation will detect
the film fragments associated with the vein structure.

Step I, Part 2. The fibers or bundles do not disappear with
crossed polars.

The possible presence of isotropic materials, including fiberglass, diatomaceous earth, perlite or any isometric mineral
has been eliminated. The substance is anisotropic. The following possibilities exist:

A. The substance may be plant fibers.

Plant fibers are usually much thicker than asbestos
fibers, the ends of branching fibrils are stubby,
internal structure can be seen with crossed polars.
Plant fibers will also go to extinction every 90°
on rotation of a stage as do asbestos fibers.

B. The substance may be textile or synthetic resin
fibers.

These fibers will be large compared to asbestos
fibers. Asbestos fibrils can be much finer than
one micron in thickness. Textile fibers will ordinarily be more than 5 micrometers in thickness.
The fibers will have a circular cross section and
the ends will break in characteristic ways. Bundles
resembling asbestos bundles will not be seen.

C. Hair or fur fibers may be present.

Human hair, depending on race, may be about 100
micrometers thick. Animal hair may show a central
canal; scales or surface patterns may be present.
It is unlikely that this type of fiber would be
mistaken for asbestos.

D. Non asbestos mineral fibers may be present.

   1. Wollastonite. Wollastonite is a fibrous
   calcium silicate sometimes used in industry
   as a substitute for asbestos. Further testing will be necessary if wollastonite is
   present. See the discussion on fiber rolling,
   and the table on identification of fibers by
   dispersion stain.

   2. Talc fibers.

   Talc fibers may be present in some talcs, especially if the talcs contain anthophyllite
   or tremolite asbestos and a metamorphosis or
   transition to talc has taken place. The
   transition is sometimes incomplete as in
   talcs from the Gouveneur district of upper
   New York State. If talc fibers are present,
   further testing as described below will be
   necessary.

   3. Gypsum.

   Due to its blocky appearance, gypsum is unlikely to be confused with asbestos by an
   experienced analyst. Gypsum will often
   show particles with aspect ratio of 3:1 or
   greater. However, gypsum can be identified
   by dispersion staining using cargille HD
   medium 1.530.

E. Asbestos fibers may be present.

If asbestos is present and the sample is not a talc
sample, it is most likely to be chrysotile since
about 90% or more of the asbestos used in American
industry is chrysotile. If the sample is taken
from a shipyard, there is a high probability that
it will be amosite asbestos. If asbestos is found
in a talc sample, it is likely to be anthophyllite
or tremolite-actinolite or an asbestos intermediate
fiber; chrysotile is a possibility, however. If
the sample is insulation, expect a variety of fibers.

Some old fiberglass insulations will contain 2 or
3% asbestos, usually chrysotile. Plant and other
organic fibers are also used in insulation.

Asbestos Fibers Identification

Rotate the stage. Note that with the polars crossed,
the fibers go to extinction every 90° and also have
positions of maximum brightness 90° apart. Take note
of morphology, chrysotile fibers appear to be fine
and are often wavy. Amosite fibers look stiff and
straight and fibrils coming off a bundle viewed at
high magnification may resemble a household broom.

Step II. Insert a first order red compensator into the
optical path. Take note of the color of fibers as the
stage is rotated. Several possibilities exist.

A. The fibers, although large enough to react with
polarized light, are visible but have no brightness
or color of their own. The color matches the red
color of the background.

These fibers are isotropic, usually amorphous, i.e.
fiberglass, etc.

B. The fibers react with polarized light but
internal structure is seen with cells of color
showing intricate patterns.

These are organic fibers, usually plant fibers.
Occasionally, plant fibers show a single color
with a retardation plate which changes in color
in a manner similar to asbestos. If morphology
suggests the possibility of plant fibers, do a
dispersion staining test.

C. Cells of color are not seen but shading of
color indicates the birefringence is too high
to be asbestos.

Especially in a talc sample, suspect the presence of talc fiber bundles. This can be verified by dispersion staining if the analyst is
uncertain.

D. Pure colors are seen, i.e., the color is the
same along the length of the bundle. Rotation
of the stage causes color change from yellow to
blue or blue to yellow.

Suspect the fibers to be asbestos. The variety
of asbestos can be determined by dispersion
staining. Chrysotile will be recognized by its
morphology.

E. Conditions are the same as "D" but rotation
of the stage shows the color changes from blue
to green or green to blue. Larger bundles are
required to clearly see the reaction with polarized light. The bundles, when viewed without crossed polars in phase contrast, have a
natural blue absorbance color.

The asbestos is crocidolite or South African
blue asbestos. The green color seen is a
combination of the yellow retardation color
and the natural blue color. Due to the low
birefringence of crocidolite, small fibers
may be mistaken for fiberglass when tested
with cross polars. If fiberglass is mixed
with crocidolite, the two can be distinguished
by dispersion staining. Another clue that crocidolite is present is that the yellow or green
retardation color will often be seen when oriented, in a direction which gives blue for
all of the other asbestos minerals.

Step III. If the identity of the fibers remains doubtful
after phase contrast and polarized light study on the membrane, remove fibers from the membrane and examine by dispersion staining. All of the optical tests described herein can be performed while the fibers are on the membrane
except fiber rolling, dispersion staining, and determination of n.

Identification of fibers by dispersion stain colors:

Three indices for Cargille high dispersion media which can be
used to distinguish between asbestos fibers are 1.550, 1.605, and
1.670. See table III for dispersion colors obtained.

TABLE III

Mineral fiber	Index of refraction of medium	Color seen with fiber oriented parallel to polarizer	Color seen with fiber oriented perpendicular to polarizer *
Chrysotile	1.546	yellow to orange	orange to magenta
Chrysotile	1.550	red to magenta	blue
Amphiboles	1.550	white	white
Talc	1.550	yellow	blue
Chrysotile	1.585	blue	blue white
Tremolite	1.585	yellow	yellow
Anthophyllite	1.585	yellow	yellow
Chrysotile	1.605	white	white
Talc	1.605	blue to white	white
Tremolite	1.605	yellow	orange to blue
Anthophyllite	1.605	yellow	orange to blue
Wollastonite	1.605	yellow	yellow orange
Amosite	1.670	yellow	red to violet
Crocidolite	1.670	yellow orange	yellow

* Color may depend on whether alpha or beta is being viewed depending on rotation of fiber about its axis.

If the asbestos appears to be chrysotile, 1.55 is the preferred medium for confirmation by dispersion staining. Paper or plant fibers which have passed screening by polarized light and first order red compensators will be screened out by dispersion staining. While both paper or chrysotile fibers give a central stop blue color if the fiber is oriented perpendicular to the vibration direction of the polarizer, when the fiber is parallel to the vibration direction of the polarizer, chrysotile will be red to magenta (centrol stop) while paper or plant fiber will be yellow. Dispersion staining gives a color only at the edge. Since chrysotile has many edges, the dispersion staining color is uniform across the bundle. The dispersion staining color of plant fibers is seen only on the outside border of the fibers. Talc fibers also give a blue central stop dispersion staining color when the fibers are oriented perpendicular to the polarizer in 1.550 medium and a yellow central stop color when the talc fibers are oriented parallel to the vibration direction of the polarizer. If chrysotile is suspected in talc, chrysotile fibers can be differentiated from talc fibers in 1.550 medium. 1.670 medium is the choice for identification of amosite or crocidolite asbestos. If only crocidolite asbestos is suspected, 1.690 medium can be used.

Tremolite and anthophyllite can be identified in 1.620 medium.
In a talc sample where talc fibers may also be present, 1.605 medium is prefered. This will distinguish between talc fibers and
asbesestos fibers by the dispersion staining colors. 1.605 medium
will also distinguish between wollastonite and asbestos.

If dispersion staining shows that a fiber is either tremolite
or anthophyllite, one can distinguish between the two by carefully
determining the slope of the dispersion staining curve or by
measuring the angle of extinction.

Rolling Fibers

The gamma index for all asbestos minerals except crocidolite
will be seen when the fiber is oriented parallel to the vibration
direction of the polarizer. The dispersion staining colors for
all asbestos minerals except crocidolite will show alpha and beta
perpendicular to the vibration direction of the polarizer. If
alpha is not seen in the perpendicular position, the fiber can be
rolled about its own long axis to bring alpha into view. If for
example, the central stop dispersion staining color goes from
reddish magenta to blue by rotation of the fiber about its own
long axis, the blue color will represent the lowest or alpha
index. If the same fiber shows a yellow central stop color when
the fiber is oriented parallel to the vibration direction of the
polarizer, one knows that the index of the fiber in this direction is high relative to the mounting medium, and the high or
gamma index of the fiber is being examined. This rolling test
and the determination that three indices of refraction are
present tells the analyst that the fiber is one of the biaxial
minerals. All asbestos minerals are biaxial. However, the rolling test is not needed in the analysis of chrysotile.

Fibers are rolled around their long axis by gently tapping
the cover slip with a dissection needle. Keep the fiber in view
at all times as this is done. If a mineral plate is seen on edge
it may resemble a fiber. Rolling the plate over reveals the true
nature of the plate. This is a useful test when platy minerals
such as talc or mica are being examined for the possible presence
of asbestos.

To test for the presence of wollastonite fibers, cross the
polars, insert a first order red compensator, orient the fiber to
be rolled in a position at an oblique angle to the vibration direction of the polarizer by rotation of the stage, then rotate
the fiber around its own long axis by gently tapping the cover
slip. If the fiber changes color from yellow to blue, then back
to yellow as it rotates about its own long axis, at the same
oblique angle, it is likely to be wollastonite. Asbestos will
not act in this way. OSHA methods (39) gives a test with hydrochloric acid for the presence of wollastonite. The treated wollastonite fibers can be reacted so that they polarize light very
weakly but retain their morphology if mounted on a slide before

treatment with acid.

Determining the Index of Refraction

If n's of a mineral are determined, Tables can be consulted to determine the identity of the mineral. These are generally listed according to whether the mineral is uniaxial or biaxial, and whether the mineral is positive or negative (40).

In phase contrast microscopy when particles are viewed in brightfield, i.e., without the use of crossed polars, if particles have an n less than n of the medium, the particles appear very white unless the particles have a strong absorbance color. If n of the particles is close to n of the medium, the particles will appear faint blue. If n of the particles is greater than n of the medium, the particles will show sharp contrast. Edges and surface features will be easily seen.

Another test to determine whether the particle or medium has the higher n is the Becke test. The Becke line is a halo around the particle. As the objective is raised or the stage is lowered, the Becke line will move into the medium or particle having the higher n. As the objective is lowered or the stage is raised, the Becke line will enter the medium or particle having the lower n. Due to dispersion or variability of n with wave length of light, this test is difficult to use with white light as n is approached. It is difficult to determine which line is the right Becke line since lines will be seen moving into both the particle and the medium. If particles are examined by dispersion staining techniques and n of the medium has matched n of the particles for the Sodium D doublet, i.e. 589.3 nanometers, the Becke lines produced by central stop dispersion staining can be examined and it will be noted that the yellow light from a white light source has been central stopped out, the blue Becke line will spread into the medium as the objective is raised and the red line will spread into the particle. The blue magenta color of the combined Becke lines produced by the central stop or the yellow color produced by the annular stop indicate that there is an index match between the particle and the medium.

The color (wavelength)of light seen in central stop dispersion staining is the complimentary color to that seen in annular stop dispersion staining. While the color seen in annular stop dispersion staining is the color at which an n match occurs between particle and medium, the central stop dispersion staining color is more easily identified by the eye. If the color seen is not 589.3 nanometers, the n of the medium at the wavelength seen is not the point of interest. The measurement of interest is to determine the wavelength of light seen (color at the edge of a particle) in a medium whose n at 589.3 nanometers is known. On a Hartman net (41) the parallel lines for n each represent a medium whose n is measured at 589.3 nanometers. The n of the medium at other wave lengths is not shown. A Hartman net is used to determine the slope of the dispersion curve for a particle of interest. If the dispersion staining color at the particle edge is plotted against the n of the medium used, the dispersion curve will cross the 589.3 nanometer line on the Hartman net. At this intersection, an n match occurs between the particle and medium at 589.3 nanometers, the wavelength at which n is usually measured. The accuracy with which the n of the particle is measured at this wavelength will depend primarily on the ability of the analyst to estimate the dispersion colors if quality media of precisely determined n is used. The ability to estimate wavelength will improve with practice and experience.

The eyeball can be calibrated to read the dispersion colors produced by the different medium-particle combinations by using Koffler glass powders as standards. The colors (wavelengths) produced by various combinations are given in tabular form by R. A. Goodman (42).

The slope of the dispersion staining curve is characteristic for each mineral. Dispersion staining curves of various minerals have been plotted in the Particle Atlas (43) and dispersion data are given by Winchell (44).

Analysis of Quartz

It is easier to analyze quartz petrographically if the sample has been cleaned up by dissolving the non-quartz minerals in hot phosphoric acid. Petrographic analysis can be used to check the phosphoric acid residue produced in the N. A. Talvitie (45) method for the gravimetric examination of quartz. If the residue is not examined petrographically, the reported results may be high.

If quartz is analyzed by X-ray diffraction and the presence of an interfering peak is suspected, it may be possible to cross check the X-ray diffraction by petrographic examination of particles picked from the sample membrane. Quartz reflects light in a characteristic way also. The parlodian film which may be used in X-ray diffraction tends to interfere in petrographic examination.

Quartz has a characteristic appearance when examined petrographically but two factors change the appearance of quartz:
1. Quartz may be perfectly clear or it may contain inclusions. The inclusions are impurities in the quartz which appear as dark or bright spots in the particles. It is possible for some quartz to contain so many inclusions that one may mistake it for some other mineral, if the examination is not carried out very carefully.
2. The quartz particles may be part of a single crystal and have a uniform appearance or the particles may be cryptocrystalline. A cryptocrystalline substance has very fine crystals. The crystalline structure is demonstrated by X-ray diffraction. By extension, the term "cryptocrystalline is used here

to refer to samples in which the crystals within a
particle are large enough to produce a visible effect.
If the particles are cryptocrystalline, they will have
a granular appearance when examined in bright field.
The cryptocrystalline quartz has cells which are
in different orientation in the particle and the shadow
effect of light passing between cell boundaries causes
the granular appearance.

Quartz is a framework or "Tectosilicate". This strong binding force on quartz in three dimensions causes quartz to lack
cleavage planes since there is no direction of greater weakness in
quartz. This causes the cleavage in the quartz to be conchoidal
(from the Greek word for shell) since there may be rings showing
the direction in which a cleavage force was applied. Another
common material which has conchoidal cleavage is glass.

The petrographic methods for examination of minerals have
been described already. In a matching n medium with crossed polars, quartz has a white appearance. If particles are 40 microns
thick, yellow birefringence color will be seen in the center
(without compensator), assuming that particle orientation is
such that one is looking through 40 microns thickness. With
smaller particles and a first order red compensator yellow and
blue particles are seen depending on orientation or rotation
of the stage. This is not a conclusive test by itself since
other minerals may have similar birefringence (0.009). In
bright field at matching n, the (quartz) particles disappear.
In bright field phase contrast quartz particles viewed at
matching n appear faint blue.

A 1.547 medium is often used for examination of quartz by
dispersion staining. This medium will show the F wave length
color golden magenta (486.0 nanometers) for epsilon and the C wave
length color blue green (656.0 nanometers) for omega as viewed
with central stop.

The dispersion staining colors described are for measurements
at room temperature (25^0 C). It is possible to vary the index of
the liquid by using a hot stage (46) and obtain a dispersion slope
with a single particle without necessity of changing the mounting
medium. This technique is also useful in analysis of other minerals including asbestos.

Summary

Asbestos, quartz or other minerals can be analyzed by consideration of mineralogical principles and crystal systems. Polarized light, compensation plates, measurement of angles of extinction and dispersion staining are useful techniques. Optical behavior of a mineral is related to the internal crystal structure of
the mineral. Tables of optical constants are useful for mineral
identification. The microscope is a powerful tool for analysis
that should not be overlooked by the industrial hygiene chemist.

References:

1. Edwards, G.H, and Lynch, J.R., "The Method Used by the U.S.
    Public Health Service for Enumeration of Asbestos Dust on
    Membrane Filters". Ann. Occup. Hyg. 2, 1-6 (1968).

2. Taylor, David G., coordinator, "NIOSH Manual of Analytical
    Methods" Second Edition, vol. 1, 239-1 to 239-21, April,
    1977. U.S. Department of Health, Education and Welfare,
    Public Health Service Center for Disease Control, National
    Institute for Occupational Safety and Health, Cincinnati, OH.

3. Leidell, N.A., Bayer, S.G., Zumwalde, R.D., and Busch, K.A.,
    NIOSH - A Technical Report "USPHS/NIOSH Membrane Filter
    Method for Evaluating Airborne Asbestos Fibers". Feb. 1979.
    DHEW (NIOSH) Publication no. 79-127. U.S. Department of
    Health, Education and Welfare, Public Health Service, Center
    for Disease Control, National Institute for Occupational
    Safety and Health.

4. Joint AIHA - ACGIH Aerosol Hazards Evaluation Committee
    "Recommended Procedure for Sampling and Counting Asbestos
    Fibers", A.I.H.A. J. 36, (2) 83-90 (1975). Note: This
    issue has 6 articles on asbestos analyses or control.

5. Code of Federal Regulations, 29 Labor, Parts 1900 - 1919
    Revised July 1, 1977; 29 CFR 1910.1001, sections (a) 1,2;
    (b) 2.

6. Gellman Filters and Holders for Air Analysis (1977). Air
    Analysis Division, Gellman Instrument Company, 600 South
    Wagner Road. Ann Arbor, MI 48106.

7. Millipore Catalog MC/1, Millipore Corporation, Ashby Road,
    Bedford, MA 01730.

8. Ibid ref. 5, section e.

9. Ibid ref. 2, 239-5 paragraph 5, Advantages and Disadvantages
    of the Method.

10. Ibid ref. 2, 239-2, paragraph 3, Interferences.

11. Bayer, S.G., Zumwalde, R.D., Brown, T.A., "Equipment and Procedures for Mounting Millipore Filters and Counting Asbestos Fibers by Phase Contrast Microscopy", 1-15 (July, 1969), U.S. Department of Health, Education and Welfare, Public Health Service, Bureau of Occupational Safety and Health, 1014 Broadway, Cincinnati, OH, 45202.

12. Ibid, ref 4, Appendix 1, page 87.

13. Zeiss Microscope illuminator 100 or equivalent.

14. Asbestos Information Association, 1745 Jefferson Davis Hwy, Arlington, VA 22202.

15. "Asbestos" published monthly since July 1919. Stover Publishing Co., 131 North York Road, (P.O. Box 471) Willow Grove, PA 19090 Phone 215-659-0134.

16. Wards Natural Science Establishment, Inc. P.O. Box 1712, Rochester, New York 14603 or P.O. Box 1749 Monterrey, CA 93940.

17. Ms. M. W. Harris, NIEHS P. O. Box 12233, Research Triangle Park, N. C., 27709.

18. McCrone, W.C. and Johnson, R.I., "Techniques, Instruments and Accessories for Microanalysts" a users manual, (1974), Price list, May 1, 1978, pp 25 - McCrone Accessories and Components, 2820 South Michigan Ave., Chicago, IL, 60616, Phone 312-842-7100.

19. Deer, W.A., Howie, R.A., Zussman, M.A., Rock Forming Minerals, Vol 2, Chain Silicates, Amphiboles, pp 203-374. Vol 3, Sheet Silicates, Serpentines, pp 170 - 190. (1974) Longman Group, Ltd., London.

20. Powder Diffraction File, Inorganic, compiled by Joint Committee on Powder Diffraction, International Center for Diffraction Data, 1601 Park Lane, Swarthmore, PA 19081.

21. Hurlbut, C.D., "Danas Manual of Mineralogy" 18th Ed. 9, (1959) John Wiley and Sons, Inc., New York.

22. Ibid, ref 16.

23. Frondell, C., "The System of Mineralogy of James Dwight Dana and Edward Salisbury Dana", 7th Ed. Vol III, Silica Minerals. 1-334. John Wiley and Sons Inc., New York.

24. Ibid, ref 21, pp 41 - 96.

25. Ibid, ref 19, Vol 3, p 170 and 174.

26. Berkely, C., Longer, A., Boden, V., "Instrumental Analysis
     of Inspired Fibrous Pulmonary Particulates" Transactions
     NY. Acad. Sci. 333 - 50 (1967).

27. Kerr, P.F., "Optical Mineralogy", 3rd edition, pages 418
     and 319. McGraw Hill Book Co. New York, 1959.

28. Ibid, ref 21, p156 - 7.

29. Bloss, F.D., An Introduction to the Methods of Optical
     Crystallography, 144 et seq. Holt Rinehart and Winston,
     (1961).

30. Ibid, ref 27.

31. Ibid, ref 13.

32. McCrone, W.C., Delly, J.G., The Particle Atlas, Edition II
     1 97-116, Ann Arbor Science Publishers Inc., P.O. Box 1425
     Ann Arbor, Michigan, 48106.

33. McCrone Research Institute, 2820 South Michigan Ave.,
     Chicago, Illinois 60616.

34. Julian and McCrone, "Identification of Asbestos Fibers by
     Microscopical Dispersion Staining". The Microscope 18 (1)
     1 - 10 (1970). Note "The Microscope" has a series of
     articles on dispersion staining.

35. Ibid, ref 32. Vol 1, pp 97 - 117, Vol 4. (tables).

36. Ibid, ref 18.

37. Cargille. 55 Commerce Road, Cedar Grove, NJ 07009, USA.

38. Ibid, ref 1, 2, 3.

39. Dixon, W.C., "Occupational Safety and Health Administration
     Methods". pp 431 - 440 in NBS Special Publication 506,
     "Workshop on Asbestos Definitions and Methods" Edited by
     Gravatt, C.C., LaFleur, P.D. and Heinrich, F.J. Nov. 1978.
     U.S. Dept. of Commerce, National Bureau of Standards, Stock
     #003-003-01993-3. U.S. Gov't Printing Office.

40. Larsen, E.S., and Berman, H., Geological Survey Bulletin 848 "The Microscopic Determination of the Nonopaque Minerals" Second Edition, United States Department of the Interior, U.S. Govt. Printing Office, Washington, 1934.

41. Ibid, ref 18, pp 173.

42 Goodman, R.A., Expanded Uses and Applications of Dispersion Staining Microscope 18, 41 - 50 (Jan. 1970).

43. Ibid, ref 32 Vol 4. 872 - 975.

44. Winchell, A.M., and Winchell H., "The Microscopical Character of Artificial Inorganic Solid Substances". Academic Press, New York, 1964.

45. Talvitie, N.A., "Determination of Quartz in Presence of Silicates Using Phosphoric Acid". Anal. Chem. $\underline{23}$ 623 (1951).

46. Mettler Instrument Corporation "Modular Instrument Systems for the Automatic Determination of Thermal Values". (FP-52). Box 71 Hightstown, NJ 08520.

RECEIVED September 25, 1979.

The views expressed in this paper do not necessarily reflect those of the Occupational Safety and Health Administration; the author is solely responsible for its content.

Occupational Health Analytical Chemistry

Quantitation Using X-Ray Powder Diffraction

DONALD D. DOLLBERG, MARTIN T. ABELL, and BRUCE A. LANGE[1]

National Institute for Occupational Safety and Health,
4676 Columbia Parkway, Cincinnati, OH 45226

Particulate contaminants are of extreme importance in occupational health because of their effect on the respiratory system. Such contaminants may be grouped into several physiological categories depending on their overall effect (1). Three categories are of importance to this discussion: (1) inert, (2) minimal pulmonary fibrosis producing, and (3) extensive pulmonary fibrosis producing. Dust aerosols which produce no known injuries when inhaled but may cause discomfort and minor irritation to the lung, are classed as nuisance and/or inert. Examples of such dusts include particulate clay, limestone, gypsum or aluminum oxide. If a dust contaminant is known to produce nodulation (discrete deposits of particulate) and diffuse fibrosis (growth of nonelastic tissue) in the lung, the material is classed as minimal pulmonary fibrosis producing. Dusts in this category include barium sulfate, iron oxide and tin oxide. The third category, extensive pulmonary fibrosis producing, includes dusts such as silica and asbestos. These dusts are known to produce a significant degree of nodulation and fibrosis in the lung.

Exposure to inorganic chemicals in the workplace has been traditionally evaluated using elemental analysis. However, in recent years some attention has been given to the toxic effects of specific compounds rather than elements, e.g., chromic acid (2), nickel subsulfide (3), zinc oxide (4), and sodium hydroxide (5). It is therefore important that the occupational health chemist develop the capability to identify and quantitate chemical compounds. To this end, X-ray powder diffraction (XRD) is a unique tool for

----

[1] Current Address: Construction Products Div., W.R. Grace, Inc., 62 Whittemore Ave, Cambridge, Mass., 02140.

crystalline particulate analysis. Every species has a unique powder diffraction pattern; thus, it is possible to identify each species in a sample by either a manual or computerized search (6) of crystalline standards. Upon identification of the compounds present in the sample, each may be quantitated since the diffracted intensity for a given profile or peak of the diffraction pattern is proportional to the amount present in the sample. Furthermore, the non-destructive nature of XRD permits additional analyses by other techniques should this be necessary.

Recognizing the applicability of XRD to occupational health chemistry, Lennox and Leroux (7) suggested a number of chemical species which would be suitable for XRD analysis: arsenic trioxide, beryllium oxide, mica, vanadium oxides, calcium fluoride in ceramic materials, as well as a number of organics such as DDT, lindane and chlordane. Unfortunately, the general application of XRD to the quantitation of industrial hygiene samples has not been realized and the majority of these analyses are restricted to free silica and to a lesser extent asbestos and talc.

Table I lists several XRD analytical methods recently developed in the NIOSH laboratories. For each analyte, the analytical range, detection limit and analytical precision are listed. The method numbers refer to the NIOSH Manual of Analytical Methods (8). As indicated in the table, there are several NIOSH methods available for free silica analysis. Method No. P&CAM 109 incorporates the internal standard approach as developed by Bumsted (9). The other two methods S-315 and P&CAM 259 are based on the substrate standard method. The major difference between the two is the direct sampling on silver membrane filters (S-315). This paper will address the various methods of quantitation, sample collection and procedures for matrix absorption corrections that have been used in this laboratory for the analysis of crystalline particulate contaminants in the workplace.

Methods of Quantitation

Because X-ray powder diffraction deals with solid samples, the analytical variables are different from those associated with the analysis of liquid or solution samples. Principle among these are particle size effects, uniform sample surface, crystallinity and X-ray absorption. Although particle size and a non-uniform sample surface are serious problems, their

TABLE I

Permissible Exposure Levels And
XRD Analytical Methods

Analyte	Standard mg/M^3	Analytical Range, mg/M^3	Relative Std.Dev.	NIOSH Method
Zinc oxide	5.0 (a)	0.03-2.4	0.10	P&CAM 222
Zirconium oxide	5.0 (b)	0.03-1.5	0.08	P&CAM 250
Chrysotile	0.15 (c)	0.025-0.25	0.07	P&CAM 309
Fibrous tremolite		0.012-0.25	0.14	
Quartz	0.05 (a)	0.030-1.3		P&CAM 109
		0.025-0.4	0.07	S 315
		0.025-2.4	0.10	P&CAM 259

(a) NIOSH recommended standard
(b) American Conference of Governmental Industrial Hygienists
(c) West German mass standard; c.f. ref. 30.

effects can be reduced or eliminated through careful sample preparation. Field sample crystallinity is, perhaps, the most uncontrollable variable which effects quantitative XRD analysis. Often the analyte is generated in the workplace under adverse conditions; conditions significantly different from those used in the laboratory for the preparation of standards. Thus, to lessen the effect of the variation in degree of crystallinity between standards and samples, the diffraction peak area rather than peak height must be measured.

Both historically and currently, X-ray absorption by the sample has had a major impact on the development of analytical methodology. While the theory of X-ray absorption is complex, the observed effect is straight forward. As X-rays pass through a material they are

absorbed; the extent of the absorption depends upon the
thickness   and   nature   of   the   absorbing   medium.
Diagramatically the specific factors influencing X-ray
absorption   are   pictured   in   Fig. I.   The   sample
thickness (t) and the diffraction angle (θ)   determine
the   path   length   of   the X-rays through the absorbing
material, while the chemical composition of the   matrix
determines   the   degree   of absorption per unit length.
By knowing the thickness (or area, mass and density) of
the   sample   and   its   exact chemical composition it is
possible to calculate the absorption effect and thereby
make corrections.   However, for an actual filter sample
collected in the workplace environment these parameters
are   rarely   known   and   often impossible to determine.
Therefore, to account for the X-ray absorption   effect
on   quantitative   analysis, two experimental procedures
have   been   utilized   in   the   X-ray   laboratory: the
internal standard procedure and the substrate standard
procedure.

     Internal Standard Procedure. The first of these
absorption   correction   methods   was   developed   by
Alexander   and   Klug (10) and involves the addition of a
known amount of an internal standard to the sample.   If
the analyte and the internal standard have diffraction
profiles   at   approximately   the   same   angle,   their
intensities will   be equivalently influenced by matrix
absorption.   Thus, the intensity ratio of the   internal
standard   to   that   of   the   analyte   can   be used as a
quantitative measure of the amount of analyte   present.
To   effectively   use the internal standard procedure, a
number   of   requirements   must   be   met.   First,   the
standard   should   have   a   strong diffraction peak near
that of the analyte, but not so close as to   interfere.
Secondly,   the   density,   particle   size   and   mass
absorption coefficient of   the   analyte   and   standard
should   be similar.   Thirdly, the analyte, standard and
any matrix must be chemically inert   relative   to   each
other   and finally, a homogeneous mixture of sample and
standard must be generated.
     The   major   drawbacks   to this method as a general
quantitative procedure   include   the   rather   stringent
requirements for the internal standard, the preparation
of a homogeneous mixture of standard   and   sample,   and
the additional time required for the measurement of the
two   phases.   Furthermore,   since   it   is   not   always
possible to know in advance whether the matrix contains
strongly   absorbing   materials,   the   internal   standard
must   be   added   to   every   sample   as   a precautionary
measure.

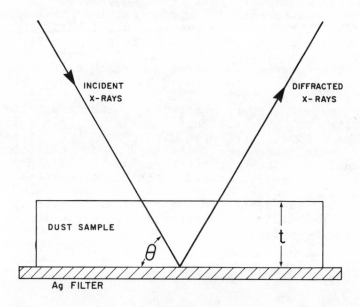

Figure 1.   Geometric factors that affect the degree of x-ray absorption

Bumstead (9) chose native fluorite as an internal standard for the analysis of quartz in coal dust. His procedure consisted of mixing 0.20 mg fluorite into each water suspension of standard and sample and depositing on silver membrane filters for a calibration curve (fluorite/quartz intensity ratio vs. mg quartz). The application of this method to coal dust samples containing less than 1% quartz produced acceptable results; relative standard deviation (RSD) was 18.2% (9).

Substrate Standard Procedure. The second method, also known as the external standard procedure, depends on the measurement of a diffraction peak from the substrate supporting the sample. This method is based on the work of two independent groups. Leroux, Lennox and Kay (11) developed a procedure for calculating an absorption correction based on the diffracted and transmitted intensities from a bulk sample. Williams (12) simplified this process by mounting the sample on a fine grained copper metal foil and measuring the intensity of the diffracted radiation from this foil with and without the sample in place. A correction factor can then be calculated from the observed attenuation of the copper diffraction peak. Leroux and co-workers (13,14) extended the Williams technique by replacing the copper foil with a silver membrane filter and applied the method to the analysis of quartz.

To calculate the absorption correction, Γ, the following equation is employed:

$$\Gamma = \frac{-R \ln T}{1 - T^R}$$

where:

$R = \sin \theta \text{ substrate} / \sin \theta \text{ analyte}$

$T = I_{Ag}/I_{Ag}^o$

I_{Ag} = diffracted intensity for the substrate with sample deposition

I_{Ag}^o = diffracted intensity for the substrate without sample deposition

The observed intensity or weight of analyte is then multiplied by Γ to give the corrected intensity or weight. The substrate standard method requires that the substrate be crystalline (such as a silver membrane filter) and assumes a uniform sample distribution. The major drawback to this approach is the possibility of overlap of the analyte profile with that of the substrate profile.

Sample Collection and Preparation

For occupational health investigations, personal sampling is done in the breathing zone of the exposed worker. To accomplish this, a portable sampling pump must be attached to the worker and a collection device positioned near the breathing zone, usually attached to the shirt collar. This device consists of a plastic holder (filter cassette) containing the membrane filter. Typical filters used for the collection of particulates include Mine Safety Appliance's (MSA) FWSB (polyvinylchloride) and Gelman Sciences DM-5000 (polyacrylonitrile-polyvinylchloride). Flow rates for personal sampling usually range from 1.0 - 2.0 L/min with 1.7 L/min being the recommended sampling rate.

When the working environment is suspected of containing dusts formed by comminution (quartz, asbestos, talc), a size selecting device (cyclone) is added to the sampling train to insure the collection of only respirable particles. The addition of the cyclone is a distinct advantage for XRD analysis since this produces a sample in which the particle size is known and a standard can be selected to match. A sampling setup with a cyclone and a closed face filter cassette is shown in Figure 2. Dust laden air entering the side of the cyclone must make an abrupt change in direction to be pulled through the filter. Larger particles impact on the sides of the cyclone and do not reach the filter.

Sampling procedures are often dependent on the method of sample preparation as well as the physical and chemical properties of the analyte. For most analytes that are collected by the above method the usual procedure is to ash the filter in either a low temperature plasma asher or a muffle furnace, disperse the residue in a suitable liquid such as isopropanol using ultrasonic agitation, and filter the suspension through a silver membrane filter. In addition, if the internal standard method is used, the chosen standard must be added to the residue suspension prior to filtration.

Regardless of the analytical procedure chosen for the analysis, several advantages are derived from the ashing/re-deposition process. These advantages include

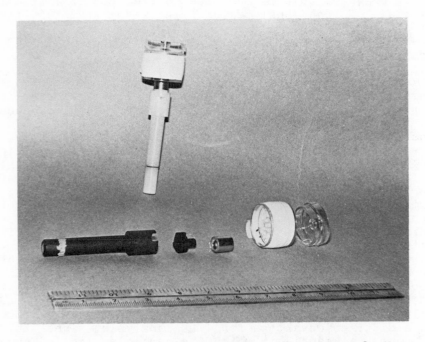

Figure 2. Personal sampling device consisting of a filter cassette and a 10-mm
nylon cyclone

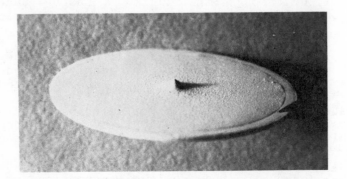

Figure 3. Illustration of a dust sample collected with a closed face cassette
showing dust deposition in the center of the filter

the elimination of most organic interferants, the formation of a uniform dust distribution on the filter, the low flat X-ray background of the silver filter (9,15) and the potential for making absorption corrections. However, if the analyte is sensitive to this preparative technique, e.g., chemically reactive during ashing, then an alternate sample collection method must be employed. Since a uniformily thick dust layer must be presented to the X-ray beam, the standard closed face filter cassette and cyclone cannot be used because of the tendency to accumulate a greater quantity of dust in the center than at the edge of the filter. Figure 3 is a good example of this problem. Although experimental evidence is lacking, the open face cassette tends to collect the required uniform dust layer. However, this collection device is more prone to abuse by the worker, is difficult to transport back to the laboratory without disturbing the uniform dust layer, and does not collect the respirable fraction.

When samples are collected with an open face filter cassette and analyzed directly, the internal standard method is not amenable to the analysis. Henslee and Guerra (16) developed a procedure for direct analysis of quartz on polyvinyl chloride filters; however, the procedure did not allow for absorption corrections. Allen, Samimi, Ziskind and Weil (17) also analyzed for quartz directly on organic membrane filters. Their method of determining matrix absorption corrections is based on the percent attentuation of the sample background compared to the background of the standards. Altree-Williams (18) modified the substrate standard method to accommodate samples collected directly on Nuclepore filters. Matrix absorption was accounted for by mounting a clean silver membrane filter beneath the Nuclepore filter. The absorption correction was then determined as described previously. In agreement with Altree-Williams, preliminary experiments in this laboratory suggested that this procedure is viable for the measurement of samples which cannot be treated by the standard preparative techniques, e.g., organic solids.

Standards Preparation

There are two basic laboratory methods for the preparation of filter standards--dust generation and the liquid suspension technique. Dust generation has a distinct advantage because of the ability to produce atmospheres similar to the workplace which can then be sampled using standard techniques. Equipment for dust generation can be as simple as the apparatus described by Leroux (19) or as sophisticated as that shown in Figure 4. This apparatus consists of a Wright Dust Feeder (20), a charge neutralizer and a dust chamber fitted with an exhaust manifold. The attachment of sampling devices to the manifold permits the collection of the generated dust on the membrane filters. A set of filter standards are prepared by varying the sampling times and the concentration of the dust in the chamber. Although dust generation may appear relatively straight forward, the technique requires considerable expertise and does not exactly match the treatment of field samples; hence, this procedure is not generally applicable in a routine analytical laboratory.

For the liquid suspension technique, a weighed quantity of the standard (particle size < 10 µm) is dispersed in a suitable liquid such as isopropanol. For most applications, suspensions in the range 10-50 mg/L are adequate. Filter calibration standards are easily prepared by pipetting aliquots of the suspension and filtering through a 0.45 µm silver membrane filter; however, classical analytical techniques must be modified when dealing with suspensions. During the pipetting operation, the aliquot must be brought up to the mark. If the suspension is treated as a solution, it is possible, due to settling within the pipette, that a highly concentrated drop of suspension will be lost when the pipette is adjusted to the mark from above. To facilitate the preparation of a uniform dust layer, a small volume of the suspending liquid (isopropanol) is added to the filtration apparatus prior to the addition of the aliquot. Vacuum is not applied until the aliquot has been added and all washings of the filtration apparatus have been accomplished.

In order to obtain a uniform suspension, the standard must be ground to a particle size < 10 µm. This can be achieved using a liquid nitrogen "freezer" mill and sieving the ground material using either dry or wet sieving. For compounds which tend to agglomerate during dry sieving, the wet sieving technique of Kupel (21) is preferable. To insure complete dispersal of the solid throughout the suspending liquid, an ultrasonic bath or probe is essential.

There has been considerable concern among XRD researchers on the errors which may result from pipeting aliquots from a suspension, errors which could

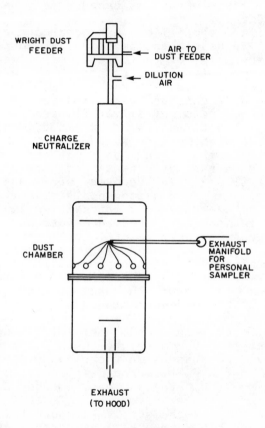

Figure 4. Dust generation system: the Wright dust feeder introduces dust into the air stream at a constant rate to produce test atmospheres.

significantly affect the overall precision and accuracy
of the method. Henslee and Guerra (16) weighed their
filters before and after deposition of the standard.
Of 30 filters, 84% agreed with dilution data to within
± 12 µg. Furthermore, calibration curves based on
weight data did not show any better precision than
those based on liquid suspension data. These authors
concluded that it would be advantageous to invest time
in multiple determinations based solely on the liquid
suspension data.
        A similar comparison has been conducted in this
laboratory. We have been specifically concerned that
the capillary tip of the pipette might generate poor
precision by promoting the formation of agglomerates.
To test for effects on the accuracy and precision,
three different techniques were used for placing pure
talc on three sets of silver filters. In the first
technique samples of talc were weighed, suspended in
isopropanol, and the entire suspension filtered through
the silver filters. In the second and third
techniques, a transfer pipette and a transfer pipette
with the capillary tip removed were used to draw
aliquots from a suspension containing 1000 µg/mL of
talc. The average talc peak intensities and associated
standard deviations were used to assess and compare the
precision and accuracy of the three methods.
Statistical tests showed that the precision and
accuracy attained with either pipette is the same as
that found with the weighed samples, demonstrating that
pipettes can be used to remove aliquots from
suspensions with concentrations as high as 1000 µg/mL
(22).
        Haartz, Bolyard and Abell (23) used atomic
absorption spectrophotometry to check filter standards
prepared by the suspension technique. Zinc oxide was
"spiked" on DM-800 filters and quantitated by AAS and
XRD. Results from these measurements are shown in
Table II. An average deviation of 2.1% was found
between the two techniques. Although this data does
give a considerable degree of confidence to the use of
the suspension procedure for standards preparation,
additional data for other analytes is needed for
conclusive proof.

Measurement and Data Analysis

        There are two methods for experimentally measuring
the diffracted intensity: peak height and peak area.
Klug and Alexander (24) have noted that peak heights
can only be used when they are known to

TABLE II

Comparison of XRD and AAS Results
For Zinc Oxide on Filters

Nominal Value µg	AAS Results µg (a)	XRD Results µg (a)	Percent Diff.
250	250.7	249.3	0.5
400	383.0	367.7	4.0
475	473.3	467.7	1.3
700	689.0	683.3	0.8
925	928.0	891.3	4.0

(a) Values reported are the average of
three samples.

be proportional to the corresponding integrated intensities. Furthermore, peak width and consequently peak height are a function of crystallite size and lattice imperfection. Thus, for samples generated in the workplace where these effects could be significant, it is essential that integrated intensities be measured.

Regardless of which quantitative procedure is chosen, i.e., internal standard or substrate standard, the measurement of the analyte profile is identical. Typically, filter samples contain light dust loadings, generally a maximum of two mg total dust, and the expected analyte weight may typically be less than 500 µg. To precisely measure the integrated intensity at this level, considerably longer counting times are required than might ordinarily be employed in XRD analysis. Experimentally, intensity measurements are usually made in one of two ways. The usual approach utilizes a scaler/timer to accumulate the diffracted radiation as the profile is continuously scanned. Alternatively, using a computer controlled diffractometer, integrated intensities are easily obtained by step scanning through the analyte profile. A counting rate of 10 sec per $0.02°$ 2θ step $(0.12°/min)$ is typical. With the exception of chrysotile, which has a very broad primary peak, the typical analyte requires step scanning through a 2θ range of $1.0-1.5°$ which requires approximately 15-20 minutes of analysis time. For chrysotile, which has a rather broad primary profile (22), the analysis time increases to approximately one hour. While it is possible to reduce the analysis time somewhat, there will be a consequent loss in sensitivity.

To account for absorption effects, an additional measurement is required. With the internal standard method, the profile for the internal standard must be measured for both calibration standards and samples. The rather small quantity of analyte present in the sample requires the addition of a similar quantity of internal standard (~ 200 μg) necessitating the measurement of the standards profile under essentially the same conditions as that of the analyte. Consequently, the internal standard method requires an additional measurement time approximately equal to that of the analyte. Under conditions noted above, this would amount to approximately thirty minutes total analysis time per sample.

In the substrate standard method the absorption effect is determined using the transmittance ratio ($T = I_{Ag}/I^0_{Ag}$). The determination of the transmittance involves additional measurements, i.e., step scanning over the silver profile, to obtain I_{Ag} and I^0_{Ag}. I_{Ag} is measured for each filter sample and I^0_{Ag} can be obtained several ways as discussed below. These additional measurements can be performed very quickly compared to the more lengthy measurements of the internal standard because the silver peak is quite intense. A step scan of the silver diffraction profile plus background counting time can be accomplished in about two minutes with better than 1% precision.

Abell, et.al. (25) considered several procedures for determining I^0_{Ag}. The simplest, an averaging method, involves one additional measurement for each sample and standard. Samples and standards are prepared using filters from the same box; I^0_{Ag} is determined for each filter by step scanning through the silver 100 line after the diffraction profile of the analyte is measured. Standards having less than 200 μg of material are essentially "clean" silver filters for absorption purposes; therefore, the diffracted intensities determined for these standards are essentially I^0_{Ag} values. The average of the individual I^0_{Ag} values is an estimate of I^0_{Ag} for an individual filter within a given box. An RSD of approximately 4% was found when this procedure was used to determine T (25).

There are two "single filter" methods for determining T. One involves measuring I^0_{Ag} on a clean filter before depositing the sample and measuring I_{Ag} and analyte intensities. The other involves measuring the analyte and silver (I_{Ag}) intensities on a dust laden filter and then measuring I^o_{Ag} on the reverse side. The latter approach was first proposed by Leroux (14). Thatcher (26) found a large difference in silver intensity from the two sides of clean filters and adopted the former method. Altree-Williams (27) also adopted the former method after finding a 7% RSD in intensities from different filters. The large differences found by these researchers disagree with that found for the smallest pore size (0.45 μm) silver filters by Abell et al. (25). They also found the front reverse method to have slightly better precision than the averaging method.

The following example illustrates a typical application of an absorption correction calculation. A dust sample containing 135 μg chrysotile asbestos and 4365 μg talc was deposited on a silver membrane filter. The net diffracted intensity for chrysotile when compared to an established calibration curve indicated only 88 μg present. Comparison of the sample's silver diffracted intensity (I_{Ag} = 42454 counts) to the established average value (I^o_{Ag} = 59379 counts) indicated that an absorption effect was present. From this intensity data the transmittance, ($T = I_{Ag}/I^o_{Ag}$), was determined to be 0.713. T can then be determined either by solving Eq. 1 or from a table of correction factors which can be prepared before hand either manually or by computer. In this case, T was 1.6. Thus, the corrected weight of chrysotile was 138 μg in excellent agreement with the amount "spiked" on the filter.

Proponents of the internal standard procedure have questioned the validity of the substrate standard method to adequately correct for matrix absorption. Leroux and coworkers (11,13,14) have presented data which support the method; in addition, several measurements were performed in this laboratory to verify the validity of the method (22). Mixtures of chrysotile in talc (1-7%) were prepared and various quantities "spiked" on silver filters. Table III illustrates the results obtained after correcting for matrix absorption as compared with the uncorrected data. Overall, there is excellent agreement between the corrected weight and the "spiked" weight.

As is the case for any quantitative analysis scheme, the precision and accuracy of the results depends significantly on the calibration standards. Because the quantities of dust to be measured correspond with the lower end of the instrumental range, long counting times, as previously noted, are

TABLE III

QUANTITATIVE MEASUREMENT OF CHRYSOTILE
USING CORRECTED & UNCORRECTED INTENSITIES

Percent Chrysotile in Talc	Uncorrected Weight	Actual Weight	Corrected Weight
7	151	175	188
7	118	140	139
7	93	105	106
5	93	125	119
7	67	70	74
7	60	63	62
7	46	49	49
7	28	28	28
5	93	125	119
5	75	100	99
5	60	75	77
5	35	50	44
5	33	40	39
5	26	30	31
3	113	180	191
3	88	135	138
3	63	90	87
3	56	72	71
3	45	54	55
3	37	45	44
3	31	36	36
1	61	150	168
1	49	100	102
1	42	70	78
1	34	50	52
1	23	30	27
7	93	105	106

necessary to compensate to some extent for the increased degree of imprecision. Thus, several filter calibration standards at each level must be prepared to obtain the best calibration curve. A linear regression analysis of the net intensity vs weight of standard data helps to insure the best precision.

Of the several parameters associated with an analytical method, detection limit is a very important but often a little understood parameter. In X-ray powder diffraction the detection limit is defined as the amount of material which will produce a net intensity that is equal to three times the standard deviation of the background as measured over a time period equal to that used in measuring the corresponding peak (28). It cannot be emphasized too strongly that the detection limit is useful only in ascertaining an analyte's presence with a reasonable degree of confidence. Quantitation is generally impossible at this level. In addition, the range of the calibration curve between the detection limit and the lowest measured standard is a "gray area". Measurements made in this region are based essentially on extrapolation of the calibration curve so that results must be considered as unreliable.

Matrix Interferences

Quantitative analysis of field samples must, of course, be performed under identical conditions to those used in analyzing the standards. Prior to the actual analysis, a powder pattern of a bulk sample such as rafter dust, an area sample, or a heavily loaded filter is obtained to determine information about the matrix. This information may necessitate some modification to the analytical method, such as quantitatively measuring the secondary peak because of a matrix interference with the primary peak. Such a modification usually results in poorer sensitivity because of the reduced intensity of the secondary peak.

The number of compounds with profiles that overlap the primary analyte profile are potentially very large, but the number of compounds which are potential interferences in occupational health usually depends on the industry in which the analyte is collected. Altree-Williams (18) collected samples at several industries where quartz and kaolinite or feldspar/mica

TABLE IV

Matrix Interferences

Analyte	Interference
Quartz	Mica, biotite, potash, feldspars, silimanite, zircon, graphite, iron carbide, lead sulfate
Zinc Oxide	α-iron oxide, $(NH_4)_3 ZnCl_5$, $(NH_4)_2 Zn(SO_4)_2 \cdot 6H_2O$, Zn
Chrysotile	Chlorite, antigorite, lizardite, anthophyllite

were present. He did not find these substances to present an interference to the quartz XRD analysis. Freedman, et. al. (29) analyzed coal dusts which contained clay minerals using infrared absorption and XRD. They noted good agreement between the two techniques particularly when the samples were ashed prior to analysis. Some potential interferences are listed in Table IV for the quartz, chrysotile and zinc oxide primary peaks. If organic interferences are present, they can usually be eliminated in the ashing step. For the case where there is significant overlap, little can be done unless the analyte has a secondary line of sufficient intensity for quantitation. For example, 20 µg of quartz can be quantitated using the primary peak; with the secondary peak, only 100 µg can be quantitated.

If the secondary or other less intense peaks are not usable and the degree of overlap is not too severe, two other approaches are possible. The simpler approach is to use longer wavelength radiation. Changing from the widely used copper radiation (1.54A) to chromium radiation (2.29A) allows a slight improvement in resolution. Figure 5 illustrates the improved resolution of zircon interference with quartz. This approach would only be practical for the situation where samples with a similar interference were regularly received. The second, and more complex, approach to the problem is the use of deconvolution or peak stripping techniques. This approach is being actively pursued by a number of researchers and shows promise as a viable solution to the interference

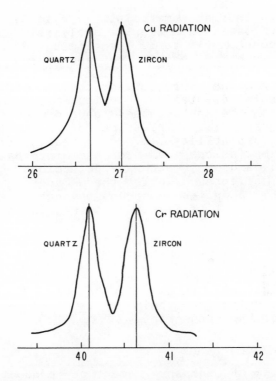

Figure 5. Effect of radiation wavelength on quartz and zircon profiles. The two profiles are better resolved with a chromium target tube ($\lambda = 0.229$ nm) than with a copper tube ($\lambda = 0.154$ nm).

problem. Thus, a combination of radiation type, a
deconvolution computer program and a judicious choice
of X-ray optics may solve many of the interference
problems.

Conclusion

The trend in industrial hygiene work is to
identify the particular species responsible for an
occupational health problem, although assessment of
exposures to inorganic materials previously has most
often been based on elemental analysis. When a solid
inorganic compound is to be identified and quantified,
X-ray diffraction should be among the approaches
considered. This paper has outlined the use of X-ray
powder diffraction as a tool for the identification and
quantitation of crystalline particulates. It has been
shown that the substrate standard method is the
preferred quantitative procedure for several reasons:
(1) easy adaptability to most analytes; (2) fast
analysis time (as compared to the internal standard
procedure); and (3) accurate determination of matrix
absorption effects. While there are a number of
reasons why a given compound may not be amenable to
this technique, it is likely that the list of analytes
will be added to in the future.

Acknowledgement

The authors wish to thank Dr. Janet C. Haartz and
Mr. John L. Holtz for their review and constructive
criticism of the manuscript.

Disclaimer

Mention of company names or products does not
constitute endorsement by the National Institute for
Occupational Safety and Health.

Abstract

X-Ray powder diffraction (XRD) has assumed
increasing importance as an analytical technique for
the identification and quantitation of contaminants in
the workplace environment. Traditionally, the major
use of this technique has been for the analysis of free
silica, talc and asbestos; however, because of the
increasing need for the quantitation of chemical

compounds as opposed to elements, the importance of XRD in the analytical laboratory has grown considerably. This paper will reveiw the application of XRD to the analysis of dust contaminants collected on membrane filters. The advantages and disadvantages of the internal and substrate (external) standard procedures are also discussed. The latter method, currently in use at NIOSH, is discussed in detail emphasizing the use of the silver membrane filter for re-deposition of the dust sample and for the correction of matrix absorption. This analytical procedure has been applied to the analysis of free silica, zinc oxide, zirconium oxide and chrysotile.

Literature Cited

1. Pritchard, J.A., "A Guide to Industrial Respiratory Protection," DHEW Publication No. (NIOSH) 76-189, p. 201, National Instiute for Occupational Safety and Health, Cincinnati, Ohio, 45226, 1976.

2. "Criteria for a Recommended Standard...Occupational Exposure to Chromic Acid," DHEW Publication No. (HSM-11021), National Institue for Occupational Safety and Health, Cincinnati, Ohio, 45226, 1973.

3. "Criteria for a Recommended Standard...Occupational Exposure to Inorganic Nickel," DHEW Publication No. (NIOSH) 77-164, National Institute for Occupational Safety and Health, Cincinnati, Ohio, 45226, 1977.

4. "Criteria for a Recommened Standard...Occupational Exposure to Zinc oxide," DHEW Publication No. (NIOSH) 76-104, National Institute for Occuptional Safety and Health, Cincinnati, Ohio, 45226, 1976.

5. Criteria for a Recommended Standard...Occupational Exposure to Sodium Hydroxide," DHEW Publication No. (NIOSH) 76-105, National Institute for Occupational Safety and Health, Cincinnati, Ohio, 45226, 1976.

6. Johnson, G.G., Jr., Joint Committee on Powder Diffraction Standards.

7. Lennox, D. and Leroux, J., Ind. Hyg. and Occ. Med., (1953).

8. Taylor, D.G., "NIOSH Manual of Analytical Methods," 2nd ed., DHEW Publication No. (NIOSH) 77-157,

National Insitute for Occupational Safety and
Health, Cincinnati, Ohio, 45226, 1977.

9. Bumsted, H.E., Amer. Ind. Hyg. Assoc. J., (1973),
   34, 150.

10. Alexander, L. and Klug H.P., Anal. Chem., (1948),
    20, 886.

11. Leroux, J., Lennox, D.H., and Kay, K., Anal. Chem.
    (1953), 25, 740.

12. Williams, P.O., Anal. Chem., (1959), 31, 1842.

13. Leroux, J. and Powers, C.A., Staub-Reinhalt Luft
    (Eng. ed.), (1969), 29, 26.

14. Leroux, J., Davey, A.B.C. and Parlard, A., Amer.
    Ind. Hyg. Assoc. J. (1973), 34, 409.

15. Peters, E.T., "Evaluation of the National Insti-
    tute for Occupational Safety and Health X-Ray
    Diffraction Method for the Determination of
    Free Silica in Respirable Dust," Final Report,
    Contract No. CDC 99-7451, May 1976.

16. Henslee, W.W. and Guerra, R.E., Advan. X-Ray
    Anal., (1977), 20, 139.

17. Allen, G.C., Samini, R., Ziskind, M., amd Weil,
    H., Amer. Ind. Hyg. Assoc. J., (1974), 35,
    711.

18. Altree-Williams, S., Lee, J., and Mezin, N.V.,
    Ann. Occup. Hyg. (1977), 20, 109.

19. Leroux, J., Staub-Reinhalt, (1969), 29, 33.

20. Wright, B.M., J. Sci. Instr., (1950), 27, 12.

21. Kupel, R.E., Kinser, R.E., and Mauer, P.A.,
    Amer. Ind. Hyg. Assoc. J., (1966), 29, 364.

22. Lange, B.A. and Haartz, J.C., Anal. Chem.,
    (1979), 51, 520.

23. Haartz, J.C., Bolyard, M.L. and Abell, M.T.,
    American Industrial Hygiene Assoc. Conf.,
    Minneapolis, MN., (1975), Paper No. 145.

24. Klug, H.P. and Alexander, L.E., "X-Ray Diffraction Procedures for Polycrystalline and Amorphous Materials," John Wiley and Sons, New York, NY, 2nd ed., 1974, p. 358.

25. Abell, M.T., Lange, B.A., Dollberg, D.D., and Hornung, R., To be presented at the 28th Annual Conference on Applications of X-Ray Analysis, Denver, Colorado.

26. Thatcher, Mine Enforcement and Safety Administration Information Report No. 1021, (1975).

27. Altree-Williams, S., Anal. Chem. (1977), 49, 429.

28. Hertoys, P and DeVries, J.L., Conference On X-Ray Spectroscopy, Swansea, 1966.

29. Freedman, R.W., Toma, S.Z. and Lang, H.W. Amer. Ind. Hyg. Assoc. J., (1974), 35, 411.

30. Schutz, A., and Wortowitz, H.J., Staub-Reinhalt Luft, (1973), 33, 445.

RECEIVED October 31, 1979.

Determination of Respirable Quartz by Infrared Spectroscopy with a Multiple Internal Reflectance Accessory

RUSSELL BROXTERMAN

Kansas Department of Health and Environment, Office of Laboratories and Research, Forbes Building 740, Topeka, KS 66620

Subsequent to the passage of the Occupational Safety and Health Act, there has been an increasing awareness among both employers and employees of occupational health hazards in the workplace environment. Correspondingly, there has also been an increase in the demand placed upon our agency and others to evaluate worksites for the presence of occupational health hazards and to recommend control measures when appropriate. In order to provide the analytical support necessary to accommodate an increasing number of requests for evaluations relating specifically to the hazard resulting from exposure to quartz in airborne dusts of respirable size, it became readily apparent that an analytical procedure would have to be developed.

In considering the three most prominent analytical techniques for quartz, i.e. colorimetric, infrared (IR) and x-ray diffraction, it was possible to immediately exclude the x-ray diffraction procedure for use because the instrument was not available and the cost of purchasing such a unit was considered to be prohibitive in view of the relatively small number of samples anticipated. The Talvite (1) colorimetric procedure has previously been employed without particular success. This method was generally considered to be unacceptably tedious, time-consuming and of questionable accuracy. For these reasons and because the infrared instrumentation was available, it was decided to focus our preliminary efforts on the development of an infrared procedure.

Although there are certain shortcomings involved in the use of any infrared technique, similar shortcomings exist in the use of colorimetric and x-ray procedures as well. For an overall review of the probelms of major analytical techniques for quartz one is referred to a critical literature review by Anderson (2). He indicated two of the major problems in the use of an IR procedure is the "effects of particle size" and "mutual line interferences". Generally the 800 cm^{-1} band of quartz is used for infrared analysis because of its sensitivity and because this segment of the IR spectra is relatively free of the common interferences expected from other mineral components of dust samples. The use of the

0-8412-0539-6/80/47-120-067$05.00/0

800 cm^{-1} band does not totally eliminate the problem of mutual
line interferrences, therefore, some knowledge of the mineral content of dust samples is necessary to assure the absence of inter-
ferring components. The sensitivity of this band, however, is
affected by particle size as has been demonstrated by Tuddenham
and Lyon (3) and others. Gade and Reisner (4) in their demonstration of this effect, have also shown that a determination of
the particle size of an unknown can be made by using the relationship between particle size and the quotients formed of the optical
density of each of the two maxima and the minimum of the quartz
doublet at 800/780 cm$_1^{-1}$. The effect of particle size can then be
negated by using standards with approximately the same particle
size as that of an unknown.

To achieve the sensitivity necessary to analyze the small
quantities of quartz collected on filters by personal respirable
dust sampling the use of Multiple Internal Reflectance (MIR) Spectroscopy was considered. According to Gilby, Cassels and Wilks
(5), internal reflectance spectroscopy "depends for its existence
on the very small penetration of a light wave beyond a totally
internal reflecting interface. If a sample is placed in contact
with this surface, the reflected beam is attenuated at the characteristic absorption frequencies of the sample". For a detailed
discussion of the theory of internal reflection spectroscopy reference number six (6) should be consulted. They further indicated
that MIR spectroscopy was a sensitive micro sampling technique and
lends itself to the analysis of solid samples such as dust on
membrane filters but cautioned that hard particles should be ground
so as to prevent damage to the crystal. Hannah and Dwyer (7) concluded that membrane filters, because of their surface retention
ability, not only accomplish a separation of particulate material
from a fluid media but also permitted a nearly ideal presentation
of the sample to an Attenuated Total Reflection crystal.

Using the background information summarized above, a procedure was developed in which the respirable dust samples were
ashed, taken up in a suspension and redeposited on a membrane
filter. The redeposited membrane filter was used to present the
sample to the MIR cyrstal. The cyclone sampler used for collecting respirable dust selectively collects particles less than 10
microns in diameter and no effect was made to grind the particles
as no problem in damaging the crystal was encountered.

Experimental

Apparatus. A Perkin-Elmer Model 467 infrared spectrophotometer was used under the analytical conditions stated in Table I.
A Mutiple Internal Reflection Accessory for use with Perkin-Elmer
infrared spectrophotometers was used to introduce the sample to
the IR beam. To correct for losses in energy transmittance through
the sample beam resulting from the use of the MIR Accessory, a
comb-type reference beam attenuator was employed. A LFE Corpora-

tion Model LTA 302 Low temperature radio frequency asher was used
to ash samples.

Table I

INSTRUMENTAL OPERATING CONDITIONS FOR QUARTZ

Instrument: Perkin-Elmer Model 467
Scan Mode: Slow (50 cm^{-1}/min)
Time Constant: 2 (Pen Response Time 2.0)
Slit: Normal (1.7 cm_1 @ 800 cm^{-1})
Scan Range: 900 to 700 cm^{-1} (11.0 to 14.0 micro-
                                        meters)
Readout: Absorbance (On chart paper)
MIR Setting: 30° angle

Reagents. Standards were prepared with 15 micron Min-U-Sil
quartz. The hydrochloric acid and isopropanol were analytical reagent grade. A 0.5% Aerosol OT solution was prepared by diluting
a commercially prepared 25% Aerosol OT solution. Water was deionized and glass distilled. Filters used for redeposition were
MSA, 0.5 micron, 37mm, polyvinyl chloride (PVC), membrane filters.
The internal reflecting plate (crystal) was a Wilks and Barnes
KRS-5 crystal, 52.5 x 20 x 2mm, with 45° ends.

Procedures. Standards are prepared by filtering suspensions
of known amounts of quartz onto a membrane filter. The desired
amount of quartz is weighed on a micro electrobalance and transferred to a one liter pyrex reagent bottle to which 500 mls of
distilled water is added. The suspension is shaken vigorously and
placed in an ultrasonic bath for 15 minutes. Prior to pipetting;
the suspension is shaken vigorously for 30 seconds, placed on
counter and 10 mls of the suspension is immediately pipeted with a
blow-out serological pipet onto a membrane filter. The pipet is
rinsed well with a forced stream of 0.5% Aerosol OT solution from
from a plastic washbottle. A blank is also prepared using distilled water. The filter is placed in a 47mm Millipore petrislide
and allowed to dry. Drying time can be facilitated by placing on
top of an oven or warm place at about 40^oC.
Samples from the field are redeposited on membrane filters by
filtering a suspension of ashed sample. To ash field samples, the
filter is placed dust side down in a 50 ml pyrex beakers and placed
in a low-temperature radio frequency asher. The asher used has
two chambers and will accommodate eight beakers at one time. The
oxygen flow is set at 15 scc per minute. Samples are initially
ashed for 15 minutes at a RF wattage of 100 watts to prevent the
filter from curling due to high heat. The RF wattage is then increased to 250 watts and the sample is allowed to ash for an additional 30-45 minutes to eliminate any carbonaceous material. The
ash is treated with one milliliter of hydrochloric acid to elimi-

nate iron oxide; diluted to the 10 milliliter mark with distilled water and placed in a sonic bath for 30 minutes. (Dust samples containing iron oxide can result in an excessive loss of crystal reflectivity. The acid dissolution step may also reduce other contaminant interferences, but this effect has not been positively demonstrated.) The suspension is swirled and filtered through a membrane filter. The beaker is initially rinsed with distilled water, followed by rinsing with 0.5% Aerosol OT solution. The filter is allowed to dry.

A simple filtration device was made with the bottom portion and center ring of a three piece Millipore, 37mm, cassette filter holder. A Millipore filter support pad and a MSA, 37mm, 0.5 micron, PVC, membrane filter is placed, smooth side up, in the bottom portion and the center ring is pressed on. The filter is wetted with 5 mls of 0.5% Aerosol OT solution, vacumn is applied, and pressure is applied to the center ring to assure the assembly is tight. Several filtration devices can be made up to save time disassembling and reassembling before each filtration. It was found that the filtration device would fit firmly on a number 7 rubber stopper with a hole drilled in it. The rubber stopper was then placed in a 250 ml filtration flask with the cassette on top.

It is important that the sample be evenly deposited onto the filter. The center well of the filtration device will hold approximately five milliters; therefore, to assure even deposition, filtration is done as follows: the center well is filled; slight vacumn is applied then released; the center well is filled again being sure not to disturb the deposit on the filter; again vacumn is applied and released. This is continued until all of the standard or sample suspensions and their rinsings are filtered.

The MIR sampler holder is assembled essentially according to the manufacturers instruction for use with solid samples with a few additional steps. The clamping plate is placed on a table so that the cut-out for liquids is against the table top and the liquid sample ports are facing to the left. A piece of aluminum foil, cut the width of one of pressure pads and long enough to overlap the ends, is placed on one of the pressure pads. (If pad is not covered with foil, loss of crystal reflectivity will occur when the pad comes in contact with the crystal.) The pad, with foil, is placed on the plate centered under the crystal with the foil face up. To assure even pressure of the filter against the crystal, half of a 37mm Millipore support pad is placed on the foil covered pad with the curve part of the support pad facing right. One half of a membrane filter is placed on the support pad with the smooth side (dust-side) facing up. The crystal holder and crystal are placed down on the plate so that the holes in the crystal holder are centered over the holes in the plate. (Sample and pad should be centered under crystal.) The other half of the membrane filter is placed (dust-side down) through the cut-out of the crystal holder against the crystal. For easy alignment of the filter on the crystal; sight down the left side of the cut-out in

crystal holder and align straight portion of membrane filter directly under the edge. The other half of the support pad is placed
on the membrane filter. A small portion of the curved side of the
support pad will have to be cut off to fit through the cut-out of
the crystal holder. This is not necessary for the membrane filter
as it is flexible enough to place through the cut-out. A piece
of aluminum foil cut slightly less than the width and length of
the cut-out is placed on the support pad. The other pressure pad
is placed on the foil through the cut-out. Align the clamping
block so that the holes in the block are centered above the holes
in the crystal holder. Insert the screws and tighten each a small
amount as uniformly as possible. When finger tight, apply as much
force as can be exerted on each screw. This will aid in applying
good even pressure on the filters to assure a good crystal interface contact. Care should be taken when assembling filters in
sample holder so that they are placed on the same areas of the
crystal each time.

    For infrared analysis, each standard quartz filter or redepos-
ited sample filter is cut in half with surgical scissors and
placed on the 30° or desired angle setting of the MIR Accessory
base. The IR is adjusted to a scan setting of 750 cm^{-1} and the
reference beam attenuator is used to bring the transmittance level
to $90-100\%$. The filter is then scanned in duplicate from 900 to
700 cm^{-1}. The spectrum is recorded on absorbance chart paper.
The 800 cm^{-1} peak of the $800/780$ cm^{-1} quartz doublet is used for
measurement by the baseline method.

    After each filter is scanned the crystal may require cleaning.
Due to the toxicity of the KRS-5 crystal, it is left in the crystal holder at all times so as to avoid unnecessary handling as
well as, scratching or damaging the crystal. The crystal, in its
holder, is flushed with a forced stream of anhydrous isopropanol
from a plastic wash bottle. A cotton swab, soaked in isopropanol,
can be used to remove deposits on the crystal. This should be
done with very light rubbing as the KRS-5 crystal scratches very
easily.

Results-Discussion

    In Figure 1, the infrared absorbance spectrum of a blank MSA
filter, a, is compared directly with that of a prepared standard
filter, b, with 100 micrograms of 15 micron Min-U-Sil quartz deposited on it. To determine the absorbance of the 800 cm^{-1} peak
it is necessary to approximate a baseline as indicated by the
dotted line of spectrum 'b'. As an indication of sensitivity the
absorption of the 800 cm^{-1} peak is 0.19 Absorbance units.

    In Figure 2, the infrared absorbance spectrum of a redeposited
blank filter, a, is compared directly with that of a redeposited
field sample filter, b, which has a calculated 59 micrograms of
quartz on it. The original filter from a foundry had 0.222 milligrams of respirable dust on it. Figure 3 is the infrared absorb-

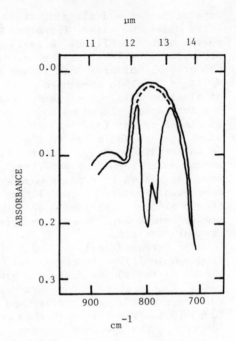

*Figure 1.   Absorbance spectra of quartz
          on MSA filter*

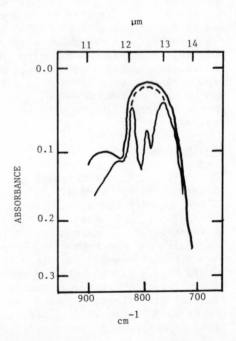

*Figure 2.   Absorbance spectra of rede-
posited respirable dust on filter*

ance spectrum of a redeposited filter which had a calculated
quartz content of 169 micrograms. The original filter from a
foundry had 1.103 milligrams of respirable dust on it. The spectrum, b, of Figure 2 provides a good baseline for absorption measurements of the 800 cm^{-1} peak. However, as the amount of dust increases, broad band spectral interferences began to show in the
850 cm^{-1} region as shown in Figure 3. With larger amounts of dust
on the filter the 800 cm^{-1} peak will eventually be masked by these
interferences. Although an adequate baseline line can be established from the spectrum shown in Figure 3; keeping the amount of
dust collected from 0.5 to 1 milligram will lessen this type of
interference. In the event the amount of dust on the field samples
is considered excessive, the "sample" filter can be cut in half or
appropriate sections and analysed separately.

Figure 4 is a spectrum of a filter from the Proficiency Analytical Testing Program (PAT) conducted by the National Institute
of Occupational Safety and Health (NIOSH) which contained 103 micrograms as determined by this lab. PAT filters are prepared with
2 mg of sodium silicate as a contaminant. A baseline approximation
as described for Figure 1 is not possible due to the interfering
peak at 845 cm^{-1}. When a spectrum of this type is encountered, a
line is drawn from the two minimums on either side of the quartz
doublet peak as illustrated by the dotted line in Figure 4.

When analyzing PAT filters it was observed that the quartz and
sodium silicate remained on the filter. This was determined by
analyzing the crystal after analyzing a PAT filter. No quartz peak
or contaminant peaks were noted. This was attributed to the use
of a wetting agent, Aerosol OT, in the preparation of Standard
Reference Filters (8). Apparently the Aerosol OT imparts a cohe-
sive quality resulting in the silica and dust staying on the filter. To demonstrate this, a single PAT filter containing 0.168
milligrams of quartz was subjected to six separate scans. Between
each scan the MIR sample holder was disassembled, and the crystal
cleaned and reassembled. The results are shown in Table II. No
significant difference was detected between first and last scan.

Table II

Standard Stability

Run Number	Absorbance @ 800 cm^{-1}
1	0.337
2	0.340
3	0.338
4	0.345
5	0.327
6	0.337

From the plot A_{800} (max)/A_{790} (min) versus particle size from

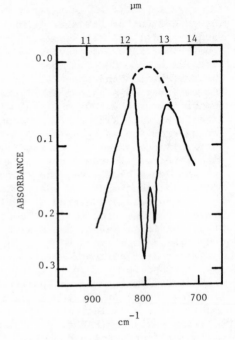

Figure 3. Absorbance spectra of redeposited respirable dust on filter

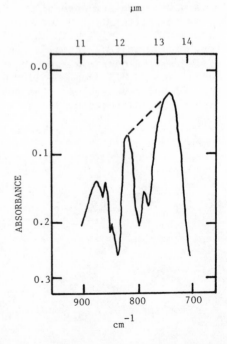

Figure 4. Absorbance spectra of PAT
filter

the work reported by Gade and Reisner ($\underline{4}$), the particle size of
the 15 micron Min-U-Sil quartz in Figure 1 is approximately 3.3
microns. For Figures 2 and 3 the particle size of the quartz is
approximately 2.3 and 2.7 microns respectively. Typically quartz
from field samples analysed by this lab are generally in the 2-3
micron particle size range. Tuddenham and Lyon ($\underline{3}$), in their study
to ascertain whether reproducible results could be obtained using
the 800 cm^{-1} quartz absorption, found that the absorbance varied
with particle size. From their plot of absorbance versus average
particle size, the absorbance is about the same in the 2-4.5 micron particle size range. Consequently, the 15 micron Min-U-Sil
quartz with an average particle size of 3.3 microns can be used as
a standard for samples which contain quartz of a particle size in
the range of 2-4.5 microns.

The linearity of a calibration curve is demonstrated by a typical calibration plot, Figure 5, of standard filters containing 10,
50, 100, 150, and 200 micrograms of quartz. A detectable peak
(2:1 peak height to noise ratio) was obtained for the 10 microgram
standard and is considered to be the minimum detectable limit.

A filter can be standardized against a calibration curve and
subsequently used as a single standard to determine quartz content
of other filters; provided appropriate quality control measures
are taken, i.e. the crystal should be checked after analyzing the
standard filter to determine if quartz was dislodged from filter
and a previously run sample should be included as a quality control sample.

The above technique is used for analyzing samples routinely in
this laboratory. Generally a filter with a concentration in the
range of 80 to 120 micrograms is used as a standardized filter.
The quantity of quartz on a sample filter is determined by multiplying the quantity of quartz on a standardized filter by the
absorbance of the 800 cm^{-1} peak of a sample filter divided by the
absorbance of the 800 cm^{-1} peak of the standardized filter. This
technique has been used to analyze 53 PAT filters and the results
are shown in Table III. Redeposition was not done due the similar
deposition technique used to prepare the Standard Reference Filters
in the PAT Program ($\underline{8}$). The first fourteen samples in Table III
were filters that had been retained by the lab from previous PAT
Rounds. The actual results on the rest were submitted in the PAT
Program to NIOSH. (PAT Filter Number S-35-2 has not been included
because half of the filter was initially analyzed backwards in the
MIR sample holder resulting in a quartz loss on the support pad.)
The % recovery was calculated based upon the PAT Geometric Mean.
An overall average percent recovery of 103.2% with a standard
deviation of 17.5% was obtained.

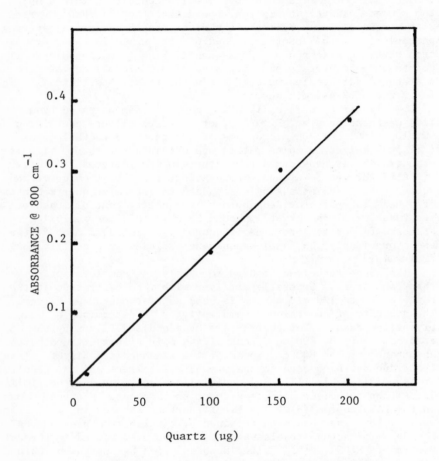

Figure 5.   *Calibration curve of 15-μ Min-U-Sil quartz*

Table III

Silica Results on PAT Filters

PAT Filter Number	PAT Geometric Mean, mg	MIR-IR Result, mg	% Recovery
S-30-2	.039	.022	56.4
S-30-3	.163	.159	97.5
S-30-4	.052	.046	88.5
S-32-1	.088	.090	102.3
S-32-2	.165	.168	101.8
S-32-3	.058	.041	70.7
S-32-4	.105	.113	107.6
S-33-1	.152	.155	102.0
S-33-2	.074	.068	91.9
S-33-3	.089	.092	103.4
S-33-4	.121	.139	114.9
S-34-2	.158	.155	98.1
S-34-3	.049	.039	79.6
S-34-4	.135	.128	94.8
S-35-1	.119	.133	111.8
S-35-3	.073	.088	120.5
S-35-4	.055	.053	96.4
S-36-1	.038	.038	100.0
S-36-2	.091	.101	111.0
S-36-3	.063	.075	119.0
S-36-4	.106	.109	102.8
S-37-1	.085	.086	101.2
S-37-2	.131	.158	120.6
S-37-3	.106	.117	110.4
S-37-4	.059	.057	96.6
S-38-1	.092	.123	139.1
S-38-2	.050	.050	100.0
S-38-3	.112	.126	112.5
S-38-4	.073	.079	108.2

continued

Table III

Silica Results on PAT Filters (cont.)

PAT Filter Number	PAT Geometric Mean, mg	MIR-IR Result, mg	% Recovery
S-39-1	.110	.129	117.3
S-39-2	.055	.064	116.4
S-39-3	.032	.031	96.9
S-39-4	.084	.080	95.2
S-40-1	.133	.121	91.0
S-40-2	.115	.087	75.7
S-40-3	.082	.051	62.2
S-40-4	.054	.039	72.2
S-41-1	.105	.091	86.7
S-41-2	.077	.084	109.1
S-41-3	.112	.096	85.7
S-41-4	.064	.056	87.5
S-42-1	.082	.093	113.4
S-42-2	.085	.103	121.2
S-42-3	.127	.121	95.3
S-42-4	.065	.073	112.3
S-43-1	.116	.132	113.8
S-43-2	.065	.073	112.3
S-43-3	.093	.131	140.9
S-43-4	.113	.133	117.7
S-44-1	.115	.159	138.3
S-44-2	.081	.084	103.7
S-44-3	.084	.100	119.0
S-44-4	.113	.142	125.7

Average	103.2
Standard Deviation	17.5

Conclusions

Experimental work has shown that the analysis of quartz in respirable dust by Infrared spectroscopy using a Multiple Internal Reflectance Accessory is a viable technique that is sensitive, accurate and simple to perform. Linearity of a calibration curve from 0 to 200 micrograms has been demonstrated. A detection limit of approximately ten micrograms of quartz was obtained. An accuracy of $\pm$ 35% at a 95% confidence level was demonstrated by data obtained from participation in the NIOSH PAT Program.

Suggested improvements in the procedure have also been recognized. The use of a second MIR Accessory in the reference beam with a blank membrane filter in place will provide a compensated spectrum and may improve the approximation of the baseline. Greater sensitivity might have been achieved had the area of contact between the sample and the crystal face been increased. While the entire procedure appears quite promising, collaborative studies are needed to positively confirm the reliability of the method when used for the analysis of varied field samples.

LITERATURE CITED

1   Talvite, N. A., J. Am. Ind. Hyg. Assoc., (1964), 25, 169.

2   Anderson, P. L., J. Am. Ind. Hyg. Assoc., (1975), 36, 767.

3   Tuddenham, W. M., and Lyon, R. J., Anal. Chem., (1960), 32, 1630.

4   Gade, M. and Reisner, M., Pneumoconiosis Proc. Internatl. Conference, (1969), 3, 636.

5   Gilby, A. C., Cassels, J., and Wilks, P. A., Jr., Appl. Spectrosc., (1970), 24, 539.

6   Harrick, N. J., "Internal Reflection Spectroscopy", Interscience Publishers (1967).

7   Hannah, R. W. and Dwyer, J. L., Anal. Chem., (1964), 36, 2341.

8   Generation of Standard Reference Silica Filter Samples for Analysis by Colorimetric Methods, Method Number CRL-001, Chemical Reference Laboratory, NIOSH, Issued 2-5-74.

RECEIVED October 15, 1979.

High Performance Liquid Chromatography and Its Application to Occupational Health Chemistry

JAMES H. NELSON and JOHN C. HOLT

UBTL Division, University of Utah Research Institute, Salt Lake City, UT 84108

PATRICK A. HEARTY

OSHA Analytical Laboratory, U.S. Department of Labor,
390 Wakara Way, Salt Lake City, UT 84108

Health hazards, both actual and potential, associated with the use of chemical compounds and mixtures in the working environment have recently received increasing attention. Activities related to the assessment of such hazards experienced significant impetus with the passage of the Williams-Steiger Occupational Safety and Health Act of 1970 (Public Law 91-596). Many subsequent events have focused on the role of occupational exposure to various chemicals with respect to the health of members of the nation's work force.

One very important aspect of research directed to the characterization of health effects involves appropriate monitoring of worker exposure to specific chemical substances. For a number of reasons, the technology required to meet the demands of recent monitoring efforts has markedly increased in both complexity and scope. These include the following: (1) There is a continuing expansion of both the quantity and variety of chemical materials used in connection with occupational pursuits. This expansion involves not only the primary chemicals used in a specific process; it also includes minor components and byproducts generated by the process itself. Accordingly, innovative analytical methods for monitoring an increasing array of chemical compounds are required to support current industrial hygiene efforts. In addition to this expanded scope, the complexity of typical analytical problems encountered in occupational health chemistry is also increasing because of the greater number of individual constituents to be resolved and analyzed from a given sample matrix. (2) It has become evident that, in some instances, the presence of even very low levels of specific chemicals in the workplace may represent significant health problems. Such instances may involve, for example, catalysts, trace contaminants in major process materials or products, or low concentrations of undesirable byproducts. The observation that carcinogenesis may possibly result from only limited exposure to extremely low levels of biologically active chemicals contributes to the current emphasis on the study of

the possible effects of low-level occupational exposure. The
requirement for quantitation of substances at very low concentrations imposes stringent demands on the sensitivity specifications of both sample collection and analytical procedures.
(3) The potential for either antagonistic or potentiating
effects for combinations of chemical compounds, in connection
with their ultimate biological activity and the related health
problems, emphasizes the importance of developing analytical
procedures which can be used to quantitate levels of specific
compounds in the presence of a wide variety of chemical substances, many of which may be present at very high concentrations.

In view of the preceding observations, it is obvious that
problems encountered by the modern industrial hygienist and the
attendant analyst are increasing in complexity and scope.
Sample collection procedures and accompanying analytical methods
must be developed for an expanding array of chemical compounds
and mixtures, methodology must be adaptable to a wide variety of
sample matrices, sensitivity levels must be lowered, and the
resolving power and specificity of applied techniques must be
improved continually such that complex mixtures, including those
which involve only a small quantity of analyte in the presence
of very large quantities of potential interfering substances,
may be effectively characterized.

Obviously, several types of analytical chemistry instrumentation are available for application to these problems. Of
the instrumental techniques currently in use for laboratory
analysis of industrial hygiene samples, perhaps the most rapidly
growing is that of high performance liquid chromatography (HPLC).
Several advantages are inherent in the use of HPLC. Of primary
importance is the fact that it may be applied successfully to
the analysis of a wide variety of compounds derived from diverse
types of sample media such as those which are essential in
industrial hygiene monitoring. For example, sample matrices for
which HPLC analyses have been effected include: filters, solid
sorbents, impinger and bubbler solutions, wipe samples, several
types of bulk materials, and biological samples (e.g., blood,
urine, and tissue). Many HPLC devices are now equipped with
detectors which enable one to determine various analytes at
nanogram and subnanogram quantities (1, 2, 3, 4). Thus, the
sensitivity of the method is an advantage for several types of
analyses. An additional advantage is the specificity which may
be achieved by appropriate selection from the diverse types of
detectors available for HPLC (1, 3). Compounds which are not
readily adaptable to gas chromatographic (GC) analysis due to
insufficient volatility or to other factors are candidates for
determination by HPLC. This is an important observation, in
view of the fact that it has been estimated that (without
derivatization or modification) only 20-25% of the known organic
compounds may be analyzed efficiently by GC (1). For example,

ionic species, high molecular weight compounds, and substances
which are labile at high temperatures are not generally amenable
to determination by GC. Since HPLC is not limited by analyte
volatility or thermal instability, analysis of such compounds
may be achieved by this method. It is also important to note
that very difficult chromatographic separations are frequently
more easily pursued by HPLC than by conventional GC. This may
be attributed in part to the observation that, with HPLC, lower
temperatures are used, and that two effective chromatographic
phases, rather than one, are employed for interaction with
analyte molecules.

Frequently industrial hygiene analyses require the identification of unknown sample components. One of the most widely
employed methods for this purpose is coupled gas chromatography/
mass spectrometry (GC/MS). With respect to interface with mass
spectrometry, HPLC presently suffers a disadvantage in comparison to GC because instrumentation for routine application of
HPLC/MS techniques is not available in many analytical chemistry
laboratories (3). It is, however, anticipated that HPLC/MS
systems will be more readily available in the future (5, 6, 7, 8).
HPLC will then become an even more powerful analytical tool for
use in occupational health chemistry. It is also important to
note that conventional HPLC is presently adaptable to effective
compound identification procedures other than direct mass
spectrometry interface. These include relatively simple procedures for the recovery of sample components from column eluate
as well as stop-flow techniques. Following recovery, a separated
sample component may be subjected to, for example, direct probe
mass spectrometry; infra-red (IR), ultraviolet (UV), and visible
spectrophotometry; and fluorescence spectroscopy. The stopped
flow technique may be used to obtain a fluorescence or a UV
absorbance spectrum of a particular component as it elutes from
the column. Such spectra can frequently be used to determine
specific properties of the component for assistance in compound
identification (9).

The factors discussed in the preceding paragraphs indicate
the fundamental importance which HPLC procedures are likely to
occupy in connection with the pursuit of occupational health
chemistry in the future. Accordingly, a consideration of HPLC
from this viewpoint is timely. This document provides a brief
summary of general HPLC methodology as well as a description of
specific procedures for the analysis of selected compounds or
groups of compounds which are currently important in occupational health hazard research studies and evaluations.

Description of General High Performance Liquid Chromatographic Techniques

HPLC technology has recently experienced a period of very
rapid growth to the extent that, along with GC, conventional LC,

and thin layer chromatography (TLC), it is now a primary tool
for separation problems (4). Generally, modern HPLC techniques
employ narrow columns, small particle column packings, high
pressure flows, and continuous detection to effect high-efficiency
separations and component quantitation (1, 4). HPLC procedures
were developed in part from previous conventional liquid
chromatography technology, existing GC theory, and the independent discovery of high-performance stationary phases and
sensitive detectors. As with other types of chromatography,
HPLC achieves separation as a direct result of an inherent
difference in the relative affinity of each type of analyte
molecule for the chromatographic stationary phase (column
packing) and the mobile phase (solvent). The mixture to be
analyzed is placed at the top of a column comprised of the
stationary phase distributed on an appropriate support medium,
and the components are selectively eluted from the column with
the mobile phase. If required, the composition and properties
of the mobile phase may be altered during the course of the run
to obtain better component separation. Substances with a
greater affinity for the mobile phase will move more readily
through the column. Specific HPLC methods may be classified on
the basis of the characteristics of the stationary and mobile
phases which are employed. Major classes of HPLC methodology
are: liquid-solid (adsorption) chromatography (LSC); liquid-
liquid (partition) chromatography (LLC); ion exchange chromatography (IEC); and gel permeation chromatography (GPC). A
brief description of each of these is presented as follows:

Liquid-Solid Chromatography. Separation by LSC, often
referred to as adsorption chromatography, is based on relative
interactions between the solute (analyte) and mobile phase
(solvent) molecules and a stationary phase comprised of active
sites dispersed on a finely divided solid adsorbent. For most
current high performance chromatographic procedures, the solid
adsorbent consists of small particles of uniform diameter
packed in a column of 1-4 mm diameter. In LSC applications,
adsorbents may be classified into two types: porous and
pellicular. The relatively large particles (40 μm diameter) of
porous packings are characterized by pores which extend deep
into the interior of the particle, while pellicular packings are
comprised of particles with solid cores and thin, porous, outer
shells. Accordingly, particles of pellicular packings have
short diffusion distances producing better efficiencies.
Packings of small porous particles (5-20 μm), however, have the
advantages of both short diffusional distances and small inter-
stitial volumes.

Compounds most efficiently separated by LSC are non-ionic
and relatively soluble in organic solvents (4). Because the
solvent (mobile phase) interacts with the surface of the
stationary phase, the separation process is influenced by

competition between solute (analyte) and solvent molecules for
surface sites. Solvent strength in LSC determines the interaction energy between solvent and surface. Although the two
properties are not equivalent, solvent strength somewhat
parallels solvent polarity. Accordingly, nonpolar solutes are
eluted by weak (nonpolar) solvents and polar solutes by polar
solvents (4).

Liquid-Liquid Chromatography. Liquid-liquid chromatographic (LLC) separations result from partitioning of solute
(analyte) molecules between two immiscible liquid phases (10).
The liquid mobile and liquid stationary phases ideally have
little or no mutual solubility. The stationary liquid phase is
dispersed on a column of finely divided support. The use of a
nonpolar mobile phase and a polar stationary phase is referred
to as normal phase LLC. Under these conditions, less polar
solutes are preferentially eluted from the column. Reverse
phase chromatography employs a nonpolar stationary phase and a
polar mobile phase. Generally, polar compounds elute more
rapidly with this technique. Reverse phase chromatography,
useful for the separation of less polar solutes, has found
increased application in occupational health chemistry. It is
optimally suited to the separation of low-to-medium molecular
weight compounds of intermediate polarity.

Some problems associated with conventional LLC (e.g., the
loss of the liquid stationary phase through dissolution in the
mobile phase) may be obviated by chemically bonding the liquid
stationary phase to the support medium. This type of liquid-
liquid chromatography is designated bonded phase chromatography
(BPC)(11). Since the properties of bonded phases may differ
substantially from those of coated phases, BPC separation
characteristics may differ from those of conventional LLC. Many
phases have exhibited increased efficiency when bonded to the
support medium. Most current reverse phase HPLC work involves
the use of stationary phases bonded to microparticles.

A special application of LLC is ion pair partition chromatography. In this procedure, the ionic form of the solute
(analyte) is paired with an appropriate counter ion of decreased
polarity, e.g. tetra-tertiary-butyl amine. This ion pair is
then partitioned between selected mobile and stationary phases
to achieve the desired separation. In practice, ion pair
chromatography is commonly conducted by utilizing a mobile phase
comprised of a miscible aqueous/organic mixture containing a
relatively high concentration of counter ion. The technique is
applicable to analysis of many types of ionic compounds (10).

Ion Exchange Chromatography. In ion exchange chromatography (IEC), the solid stationary phase is comprised of ionic
material. This serves as an ion exchanger and separation is
achieved primarily on the basis of the relative affinities of

each solute for the ionic stationary phase. Obviously, ion
exchange chromatography is well suited to the separation of
ionized or ionizable moieties. Stationary phases are generally
comprised of porous polymeric organic resins with attached
cationic or anionic exchange groups. Active sites in anion
exchangers are frequently quartenary ammonium or alkyl ammonium
groups. Cation-exchange groups are usually carboxylic or
sulfonic acids. In IEC, separation is effected by altering the
ionic strength or the pH of the mobile phase. IEC is particularly adaptable to the analysis of weak organic acids and bases
as well as inorganic ions (12).

Gel Permeation Chromatography. In gel permeation chromatography (GPC), sometimes referred to as exclusion chromatography or gel chromatography, separation is accomplished
primarily on the basis of molecular size. Molecules of
sufficient size are sterically excluded from the pores of the
matrix of the stationary phase. Accordingly, these solutes are
eluted most rapidly from the column. Smaller molecules, which
can diffuse into the pores of the stationary phase, are temporarily retained. Their movement through the column is thus
retarded and they are eluted less rapidly. The usefulness of
GPC has been enhanced significantly by the advent of high
pressure technology and it is now applied to a wide variety of
analytical problems. The exclusion technique is, however, most
useful for compounds of molecular weight 500 or more. It is
effective with respect to the separation of very high molecular
weight compounds, such as polymers, and to the separation of
components differing extensively in molecular weight. In the
practice of industrial hygiene chemistry, GPC is particularly
useful for preliminary chromatographic procedures designed to
explore the separation of mixtures of unknown composition.

Apparatus for HPLC. The equipment required to conduct HPLC
analyses is relatively sophisticated. The basic components of a
typical modern high performance liquid chromatographic system
are illustrated in Figure 1. The system includes reservoirs to
accomodate components of the mobile phase; a solvent delivery
system for pumping the mobile phase; gradient elution equipment
for changing the composition of the mobile phase during the
course of the chromatographic run; an injection device for
introduction of the sample onto the analytical column; a column
appropriately packed to effect the required separations; a
detector; a recorder; and a data processor (1, 2, 3, 4).

Reservoirs. Most analytical work with HPLC can be accomplished with reservoirs of approximately one-liter capacity. A
vessel should be available for each component of the mobile
phase if gradient programming (changing mobile phase composition)
is employed. Ideally, reservoirs should be unbreakable and

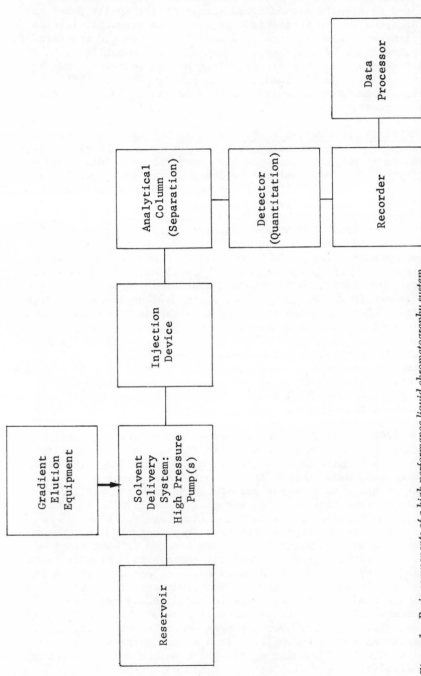

Figure 1. Basic components of a high performance liquid chromatography system

resistant to attack by mobile phase solvents. Some sophisticated reservoirs are designed such that the mobile phase may
be degassed in the reservoir. Degassing is essential in order
to eliminate potential problems associated with the reaction of
dissolved gases (e.g., oxygen) with either the mobile or
stationary phase, to obviate fouling of the detector, and to
prevent vapor lock in reciprocating pumps. For many HPLC
applications, simple reservoirs such as glass flasks or bottles
are adequate.

   Solvent Delivery Systems. A means by which the mobile
phase may be moved through the column at relatively high
pressure is required for most high performance liquid chromatography. The ideal solvent delivery system would provide a
constant reproducible flow of any of a number of different
mobile phases. High pressure is mandated by the use of high
efficiency columns packed with small particles. Solvent
delivery systems should have the capability of performing at
4000-6000 psi although most work is presently accomplished at
lower pressures (e.g., 1000-2000 psi). Pumps conventionally
employed for HPLC purposes may be classified into two general
types: constant flow or constant pressure. Constant flow pumps
are generally mechanical reciprocating devices or syringe-drive
systems. Reciprocating pumps are less expensive and also convenient to use with a gradient elution system, but suffer the
disadvantages associated with a pulsating flow. Such flows can
result in instability with the use of specific types of detectors. Solvent flow pulsation can be moderated, however, with
the use of several types of damping apparatus. Screw-driven
syringe (constant displacement) pumps are expensive, but ad-
vocates of this type of pump emphasize their ability to generate
accurate, reproducible pulseless flow rates at high pressures
(3000-7000 psi) independent of column resistance. A disadvantage of this type of pump is its limited solvent capacity
(300-500 ml) which necessitates frequent refilling. The second
type of pump used in HPLC is the constant pressure pump. Constant pressure devices are pulseless and flow is relatively
constant, resulting in a low detector noise level. A disadvantage of these pumps is that the flow rate (elution volume)
may change with changes in pressure drop across the column or
changes in solvent viscosity. There are two primary types of
constant pressure pumps. The first employs gas cylinder pressure
to drive the solvent from a metal coil. These devices are inexpensive but also inflexible. The other type of constant
pressure pump commonly employed for HPLC is the pressure in-
tensifier. This is a pneumatic amplifier pump in which a gas-
driven piston of large surface area operating at relatively low
pressure acts on a hydraulic piston of low surface area.

   Each type of pumping system has a unique set of advantages
and disadvantages and selection of the most appropriate pump is

dependent on the nature and specifications of the HPLC work to be accomplished.

Gradient Elution Equipment. Gradient elution, as used in HPLC, is applied to solve difficult separation problems and to achieve improved resolution of sample components. It is somewhat analogous to temperature programming in gas chromatography, except that the relative retention times of sample components are altered by changing the characteristics (e.g., polarity, pH, ionic strength) of the mobile phase rather than by altering temperature. Changes in composition of the mobile phase may be continuous or step-wise. A research-grade gradient elution system should be capable of generating a wide variety of changes in the carrier solvent, including relatively rapid changes. Such changes can be used for preliminary chromatographic runs to determine optimal operating conditions for the ultimate solution of a difficult analytical problem.

Gradient generating systems may be classified as either high pressure or low pressure systems. The use of a particular type of gradient elution system is dependent on the type of pump which is employed. With a low pressure gradient system, solvents are mixed at atmospheric pressure, after which the final solvent mixture is pressurized. These devices are simple, relatively inexpensive, and accomodate extensive changes in solvent composition. Small-volume reciprocating pumps are generally required for low pressure gradient systems. Low pressure systems are more versatile because mobile phase of any reasonable composition may be fed to the pump.

High pressure gradient systems mix the mobile phase solvents at high pressure to achieve the desired solvent composition. The gradient is produced by controlling the delivery of the high pressure pumping system. This process normally involves the use of two high pressure pumps, with controlled outputs from each. Therefore, high pressure gradient systems are relatively expensive. In principle, virtually any type of gradient may be generated with these systems because outputs from each pump may be carefully controlled electronically. The pumps employed in this procedure are usually of the constant flow type. High pressure mixing systems are particularly useful for operation in the constant solvent-composition (isocratic) mode because rapid changes between two different constant-composition mobile phases are easily effected.

Choice between low pressure and high pressure gradient systems is based on specific analytical requirements.

Injection Devices. Sampling, i.e., introduction of the sample onto the analytical column, is of critical importance in HPLC. This is particularly valid in connection with obtaining high column performance. There are two basic designs for injection systems: syringe and valve.

With the use of a syringe-type device, samples are generally injected with a microsyringe through a septum mounted in
a low volume inlet system. Injection may involve direct
sampling onto the packing at the inlet of the column or into a
swept-port injection device in which sample is introduced onto a
rigid column plug rather than column packing. Direct injection
onto the packing results in maximum column efficiency, but
problems associated with plugging of the needle with particles
of packing and disturbance of the packing are eliminated with
swept-port injection. Under normal operating conditions,
syringe/septum injections are generally limited to pressures of
1500 psi or less. Injections may be accomplished, however, at
higher pressures by employing stop-flow techniques. In a simple
system, this involves discontinuation of pumping, equilibration
of column inlet pressure to atmospheric pressure, injection, and
resumption of pumping. Since diffusion of liquids is very slow,
stop-flow injection procedures generally do not affect the
efficiency of HPLC separations.

Sampling can also be accomplished using sliding or rotating
valves. In this procedure, the sample is placed in an internal
cavity or in an external loop in the valve. By appropriate
changing of the configuration of the valves, the sample is swept
onto the column by the mobile phase. Sampling valves (loops)
initially applied in HPLC work suffered the disadvantage of
fixed volume. Newer designs employing large sample loops and
back-filling techniques provide required flexibility for injection volume, permitting sample volumes from as low as 0.5 µl
up to several milliliters. These valves are operable at high
pressure and minimize problems with contamination.

Columns. High performance columns characterized by minimum
band broadening comprise the most crucial component of a high
performance liquid chromatographic system.

Column Hardware. The unpacked column is important in
achieving good separation efficiency. Column construction must
be such that the column will withstand high pressure and resist
corrosive activity of solvents. Most modern HPLC columns are
constructed of stainless steel tubing. Precision-bore tubing is
frequently employed because the smoothness of the interior
surface evidently reduces band spreading attributable to wall
irregularities. The interior diameter of the column influences
its efficency. Typical HPLC analytical separations are accomplished with columns of 1-4 mm i.d. Columns of 2-3 mm i.d.
represent a reasonable compromise between efficiency and convenience, as columns of 1 mm diameter or less are difficult to
pack. Straight columns 25-150 cm in length are normally employed. Minimum dead volume is essential with respect to
fittings and connectors.

Column Packings. Several important factors related to
column packings for HPLC have been noted in the preceding
section detailing types of elution chromatography.

Commercial packings for high performance liquid chromatography may be classified according to shape (spherical or
irregular), rigidity (rigid solids, hard gels, or soft gels),
and porosity (porous or pellicular). The specific type of
packing material employed depends on application.

Better reproducibility and higher efficiencies are
generally obtained with spherical particles in comparison to
irregular particles. Particle size influences column efficiency
because more efficient columns can be prepared with small
diameter particles. Use of smaller particles results, however,
in the disadvantage of decreased column permeability with the
consequential requirement for operation at higher pressures.
Additional disadvantages of small particle columns are the
requirement for smaller dead volumes and the increased difficulty in packing. For particles < 10 μm, special procedures
must be used. Current applications of HPLC employ a particle
size in the range 5-50 μm, depending on specifications. Very
high-performance HPLC separations can be achieved with particles
of diameter < 10 μm.

Detectors. A detector capable of continuously monitoring
effluent from the column is essential for efficient HPLC
analyses. Considerations in connection with detector performance include absolute and relative sensitivity, drift characteristics, noise, linearity, specificity, and band spreading resulting from detector design. The selection of a proper
detector is essential for successful analysis, both from the
standpoint of sensitivity and elimination of effects of interfering compounds (specificity).

Generally, HPLC detectors are classified as either of two
types: (1) Those which monitor bulk properties of the mobile
phase and (2) Those which are sensitive to solute properties.
Bulk property detectors, which are universal detectors, operate
by comparing a property of uncontaminated mobile phase with the
corresponding property of solute-containing column effluent.
These detectors are less sensitive than solute property detectors with a maximum sensitivity of 1 in 10^6. Examples of
this type of detector include those which monitor refractive
index (RI), dielectric constant, or eluant density. The latter
two are relatively insensitive and not generally used.

Solute property detectors measure a characteristic of the
solute alone. These detectors are generally more sensitive
yielding a detectable signal for nanogram quantities of solute.
Representative detectors of this type include, for example,
ultra-violet (UV), solute transport, fluorescence, and conductivity monitors. Other less frequently employed detectors of
this nature are those based on radioactivity, polarography, and

infra-red radiation. Currently, the most widely used detectors
for HPLC are UV, RI, fluorescence, transport, and conductivity
detectors.
    Derivatization of solute molecules can be utilized to
modify properties of analytes of interest such that they may be
more readily identified by a specific type of HPLC detector.
The emergence of a sensitive universal detector for HPLC is yet
forthcoming. Mass spectrometry is an obvious candidate for such
and this research area is currently one of high activity.

    Recorders and Data Processors. Conventional recorders
serve adequately for the generation of hard-copy data obtained
from most detectors utilized in HPLC. A discussion of automated
data processors is beyond the scope of this presentation. It is
important to note, however, that automated systems are available
which can integrate the chromatographic peaks, generate standard
curves from the results of runs of appropriate standard
materials, and calculate the quantity of a specified compound in
a sample utilizing preprogrammed mathematical models. This is
of significant importance since the reduction of HPLC data can
be very time consuming and tedious.

Specific Procedures for HPLC Analysis of Industrial Hygiene Samples

    This section summarizes specific HPLC procedures which we
have recently used for the analytical characterization of
several substances, all of which are currently important in
occupational health studies. The methods described have not
been approved or adopted as standard methodology by any agency
of the government. We have selected these examples to indicate
the types of problems which may be addressed by high performance
liquid chromatography. Information concerning the analytical
methods discussed in the following is neither comprehensive nor
exhaustive, but rather representative of applications of HPLC.
Accordingly, only basic essentials of each method are provided.
With this approach, we present only limited data for each of
several different methods rather than a comprehensive treatment
of a selected few. Much of the data and many of the chromatograms which are presented are derived from actual work conducted during recent field studies. Such studies are frequently
pursued under the duress of stringent time constraints. Often
the objective of such analytical work is to provide accurate
data in a very short time. Accordingly, the methodology and
attendant chromatograms may not represent the absolute or
aesthetic quality that would be expected from prolonged research
directed to specific methods development problems. In no instance, however, is the integrity of results compromised. For
purposes of discussion, we have arbitrarily classified procedures presented in the following into three parts: Those

concerned with the analysis of (1) Carcinogens, (2) Pesticides, and (3) Substances associated with various different working environments. The determination of carcinogens and potential carcinogens is of primary importance in industrial hygiene work today. The analysis of pesticides is currently a challenging analytical problem because new pesticide compounds are frequently introduced and knowledge of appropriate sampling and analytical methods for assessing worker exposure is relatively modest. This problem is compounded by the high level of sensitivity required for the work and the wide variety of sample matrices which are encountered. HPLC is well suited to the characterization of carcinogens, pesticides, and a wide range of other industrial chemicals. Examples of such analyses are presented.

   Analysis of Carcinogens. HPLC methods for the determination of polynuclear aromatic hydrocarbons; benzidine and 3,3'-dichlorobenzidine; and 4,4'-methylenebis(2-chloroaniline) (MOCA) are discussed.

   Polynuclear Aromatic Hydrocarbons. Polycyclic aromatic hydrocarbon (PAH) compounds are frequently formed when organic substances are exposed to high temperatures (13). The potential for exposure to PAHs exists in a number of working environments including, for example, coking operatings (14, 15), aluminum reduction plants (16), and coal gasification and liquefaction processes (17). Concern related to the prevalence of PAHs derives from the demonstrated carcinogenicity of compounds of this type (18). One methodology for assessing exposure of workers to PAH compounds consists of sampling of airborne particulate (containing PAH) on glass-fiber/silver membrane filters, ultrasonic extraction of the filters with benzene or another suitable solvent such as cyclohexane, and analysis of the extract by HPLC. A description of this procedure follows. The chromatographic technique separates various PAH compounds such that each may be tentatively identified by a comparison of its relative retention time with those of known standards. In principle, this HPLC method is applicable to the analysis of any PAH for which acceptable resolution and peak area are achieved. In practice, we have utilized it for the analysis of molecular systems comprised of 3 to 5 fused benzene rings. Our discussion in this document is limited to the following compounds: phenanthrene, anthracene, fluoranthene, pyrene, benz(a)anthracene, chrysene, benzo(e)pyrene, benzo(a)pyrene, and dibenz(a,h)anthracene. The structures for these compounds are presented in Table I. It is important to note that the method has also been adapted to the determination of several other PAH compounds (e.g., benzo(c)phenanthrene, perylene, 3-methylcholanthrene, carbazole, 7H-dibenzo(c,g)carbazole, and indeno(1,2,3-cd)pyrene).

The analytical procedure is as follows. Filter samples (both the glass fiber and the silver membrane) are placed in a screw-cap vial and five ml benzene (or alternative solvent) is added. The sample is extracted ultrasonically for 15 minutes. The extract is filtered through a 0.45 μm silver membrane filter and collected in an evaporator tube. The sample is extracted (2 ml solvent) two additional times and these extracts are collected in the evaporator tube. The combined extracts are concentrated to 1.0 ml under a stream of clean, dry nitrogen at 40°C. An appropriate aliquot of the extract is injected for HPLC analysis. Depending on the properties of the sample (e.g., analyte concentration), injection volumes may range from 1-50 μl. In our laboratory, samples are chromatographed utilizing the following conditions and parameters:

Pumping System: Model ALC 204 (Waters Associates)
                  M6000A Pumps (2)
                  Model 660 Solvent Programmer

Injector: Model U6K (Waters Associates)

Column: 25 cm x 3.9 mm i.d.
                  Packing: 10 μm Vydac 201 TP C_{18}
                  (Separations Group)

Solvent System: 78% Methanol/22% Water to
                  95% Methanol/5% Water
                  Time: Twenty (20) Minutes
                  Gradient: Concave (Curve 8 on
                    Model 660 Solvent Programmer)
                  Flow: 0.8 ml/min.
                  Temperature: Ambient

Detector: Model 440 UV Detector (Waters Associates)
                  λ_1: 365 nm Range: 0.01 AUFS
                  λ_2: 280 nm Range: 0.02 AUFS

As noted in the preceding table, elution of PAHs is detected by UV absorbance at two different wavelengths: 280 nm and 365 nm. Fluorescence detectors are also applicable to the HPLC analysis of PAHs (9, 19). The UV detector monitors the sample simultaneously at two wavelengths, aiding in compound identification. For a specific compound, the ratio of absorbances at two different wavelengths is an intrinsic physical characteristic. Therefore, it is possible, in principle, to identify a sample analyte by this characteristic ratio. The chromatographic retention time of each of the specific peaks observed in the sample eluate is compared with those of known standard compounds for tentative analyte identification. For quantitation, peak areas of each standard, at each of six

different concentration levels, are determined and standard
curves of concentration versus peak area are constructed. The
concentration of each analyte is determined by a comparison of
its observed peak area with the appropriate standard curve.

A chromatogram of a standard mixture of nine selected PAHs
is presented in Figure 2. This chromatogram, typical of the PAH
analyses conducted in our laboratory, was obtained from a single
chromatographic run. No recycling is necessary. For this
injection, each of the nine compounds was present at the amount
indicated. Amounts range from 5-25 ng and the chromatogram
clearly illustrates the variation in sensitivity with compound.
These sensitivities are also illustrated by the approximate
limits of detection listed in Table I. The listed detection
limits apply to monitoring of UV absorbance with a Waters Model
440 Detector. They are based on a 1 µl HPLC injection volume
and a 1 ml sample of solvent extract. Obviously, detection
limits may be varied by altering these two parameters, i.e., the
solvent extract may be concentrated by evaporation or the amount
of sample injected for HPLC analysis may be increased. In
Figure 2, the lower chromatogram is that resulting from UV
detection at 280 nm at a detector sensitivity setting of 0.02
absorbance units full scale (AUFS). The upper chromatographic
trace was obtained at 365 nm and 0.01 AUFS. Note that the
recorder pens for the 280 nm and 365 nm chromatograms are
offset by one minute. The separation of different PAHs is well
illustrated by these chromatograms. In many instances, excellent chromatograms are obtained for solutions of standard
mixtures, but field sample chromatograms are unacceptable due to
matrix effects or interferences. This generally is not the case
with respect to our HPLC method for PAH analysis. The utility
of the method for actual field samples is demonstrated by the
data presented in Figures 3 and 4. Figure 3 is a chromatogram
obtained from a benzene extract of a glass fiber/silver membrane
filter combination used for air sampling in an aluminum reduction plant. Conditions for this analysis were similar to
those represented in Figure 2. Phenanthrene, fluoranthene,
benz(a)anthracene, chrysene, benzo(e)pyrene, benzo(a)pyrene, and
dibenz(a,h)anthracene are readily separated and identified in
this chromatogram. In addition, several other UV-absorbing
compounds are present in the sample. These also may possibly
be polynuclear aromatic hydrocarbons (16). Figure 4 presents
chromatographic results obtained for an air sample derived from
a coke oven operation. Phenanthrene, fluoranthene, pyrene,
benz(a)anthracene, chrysene, benzo(e)pyrene, and benzo(a)pyrene,
are readily identified in this chromatogram. Again, many unidentified peaks are observed, indicating the possible presence
of several additional PAH compounds. These chromatographic
results along with other pertinent observations demonstrate that
possible exposure to PAH compounds in industry today is a
justifiable concern for workers and for occupational health

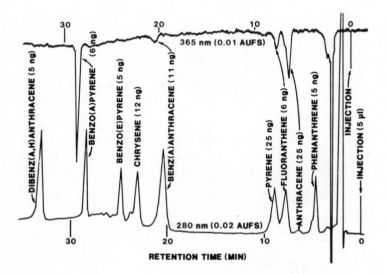

Figure 2. Chromatogram of a standard mixture of nine selected polynuclear aromatic hydrocarbons

Table I. HPLC Detection Limits for Selected PAH Compounds

Compound	Structure	Detection Limit (µg/sample)
Phenanthrene		2
Anthracene		5
Fluoranthene		1
Pyrene		5
Benz(a)anthracene		2
Chrysene		2
Benzo(e)pyrene		1
Benzo(a)pyrene		1
Dibenz(a,h)anthracene		1

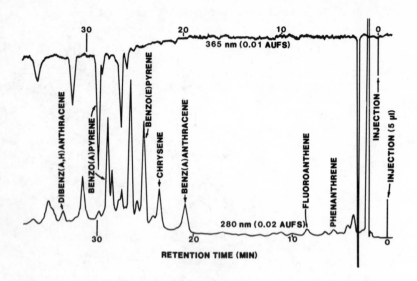

Figure 3.   Chromatogram of HPLC analysis of an air sample from an aluminum reduction plant; sample was collected on a glass fiber/silver membrane filter combination.

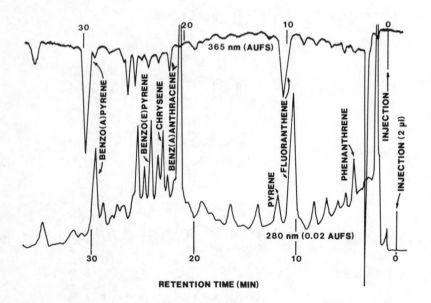

Figure 4.   Chromatogram of HPLC analysis of an air sample from a coke oven operation; sample was collected on a glass fiber/silver membrane combination.

professionals.

More definitive compound verification may be achieved by (1) Additional HPLC analyses under altered chromatographic conditions with an accompanying comparison of retention times of standards and unknowns or (2) Collection of component HPLC peaks and subsequent analysis by, for example, mass spectrometry, fluorescence spectroscopy, or optical absorbance spectrophotometry.

Benzidine Compounds. Both benzidine and derivatives such as 3,3'-dichlorobenzidine, *o*-tolidine, and *o*-dianisidine, are carcinogenic. Epidemiological studies have implicated benzidine as a human carcinogen (20, 21) and it has also exhibited carcinogenic activity in various animal studies (22, 23). The noted benzidine derivatives have been investigated extensively in experiments with rats and each compound induces tumors in such experiments (24). Accordingly, benzidine and 3,3'-dichlorobenzidine began to be regulated as carcinogens by OSHA in 1974 (25). Benzidine and its derivatives are important dye intermediates; they may also be used as plastic and rubber compounding ingredients. Their biological activity and use in industry mark them as suitable study subjects for health hazard evaluations. The analysis of these materials in air, wipe samples, and bulk materials is of primary importance in current efforts.

Reverse phase HPLC offers a simple, direct, sensitive method for the determination of 3,3'-dichlorobenzidine collected on sample filters (air or wipe). Conditions and parameters used for the analysis are summarized as follows:

Pumping System: Model ALC 204 (Waters Associates)
                        M6000A Pump (1)

Injector: Model U6K (Waters Associates)

Column: 30 cm x 3.9 mm i.d.
                Packing: 10 μm μBondapak C_{18}
                (Waters Associates)

Solvent System: 60% Acetonitrile/40% Water;
                  Isocratic
                Flow: 1 ml/min.
                Temperature: Ambient

Detector: Model 440 UV Detector (Waters Associates)
                λ_1: 254 nm Range: 0.005 AUFS
                λ_2: 313 nm Range: 0.005 AUFS

A mixture of 60% acetonitrile and 40% water elutes 3,3'-dichlorobenzidine from a μBondapak C_{18} column in approximately seven minutes. The minumum detectable amount is 1 ng. A

peak height ratio of 1:0.67 at wavelengths of 254 nm and 313 nm,
respectively, is used to confirm the presence of dichlorobenzidine
in samples. The analyte is extracted from air or wipe sample
filters with ten ml methanol containing 0.1% trimethylamine.
Figure 5 illustrates the results of the analysis of a standard
sample containing 5.9 ng dichlorobenzidine as well as the
analysis of a wipe sample from the field. The sensitivity and
effectiveness of HPLC in such analyses are readily apparent.

   The HPLC analysis of benzidine in bulk dyes is accomplished
by dissolving the bulk material in 0.12 $\underline{N}$ NaOH and extracting
the benzidine with chloroform. The extraction efficiency is
approximately 100% for benzidine concentrations of 20 ppm or
more. Less efficient extraction is achieved at lower concentrations (See below). The chloroform extract is passed through
a small column containing anhydrous sodium sulfate and the
column is thoroughly rinsed with additional chloroform. The
combined rinses and extracts are evaporated at approximately
50°C in a clean dry nitrogen stream. The residue is redissolved
in 1.0 ml methanol. The methanol solution is analyzed for
benzidine by HPLC as follows:

Pumping System: Model ALC 204 (Waters Associates)
                   M6000A Pumps (2)
                   Model 660 Solvent Programmer

Injector: Model U6K (Waters Associates)

Column: 30 cm x 3.9 mm i.d.
                   Packing: 10 μm μBondapak C_{18}
                   (Waters Associates)

Solvent System: 45% Methanol/55% Water;
                   Isocratic
                   Flow: 1 ml/min.
                   Temperature: Ambient

Detector: Vari-Chrom UV-Visible (Varian)
                   λ_1: 280 nm   Range: 0.01 AUFS

   The injection volume for these analyses is 1–50 μl. Under
the conditions noted in the preceding table, benzidine elutes
from the column in approximately 8.5 minutes. Following the
elution of benzidine, a gradient elution program to 100%
methanol in 5 minutes is effected to clean the column of later
eluting compounds. This cleanup step is of critical importance
in the analysis of bulk dye samples because of the presence of
extensive contaminating material in the chloroform extract. For
quantitation, the area of the sample peak is compared with that
of appropriate standards. The limit of detection is 10 ng
benzidine/injection. However, due to the relatively poor ex-

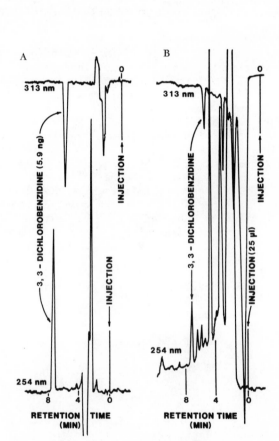

Figure 5. HPLC chromatograms of (a) standard of 3,3'-dichlorobenzidine and (b) wipe sample (filter) from the field

traction efficiency at low benzidine concentrations, the limit
of detection for bulk dyes is approximately 2 ppm. It is
necessary to correct for decreasing extraction efficiency in the
range 2-20 ppm. This method has been effectively applied in our
laboratory to the analysis of several azodyes containing 10-25
ppm benzidine. The method is also useful for the analysis of
air samples collected on glass fiber filters. In this analysis
the filter is extracted with 0.12 N sodium hydroxide, after
which the procedural approach is identical to that detailed for
bulk samples.

   4,4'-Methylenebis(2-chloroaniline). A carcinogenic compound used extensively in the plastics industry is
4,4'-methylenebis(2-chloroaniline)(MOCA)(26). The simplicity of
the HPLC method for determination of MOCA renders it particularly
useful. For example, the recommended gas chromatographic (GC)
procedure for analysis of MOCA involves collection in a midget
impinger, extraction with ethyl ether, evaporation to dryness,
esterification, and analysis by GC. This time-consuming procedure is not only difficult, but frequently yields an unstable
product for GC analysis. The HPLC methodology is a significant
improvement. Silver membrane filters have been used successfully
for sampling. An alternative approach involves use of a glass
fiber filter backed by a bed of silica gel sorbent. The samples
are desorbed in 1 ml of methanol and this solution may be injected directly into the HPLC system. Liquid chromatographic
conditions are as follows:

Pumping System: Model ALC 204 (Waters Associates)
                  M6000A Pumps (2)
                  Model 660 Solvent Programmer

Injector: Model U6K (Waters Associates)

Column: 30 cm x 3.9 mm i.d.
                  Packing: 10 µm µBondapak C_{18}
                  (Waters Associates)

Solvent System: 75% Acetonitrile/25% Water;
                  Isocratic
                  Flow: 0.7 ml/min.
                  Temperature: Ambient

Detector: Model 440 UV Detector (Waters Associates)
                  λ_1: 254 nm Range: 0.01 AUFS

   Under these conditions, MOCA elutes in approximately six
minutes. The sensitivity of the method is 0.5 ng MOCA/injection.
Assuming a 20 µl injection, this sensitivity corresponds to a
lower limit of detection of 0.5 $\mu g/M^3$ for a 50 liter air sample.

An alternative approach for MOCA analysis by HPLC, also involving reverse phase chromatography on a µBondapak C_{18} column, utilizes the paired ion technique. Paired ion chromatographic (PIC) analysis is effective for the determination of compounds which may exist as ionic species in the polar mobile phase. A counter ion, such as an alkyl sulfonate for cations or tetrabutylammonium phosphate for anions, is added to the mobile phase at a concentration of approximately 0.005 $\underline{M}$. This technique generally affords improved efficiencies in comparison to ion exchange chromatography. For the analysis of MOCA by PIC, the following conditions apply:

Pumping System: Model ALC 204 (Waters Associates)
                 M6000A Pumps (2)
                 Model 660 Solvent Programmer

Injector: Model U6K (Waters Associates)

Column: 30 cm x 3.9 mm i.d.
                 Packing: 10 µm µBondapak C_{18}
                 (Waters Associates)

Solvent System: 55% Acetonitrile with 0.005 $\underline{M}$
                 PIC B-7 (Waters Associates)/45%
                 Water with 0.005 $\underline{M}$ PIC B-7
                 Flow: 1 ml/min.
                 Temperature: Ambient

Detector: Model 440 UV Detector (Waters Associates)
                 λ_1: 280 nm Range: 0.005 AUFS

Representative chromatograms obtained with this procedure are presented in Figure 6.

Analysis of Pesticides. Organophosphates, carbamates, atrazine derivatives, and other types of compounds are receiving expanded use in comparison to classical organochlorine pesticides. Many of these compounds are not amenable to GC analysis due to thermal instability or other factors. HPLC holds promise for analysis of such substances. HPLC procedures for selected pesticide analyses are presented in the following.

Warfarin. Warfarin is a popular rodenticide particularly common in rat poison preparations. Because of its toxic nature, assessment of workplace and environmental exposures is of concern. Warfarin can be quickly and easily determined by reverse phase HPLC. Details of the procedure applied in our laboratory are as follows:

Pumping System: Model ALC 204 (Waters Associates)
                   M6000A pump (1)

Injector: Model U6K (Waters Associates)

Column: 30 cm x 3.9 mm i.d.
                   Packing: 10 μm μBondapak C_{18}
                   (Waters Associates)

Solvent System: 56% Methanol/44% Water;
                   Isocratic
                   Flow: 1 ml/min.
                   Temperature: Ambient

Detector: Model 440 UV Detector (Waters Associates)
                   λ_1: 313 nm Range: 0.005 AUFS

Under these conditions, warfarin elutes in approximately eight minutes. The minimum detectable quantity of material is approximately 5 ng. Warfarin can be extracted from rodent baits or from field wipe samples using a mixture of dioxane plus 15% water and 1% $Na_4P_2O_7$ (27). The extract is injected directly into the HPLC system. Figure 7 is comprised of chromatograms of (a) warfarin standard and (b) an extract of commercial rat bait.

Dialifor. The organophosphate pesticide, dialifor, is registered for use in control of insects on such crops as grapes and citrus. Significant exposure to this toxic compound is feasible for pesticide formulators, and applicators, and for field workers who harvest the crops. We have applied reverse phase HPLC for analysis of this compound on wipe (filter) samples taken in the field. For this analysis, the following conditions and parameters are employed:

Pumping System: SP3500 (Spectra-Physics)

Injector: Model U6K (Waters Associates)

Column: 30 cm x 3.9 mm i.d.
                   Packing: 10 μm μBondapak C_{18}
                   (Waters Associates)

Solvent System: 70% Acetonitrile/30% Water;
                   Isocratic
                   Flow: 1 ml/min.
                   Temperature: Ambient

Detector: Model 770 Spectrophotometric Detector
                   (Schoeffel Instr.)
                   λ_1: 230 nm Range: 0.02 AUFS

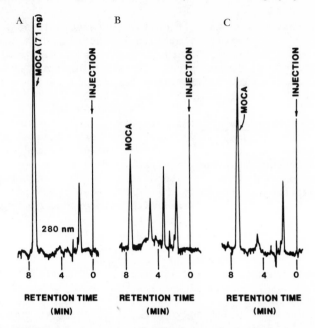

Figure 6.   *HPLC chromatograms of (a) MOCA standard and (b, c) wipe samples (filters) from the field*

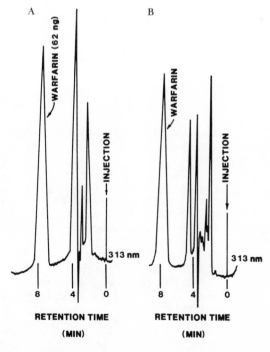

Figure 7.   *HPLC chromatograms of (a) warfarin standard and (b) sample of rat bait*

Under these conditions, the minimum detectable quantity of
dialifor is approximately 15 ng. The compound elutes in
approximately 9 minutes. Efficient analyses of wipe samples
taken on Whatman 41 filter paper has been achieved. Quantitative recovery with minimum interference is obtained by
extraction of the filters with ethyl acetate.

Atrazine Herbicides. The herbicides, atrazine and
cyanazine, may be analyzed by HPLC. Samples collected as filter
wipes (Whatman 41), on Florisil tubes, or in ethylene glycol
impinger solutions have been analyzed. Florisil tubes and wipe
samples are extracted with acetonitrile and the resulting extracts injected directly into the HPLC system. Ethylene glycol
impinger solutions are extracted with chloroform, concentrated
by evaporation, and taken up in acetonitrile and the resulting
solution used for HPLC injection. HPLC analyses are achieved as
follows:

Pumping System: Model ALC 204 (Waters Associates)
                 M6000A Pump (1)

Injector: Model U6K (Waters Associates)

Column: 30 cm x 3.9 mm i.d.
                 Packing: 10 μm μBondapak C_{18}
                 (Waters Associates)

Solvent System: 45% Acetonitrile/55% Water;
                 Isocratic
                 Flow: 1.0 ml/min.
                 Temperature: Ambient

Detector: Vari-Chrom UV-Visible (Varian)
                 λ_1: 235 nm **Range:** 0.02 AUFS

Atrazine and cyanazine elute at approximately 9.5 and 7
minutes, respectively. The limit of detection is approximately
15 ng for each compound.

Analysis of Components Pertinent to Various Industrial
Processes. HPLC has been used for various analytical problems
related to a wide range of industrial processes. The following
briefly summarizes information relative to selected examples of
such analyses.

Pentachlorophenol. Pentachlorophenol, a component of many
wood preservatives, is also encountered in the pulp and paper
and in other industries, and is sometimes used as a pesticide.
Exposure to pentachlorophenol may result in serious toxic effects.
Reverse phase HPLC coupled with a special technique referred to

as ion suppression provides a simple analytical method for
determination of this compound. In this technique, acidification
of the mobile phase (usually with acetic acid) suppresses
formation of the polar pentachlorophenolate anion and greatly
reduces peak tailing. Pentachlorophenol levels in the air of a
working environment may be assessed by collection on glass fiber
filters or in impingers containing 0.1 N NaOH. Pentachlorophenol
may be extracted from the filters with a suitable organic solvent
such as methanol. The NaOH impinger solutions are acidified to
a pH of 4 to 6, and the analyte extracted into a nonpolar organic
solvent such as benzene. Direct injection of the methanol or
benzene solution onto an HPLC column is used for analysis as
follows:

Pumping System: Model ALC 204 (Waters Associates)
                 M6000A Pump (1)

Injector: Model U6K (Waters Associates)

Column: 30 cm x 3.9 mm i.d.
                 Packing: 10 μm μBondapak C_{18}
                 (Waters Associates)

Solvent System: 75% Methanol/24% Water/
                 1% Acetic Acid;
                 Isocratic
                 Flow: 1 ml/min.
                 Temperature: Ambient

Detector: Model 440 UV Detector (Waters Associates)
                 λ_1: 254 nm Range: 0.005 AUFS
                 λ_2: 280 nm Range: 0.005 AUFS

At 280 nm, the minimum detectable quantity of pentachlorophenol is approximately 50 ng. Greater sensitivity may be
achieved by monitoring at 254 nm. With samples extracted into
benzene, however, 280 nm is preferred because of the large
extinction coefficient of benzene at 254 nm.

Isocyanates. Various isocyanates are employed in the
polymer industry. These compounds are powerful irritants and
they are highly toxic. Of particular interest are methylene-di-
paraphenylene isocyanate (MDI) and toluene-2,4-diisocyanate
(TDI). Various alkyl isocyanates (e.g., methyl, ethyl, propyl,
butyl, and cyclohexyl) derivatives may also be of current interest with respect to potential occupational health hazards.
Simultaneous analysis of MDI and TDI by HPLC has been accomplished
by a modification of the method of Dunlap et al. (28). Air
samples are collected in impingers containing p-nitrobenzyl-n-

propylamine reagent in toluene. This reagent forms a stable
derivative with isocyanates. Prior to analysis, the samples are
dried under nitrogen and brought to volume with methylene
chloride. This drying and reconstitution procedure is essential
because toluene interferes with the HPLC procedure. The
methylene chloride solutions are analyzed as follows:

Pumping System: Model ALC 204 (Waters Associates)
                   M6000A Pump (1)

Injector: Model U6K (Waters Associates)

Column: 30 cm x 3.9 mm i.d.
                   Packing: 10 µm µBondapak CN
                   (Waters Associates)

Solvent System: 60% Isooctane/33% Methanol/7% Isopropanol;
                   Isocratic
                   Flow: 1 ml/min.
                   Temperature: Ambient

Detector: Model 440 UV Detector (Waters Associates)
                   λ_1: 254 nm Range: 0.005 AUFS

     At 254 nm, the minimum detectable amount for each analyte
(TDI or MDI) is approximately 5 ng. Under the conditions
described in the preceding and at a flow rate of 1 ml/min., the
TDI and MDI derivatives elute in approximately 11.5 and 14.5
minutes, respectively. Interference problems resulting from
excess derivatizing reagent have been encountered occasionally,
the retention time of this interfering peak varying according to
age and condition of the column. It is suggested that this
interference problem may be avoided by preconditioning a new
µBondapak CN column with reagent prior to the analytical runs.
This treatment does not appear to alter the performance of the
column with respect to the isocyanate derivatives or other polar
organic analytes. Figure 8 presents chromatograms resulting
from the analysis of a standard mixture of TDI and MDI and of an
air sample collected by impinger.

     Mandelic Acid. Occupational exposure to styrene monomer is
of concern due to its extensive use in the manufacture of
plastics, synthetic rubber, resins, and insulator materials. In
addition to monitoring air of the working environment for styrene,
occupational exposure to this compound may also be investigated
by determining the concentration of metabolites of styrene in
the urine of workers. This technique is particularly advantageous for many types of industrial hygiene work because it
offers a means of assessing the quantity of a given compound
which is physiologically absorbed. One of the primary urinary

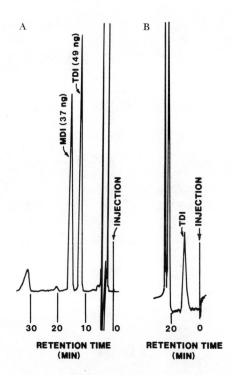

Figure 8. HPLC chromatograms of (a) standard mixture of TDI and MDI and (b) air sample (impinger)

metabolites of styrene is mandelic acid. We have recently
developed an innovative HPLC method for the analysis of mandelic
acid in urine.

A 24-hour urine sample is collected with hydrochloric acid
as preservative (1.25 ml 6 $\underline{M}$ HCl per each 100 ml urine). A 10-
ml aliquot of the sample or of a corresponding mandelic acid
standard (in water or uncontaminated urine) is processed through
a cleanup procedure involving partitioning on a column packed
with Amberlite XAD-2. The eluant fraction containing mandelic
acid is evaporated to dryness, reconstituted in water, and
subsequently extracted into ethyl acetate. The extract is dried
and the residue dissolved in water. The water solution is
analyzed for mandelic acid by HPLC. This cleanup procedure
lends itself well to processing of large sample batches. The
following chromatographic conditions are used for the analysis
of prepared samples:

Pumping System: Model ALC 204 (Waters Associates)
                    M6000A Pumps (2)
                    Model 660 Solvent Programmer

Injector: Model U6K (Waters Associates)

Column: 30 cm x 3.9 mm i.d.
                    Packing: 10 μm μBondapak C_{18}
                       (Waters Associates)

Solvent System: 0.05 $\underline{M}$ KH_2PO_4 in water, resulting
                    in a pH of 4.5; pH unadjusted
                    Flow: 1.5 ml/min.
                    Temperature: Ambient

Detector: Model 440 UV Detector (Waters Associates)
                    λ_1: 254 nm   Range: 0.005 AUFS

The μBondapak C_{18} column is preceded by a C_{18} pellicular
guard column. Mandelic acid elutes in approximately six minutes.
Following the elution of mandelic acid, it is necessary to run a
short gradient to 60% methanol/40% 0.05 $\underline{M}$ potassium hydrogen
phosphate (pH 4.5) to remove retained compounds from the column
in preparation for the next sample injection. Four or five
samples may be processed per hour. The sensitivity of this
method is 10 mg mandelic acid per liter of urine. Results of
urinary levels of mandelic acid have correlated well with the
degree of exposure to styrene.

Anhydrides. Anhydrides are important reactants and intermediates in many industrial chemical processes. Among the most
important compounds of this class are maleic anhydride and
phthalic anhydride. Exposure to either of these compounds may

produce toxic reactions as well as irritation. Both maleic and
phthalic anhydride are analyzed by HPLC as the isopropyl ester.
Samples collected on glass fiber filters are desorbed in
isopropanol, allowing sufficient time for the esterification
reaction to proceed. Impinger or bubbler samples, collected in
isopropanol, are analyzed without additional treatment. HPLC
analysis is effected as follows:

Pumping System:	Model ALC 204 (Waters Associates) M6000A Pump (1)
Injector:	Model U6K (Waters Associates)
Column:	30 cm x 3.9 mm i.d. Packing: 10 μm μBondapak C_{18} (Waters Associates)
Solvent System:	For Maleic Anhydride: 25% Methanol/ 74% Water/1% Acetic Acid; Isocratic For Phthalic Anhydride: 49.5% Acetonitrile/49.5% Water/1% Acetic Acid; Isocratic Flow: 1.5 ml/min. Temperature: Ambient
Detector:	Model 440 UV Detector (Waters Associates) λ_1: 254 nm Range: 0.005 AUFS

Quantities of anhydrides less than 50 ng are detectable
under these conditions.

Conclusion

HPLC is currently a powerful instrumental tool for
achieving rapid, sensitive, accurate analyses of many compounds
associated with occupational health problems. It is anticipated
that the analytical demands encountered with the practice of
industrial hygiene and related activities will expand significantly during the next few years. Because of the unique
capability of HPLC methodology, particularly with respect to
versatility (number of different types of compounds analyzed)
and resolving power (purification and separation of substances),
HPLC procedures are likely to be applied to an increasingly
greater fraction of the organic quantitative analyses required
in the future. In fact, with the anticipated development of
detectors with high sensitivity and the capability for compound
identification, HPLC could become the dominant analytical tool
applied in support of occupational health investigations.
Detector systems which involve radioactivity measurements to

achieve high sensitivity or mass spectrometry for compound identification are particularly promising. The improvement of detector technology coupled with the development of column materials with better separation characteristics will render HPLC procedures invaluable in the future.

The views in this paper do not necessarily reflect those of the Occupational Safety and Health Administration (OSHA). The authors are solely responsible for the contents of this paper.

LITERATURE CITED

1. Snyder, L.R., Kirkland, J.J., "Introduction to Modern Liquid Chromatography," pp. 1-237, Wiley, New York, 1974.
2. Krejci, M., Pechan, Z., Deyl, A., "Instrumentation for Liquid Chromatography," "Liquid Column Chromatography," D. Zdenek, K. Macek, J. Jaroslar, Eds., pp. 101-168, Elsevier, Amsterdam, 1975.
3. Done, J.N., "Idealized Equipment Design for HPLC," "Practical High Performance Liquid Chromatography," C.F. Simpson, Ed., pp. 69-88, Heydon, London, 1976.
4. Saunders, D.L., "Techniques of Liquid Column Chromatography," "Chromatography A Laboratory Handbook of Chromatographic and Electrophoretic Methods," 3rd Ed., E. Heftman, Ed., pp. 77-109, Van Nostrand Reinhold, New York, 1975.
5. Lovins, R.E., Ellis, S.R., Tolbert, G.D., McKinney, C.R., Anal. Chem. (1973) 45, 1553.
6. Scott, R.P.W., Scott, C.G., Munroe, M., Hess, J., Jr., J. Chromatog. (1974) 99, 395.
7. Horning, E.C., Carroll, D.I., Dzidic, I., Haegele, K.D., Horning, M.G., Stillwell, R.N., J. Chromatog. (1974) 99, 13.
8. Arpino, P.J., Dawkins, B.G., McLafferty, F.W., J. Chromatog. Sci. (1974) 12, 574.
9. Fox, M.A., Staley, S.W., Anal. Chem. (1976) 48, 992.
10. Majors, R.E., "Liquid-Liquid (Partition) Chromatography," "Practical High Performance Liquid Chromatography," C.F. Simpson, Ed., pp. 109-119, Heydon, London, 1976.
11. Majors, R.E., "Bonded Phase Chromatography," "Practical High Performance Liquid Chromatography," C.F. Simpson, Ed., pp. 121-131, Heydon, London, 1976.
12. Bristow, P.A., "Liquid Chromatography in Practice," pp. 73-80, hetp, Cheshire, 1976.
13. Blumer, M., Scient. Amer. (1976) 234, 35.
14. Criteria Document: Recommendations for an Occupational Exposure Standard for Coke Oven Emissions, U.S. Department of Health, Education, and Welfare, Public Health Service, National Institute for Occupational Safety and Health, Report No. HSM 73-11016, 1973.

15. Mazumdar, S., Redmond, C., Sollecito, W., and Sussman, N., J. Air Poll. Control Assoc. (1975), 25, 382.

16. Bjorseth, A., "Analysis of Polycyclic Aromatic Hydrocarbons in Environmental Samples by Glass Capillary Gas Chromatography," "Carcinogenesis-A Comprehensive Survey," Vol 3., "Polynuclear Aromatic Hydrocarbons, D.W. Jones and R.I. Freudenthal, Eds., pp. 75-83, Raven Press, New York, 1978.

17. Guerin, M.R., Epler, J.L., Griest, W.H., Clark, B.R., Rao, T.K., "Polycyclic Aromatic Hydrocarbons from Fossil Fuel Conversion Processes," "Carcinogenesis-A Comprehensive Survey," Vol. 3., "Polynuclear Aromatic Hydrocarbons," D.W. Jones and R.I. Freudenthal, Eds., pp. 21-33, Raven Press, New York, 1978.

18. Dipple, A., "Polynuclear Aromatic Hydrocarbons," "Chemical Carcinogens," C.E. Searle, Ed., pp. 245-314, American Chemical Society, Washington, D.C., 1976.

19. Wise, S.A., Chesler, S.N., Hertz, H.S., Hilpert, L.R., May, W.E., Anal. Chem. (1977) 49, 2306.

20. Case, R.A.M., Hosker, M.E., McDonald, D.B., Pearson, J.J., Br. J. Ind. Med. (1954) 11, 75.

21. Goldwater, L.J., Rosso, A.J., Kleinfeld, M., Arch. Environ. Health (1965) 11, 814.

22. Bonser, G.M., Clayson, D.B., Jull, J.W., Br. J. Cancer (1956) 10, 653.

23. Walpole, A.L., Williams, M.H.C., Br. Med. Bull. (1958) 14, 141.

24. Stula, E.F., Sherman, H., Zapp, J.A., Clayton, J.W., Toxicol. Appl. Pharmacol. (1975) 31, 159.

25. Federal Register (1974) 39, Part III, 3757.

26. Clayson, D.B., Garner, R.C., "Carcinogenic Aromatic Amines and Related Compounds," "Chemical Carcinogens," C.E. Searle, Ed., pp. 366-461, American Chemical Society, Washington, D.C., 1976.

27. Billings, T.J., Hanks, A.R., Colvin, B.M., J. Assoc. Off. Anal. Chem. (1976) 59, 1104.

28. Dunlap, K.L, Sandridge, R.L., Keller, J., Anal. Chem (1976) 48, 497.

RECEIVED October 17, 1979.

Analysis of Aromatic Amines by High Performance Liquid Chromatography

JOHN O. FROHLIGER, KARROLL S. BOOTH[1], and NANCY KOTSKO

Department of Industrial Environmental Health Sciences, Graduate School of Public Health, University of Pittsburgh, PA 15261

Aromatic amines are used in the manufacture of rubber chemicals, drugs, dyes, isocyanates, and many other miscellaneous chemical products. The toxicity of aromatic amines has been known and studied for many years.[1] They all penetrate the skin and all produce methemoglobinemia.[2] Recently, the Occupational Safety and Health Administration (OSHA) established exposure limits for 14 human carcinogens, several of which are aromatic amines[3]

There is a need for Industrial Hygienists to measure concentrations of aromatic amines in the working environment. Most Industrial Hygienists prefer to use impingers containing water or a weak acid as the absorber solution since they are readily available, are not flammable, and are less likely to evaporate in comparison to organic solvents. The collection of amines in aqueous acid solutions suggests that a ion exchange chromatographic method of analysis would reduce the need for extensive sample preparation.

The liquid chromatograph used in this study consisted of a Cheminert Model CMP-2K (Laboratory Data Control, Riviera Beach, Fl.) which is capable of a maximum flow rate of 2 ml/min at a maximum pressure of 500 PSI. This pump has all liquid contact parts limited to glass, teflon or KEL-F materials to reduce corrosion to a minimum. The injection valve is a Laboratory Data Control Model SU 8031 slider valve with a 0.5 ml sample loop. The injection valve is located at the top of the column to minimize dead volume. The separating column is a Laboratory Data Control type MB glass column, 30 cm long with a 2 mm bore capable of a maximum pressure of 500 PSI. The column is packed with surface sulfonated cation exchanger resin prepared in this laboratory in the following manner.

Concentrated sulfuric acid is heated to 100°C on a water bath. Styrene-Divinyl Benzene-2x (Dow Chemical Company, Midland, MI) 200-400 mesh is added to the acid so that the final mixture is 1 μg copolymer per ml of acid. The mixture was maintained at 100°C and stirred with a glass stirring rod for 15 minutes. The

[1] Current Address: Mobay Chemical Corporation, Pgh, PA 15205

reaction was quenched by pouring the mixture into 500 ml of water for each 10 ml of acid. The material was allowed to settle for 20 minutes and the fines decanted off. The resin was washed and decanted three times to remove the excess acid and the fines. The resin was filtered through a Buchner funnel and air dried. The resin will have a capacity of 0.03 meq/gm. The resin is slurry packed onto the column. These columns usually have a back pressure of 200-300 PSI which is well within the range of the system. The outlet of the column is connected to a Waters Associates, Model 440 U.V. Detector (Waters Associates, Milford, MA). The wavelength of the detector is 254 nm. The output of the detector is obtained on a 10 m.v. strip chart recorder. The chromatographic system is shown in Figure 1.

Acid eluents serve a dual function. First, the acid will protonate the amine so that the amine will interact with the resin and the hydrogen ion will serve as the exchange ion in the chromatographic process. The eluent suitable for the separation of aromatic amines is an aqueous perchloric acid solution. Other mineral acids can also be used but may form complexes with metals in the sample or the chromatograph or oxidize components of the sample.

Each amine was dissolved in dilute (1×10^{-3} $\underline{M}$ HCl). The working solution used in this study was 50 µg/ml amine. This is high concentration for the detector but assists in determining the effect of eluent concentration on retention time. The working solutions were protected from the light and fresh solutions were prepared weekly.

A series of perchloric acid solutions were prepared as the eluent. Each eluent was flushed through the chromatograph until a stable baseline was obtained. Each individual amine was injected onto the column using the 0.5 ml sample loop. The amine was allowed to elute if possible. If after sixty minutes the amine had not eluted, the system was flushed with 1 $\underline{M}$ HClO$_4$ to remove the compound. The order of elution of the amine and the effect of eluent concentration on the retention time were determined. The retention volume was plotted against the eluent concentrations to determine the optimum concentration of eluent to obtain the desired separation. Figure 2 is the plot of the retention volumes of four amines versus eluent concentrations.

The graph shows that 2-methylaniline cannot be separated from 3-methylaniline and that aniline can be separated from the methylaniline isomers using an eluent concentration of 5×10^{-3} [H$^+$]. The separation of 2-naphthylamine from 1-naphthylamine can be carried out at 8×10^{-3} [H$^+$] in less than 20 minutes. The separation of aniline and 2-methylaniline using 5×10^{-3} [H$^+$] is shown in Figure 3. The concentration of aniline is 5 ppm while the 2-methylaniline is 10 ppm

Figure 4 shows the separation of 1 and 2-naphthylamines using 8×10^{-3} [H$^+$]. The 1-naphthylamine is 5 ppm while the 2-naphthylamine is 10 ppm.

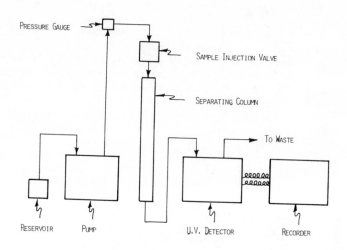

Figure 1.   Schematic of the liquid chromatograph

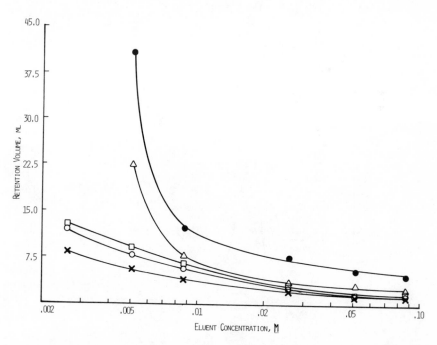

Figure 2.   Effect of low eluent concentration on retention volumes: (×) aniline, (○) 2-methylaniline, (□) 3-methylaniline, (△) 1-naphthylamine, (●) 2-naphthyl-amine.

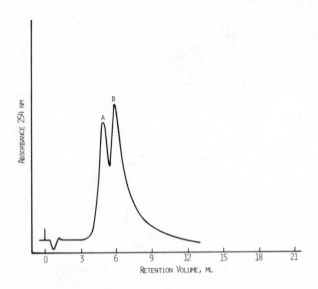

Figure 3. Liquid chromatogram of aniline and 2-methylaniline: flow rate, 90 mL/hr; eluent, 0.005M HClO₄; (a) 5 ppm aniline, (b) 10 ppm 2-methylaniline.

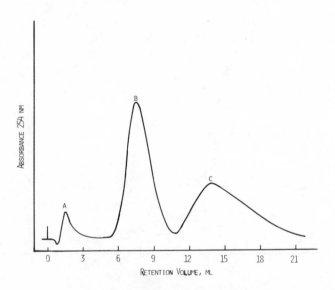

Figure 4. Liquid chromatogram of 1-naphthylamine and 2-naphthylamine: flow rate, 90 mL/hr; eluent, 0.080M HClO₄; (a) impurity, (b) 10 ppm 1-naphthylamine, (c) 5 ppm 2-naphthylamine.

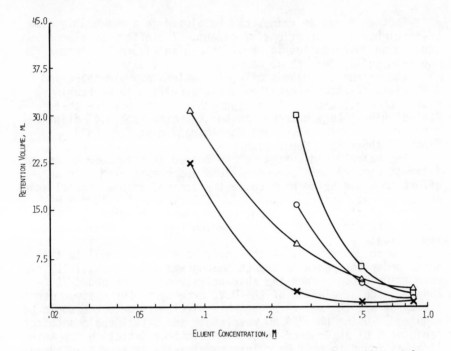

Figure 5.   Effect of high eluent concentration on retention volumes: (×) 2,4 di-aminotoluene, (○) 4,4′ diaminodiphenylmethane, (□) 4,4′ diaminodiphenylether, (△) 2-aminofluorene.

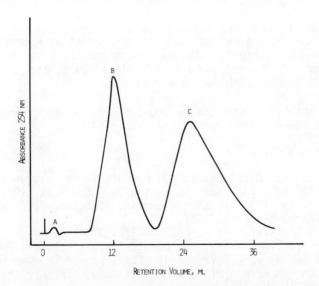

Figure 6.   Liquid chromatogram of 4,4′-diaminodiphenylmethane and 4,4′-di-aminodiphenylether: flow rate, 90 mL/hr; eluent, 0.25M HClO₄, (a) impurity, (b) 4,4′ diaminodiphenylmethane, (c) 4,4′ diaminodiphenylether.

Another group of amines can be eluted in a reasonable time using higher concentrations of eluent. The effect of eluent concentration on retention volume is shown in Figure 5. Except for the 2-aminofluorene, these compounds are all diamines.

The retention volumes of 4,4'-Diaminodiphenylmethane and 4,4'-diaminodiphenylether show a rapid shift with decreasing eluent concentrations. From Figure 5, one can predice that 4,4'-diaminodiphenylmethane can be separated from 4,4'-diamino-diphenylether using an eluent concentration of 0.25 [H^+]. Figure 6 shows this separation.

The major disadvantage to the method is that some amines of interest require acid concentrations approaching 1 $\underline{M}$. In an effort to avoid using high concentrations of strong mineral acids as the eluent, tetramethylammonium chloride in 1 x 10^{-3} $\underline{M}$ HCL was investigated. This eluent would elute the amines but the column life was greatly reduced making the use of this eluent impractical.

The concentrations of the amines are proportional to the areas under the peaks in the chromatograms. The sensitivity of each amine depends upon the absorbtivity of the compound at 254 nm., the wavelength of the U.V. detector. For optimum sensitivity of all the amines a variable wavelength detector would be required. Using the 254 nm wavelength and a full scale detector range of 0.01 absorbance units, the limit of detection for aniline was found to be 1 µg. This sensitivity is more than adequate for industrial hygiene sampling. For example, if an air sample is collected for 8 hours at one liter per minute through a midget impinger containing 10 ml of absorbing solution and 0.5 ml is injected on the chromatograph, the limit of detection of aniline in the air sample is 0.01 ppm (µl/l). The TLV for aniline is 5 ppm.[4]

The use of low capacity surface sulfonated cation exchange resin for the liquid chromatographic separation of aromatic amines provides a rapid analytical technique for industrial hygiene surveys. A wide variety of amines can be analyzed by the same technique with good sensitivity.

This work was supported by a grant from the Environmental Protection Agency (R80-5298010).

Literature Cited.

1. T. S. Scott, "Carcinogenic and Chronic Toxic Hazards of Aromatic Amines", Elsevier Publishing Co., New York, 1962.
2. F. A. Patty, "Industrial Hygiene and Toxicology", Interscience Publishers, New York, 1967.
3. Federal Register, Volume 39, No. 125, 3756, 1974.
4. "Threshold Limit Values for Chemical Substances and Physical Agents in the Work Environment with Intended Changes for 1977". American Conference of Governmental Industrial Hygienists, Cincinnati, OH, 1977.

RECEIVED November 16, 1979.

A New Fluorescence Procedure for the Determination of Methyl Isocyanate in the Occupational Environment

W. J. VINCENT and N. H. KETCHAM

Union Carbide Corporation, Chemicals and Plastics, Research and Development Department, P.O. Box 8361, South Charleston, WV 25303

Methyl isocyanate and all isocyanic acid esters are an interesting and highly reactive class of organic compounds, since the isocyanate group (-NCO) reacts readily with a wide variety of compounds as well as with itself to form dimers, trimers, ureas, and carbodi-imides. Methyl isocyanate (MIC) is an intermediate in the preparation of carbamate pesticides and conceivably could be applied to the production of special heterocyclic polymers and derivatives.

Methyl isocyanate is a hazardous chemical by all means of contact. Inhalation of the material can result in severe bronchospasms and asthmatic breathing. Because of its high vapor pressure, the possibilities of inhalation are greatly enhanced. The threshold limit value (TLV) is a 0.02 parts per million time weighted average (1).

A search of the literature indicated that several methods for determining MIC in air have been developed. These methods involve the use of (a) silica gel impregnated with p-aminoazobenzene (b) two midget impingers in series containing a dimethyl sulfoxide-hydrochloric acid absorber solution and reaction with 1-fluoro-2,4-dinitrobenzene (c) and collection on an adsorbent, thermal desorption, and subsequent reaction 1-fluoro-2,4-dinitrobenzene (2). These air sampling and analytical procedures have a variety of shortcomings. They are inconvenient and cumbersome, and lack the necessary sensitivity and specificity to determine methyl isocyanate accurately for an eight hour time weighted average as required under the Occupational Safety Act of 1970. The analytical phase of these procedures are time consuming and are very difficult to use in determining personnel exposure to MIC in the industrial environment.

Scope of the Development Work

The scope of the work includes the steps taken towards the development of a sound air sampling and analytical method for

0-8412-0539-6/80/47-120-121$06.75/0

determining MIC in air. These steps included the development
and evaluation of two fluorogenic assay procedures. The early
work used silica gel as the solid adsorbent for sampling.
Later it was found that Amberlite XAD-2 ion exchange resin made
it possible to significantly improve the sensitivity of the
method. The development work described in this report is given
in the chronological order in which it was performed in order
to show the sequence of the experimental work. The XAD-2
procedure will be the preferred method for most industrial
hygiene uses. Information about collection on silica gel is
included as this might be the preferred adsorbent in some cases.

Search for a Suitable Analytical Procedure

     Initially, analytical feasibility studies were conducted to
determine if methyl isocyanate could be recovered quantitatively from adsorbents and analyzed by any means of analysis.
Gas chromatographic, spectrophotometric, gravimetric, and
colormetric analytical methods were investigated but all
possessed inadequacies that led to their disqualification as a
method of analysis for MIC.
     During these tests, it was discovered that silica gel,
Amberlite XAD-2 ion exchange resin, and Columbia JXC carbon
retained the isocyanate efficiently, but did not release the
compound at all or were not releasing the compound in a form
that could be analyzed. Since isocyanates react with water of
ordinary temperatures to give disubstituted ureas and carbon
dioxide, analytical methods for ureas were investigated as a
means of analysis.
     It was discovered that the reaction product of urea and
diacetylmonoxime when heated in the presence of sulfuric acid
fluoroscences at a wavelength of 415 mu at an activation
wavelength of 380 mu (3). Since fluorescence methods are
usually quite sensitive, this approach was investigated as
means of determining MIC in air at the TLV.
     The diacetylmonoxime method was evaluated by placing known
concentrations of MIC on the candidate absorbents, aspirating
laboratory air through the adsorbents to facilitate any
reaction that might occur, desorbing and reacting with
diacetylmonoxime to produce fluorophors, and determining the
fluorescence on a spectrofluorometer. Table I shows the amount
of fluorescence obtained from several adsorbents using the
diacetylmonoxime method. These results indicated that silica
gel and Amberlite ion exchange resin were the best
adsorption/desorption mediums under these conditions. Since
silica gel had the highest fluoroescence, it was selected as
the primary solid adsorbent for MIC.

TABLE I

Relative Fluorescence Obtained From Various
Adsorbents Using The Diacetylmonoxime Procedure

Adsorption Medium	Amount of MIC Placed on Adosrbent, ug	Percent Transmittance
Silica Gel, GC Grade 20/40 mesh	925	51
1% HPO$_4$ Silica Gel	1850	40
Porapak N, 50/80 mesh	925	0
Porapak T, 50/80 mesh	925	0
Amberlite XAD-2	925	30

Because MIC is thought to react with water to form dimethylurea (DMU), standard solutions of DMU were prepared and analyzed using the diacetylmonoxime method. The purpose was to determine whether or not DMU could be used to make standards which were representative of the behavior of MIC on the adsorbent and in air. The results indicated that the urea may not be produced on silica gel or that the reactions were not stoichiometric, because more fluorescence was obtained from MIC standards than urea. Good recoveries were obtained when the results were compared with MIC standards. Because of the limited range of the spectrofluorometer for quantitative analysis, high performance liquid chromatography (HPLC) with fluorescence detection was investigated as a method of analysis for MIC and diacetylmonoxime.

Several unsuccessful attempts were made to analyze the fluorophor produced by the reaction of MIC with diacetyl-monoxime using HPLC and a multiwavelength fluoroescence detector. Because of a series of analytical problems, a search was initiated for a method that would lend itself to liquid chromatographic analysis more readily. Since methylisocyanate probably reacts with water according to the following equation:

$$CH_3NCO + H_2O \longrightarrow CH_3NHCOOH \xrightarrow{-CO_2} CH_3NH_2 \xrightarrow{CH_3NCO} CH_3NHCONHCH_3,$$

to produce monomethylamine as an intermediate product, a highly sensitive fluorescent procedure was investigated as a means of determining MIC in air.

Reaction of Fluorescamine with MIC

A search of the literature revealed that there were several sensitive assay procedures for primary amines, but none of these procedures possessed the capabilities of determining concentration in the picomole range. The literature search did reveal that fluorescamine (Fluram) reacts with aliphatic amines to produce intense fluorophors that can be detected in the picomole range. Known quantities of the organoisocyanate were placed on silica gel tubes. Lab air was aspirating through the tubes, and reacting with Fluram. It was discovered that fluorescamine reacted with MIC on silica gel to produce highly fluorescent products at microgram concentrations (>100). These fluoroscent products emitted a greater fluorescence than the diacetylmonoxime fluorophors and were found to be easy to analyze and quite stable compounds. Fluram in tetrahydrofuran is nonfluoroescent and the reaction with primary amines is stated to be proportional to the actual amine content. This procedure was further evaluated by placing known quantities of

MIC in flexible bags, evacuating the content of the bag through silica gel, desorbing with Fluram solution, and analyzing by HPLC using a multiwavelength fluorescent detector. Table II illustrates the recoveries of MIC that were obtained at several concentrations. Statistical analysis of the results revealed that the accuracy and the precision of the method within the range of 41 to 2 ppm was 4.9% and 4.4% respectively. Standards were prepared by applying identical concentrations on silica gel and analyzing in the same way as the sample tubes.

Chemistry of the Fluram-MIC Reaction

Fluorescamine is 4-phenylspiro[furan-2(3H),1-phthalan] 3,3'dione. MIC should react with fluram according to the following equation:

This reaction takes place in a matter of seconds and produces significantly more fluorescence than the diacetylmonoxime fluorophors. Excess reagent is quickly hydrolyzed to form nonfluorescent water soluble products. Secondary, tertiary, and aromatic amines did not react with fluram to produce any measureable fluorescence. The reaction did not occur when ammonia and ammonium salts were tested for fluorescence. Mass spectrometry of an actual field sample confirmed that the substitution product is the fluorescent species that is shown above. Further mass spectra studies indicated that dimethylurea is not produced during this reaction. This was later confirmed by introducing known quantities of the urea and little or no fluorescence was noted. These tests indicate that Fluram does react with the primary amine intermediate on the adsorbent according to the above equation, and that monomethylamine and other primary aliphatic amines would interfere.

TABLE II

Recovery Of MIC From Flexible Bags On Silica Gel

Expected Concentration, ppm	Recovered Concentration, ppm	% Recovery
40.8	43.2	106
40.8	34.6	85
40.8	33.7	83
40.8	41.2	101
40.8	52.4	128
20.4	16.5	81
20.4	16.8	83
20.4	21.3	104
20.4	18.1	89
20.4	20.0	98
4.1	4.4	107
4.1	3.8	93
4.1	3.8	93
4.1	3.5	85
4.1	4.0	98
2.04	1.98	97
2.04	1.76	86
2.04	1.84	90
2.04	2.21	108
2.04	1.98	97

Total $\overline{X}$ Recovery = 95.6
S = 3.9
A = 4.4%
P = 4.0

Evaluation of the Liquid Chromatographic Columns

Several high performance liquid chromatographic columns were evaluated according to their capabilities to separate and release the MIC-Fluram fluorophor. Reverse phase, normal partition, and amine bonded columns were tested. The reverse phase columns performed the separation and analysis more proficiently than the other columns. A Varian CH-10 column was the best column from among the several ones that were tested.

Limit of Detection and Sensitivity

The limit of detection of the silica gel adsorption/desorption procedure was determined by placing known concentrations on the adsorbent, pulling lab air through the adsorbent at 500 cc per minute for 15 minutes, and analyzing using the fluorogenic assay method. Figure 1 illustrates a typical calibration curve that can be obtained using the procedure. The limit of detection with linearity was determined to be 4.76 micrograms per milliliter which is to 0.02 ppm in a 180 liter air sample (6 hr).

Humidity Effects Upon Sample Retention

The effects of moisture upon sample retention were evaluated by aspirating moist air at 90% relative humidity through adsorption tubes containing known concentrations of MIC. The samples were analyzed in the usual manner. No significant effects of moisture upon sample retention were noted. Table III contains the pertinent statistical data which was obtained during the humidity effects evaluation.

Elimination of Interferences

Since earlier studies revealed that monomethylamine would interfere, further studies were conducted to determine if the removal of this interference could be accomplished. A brief literature survey revealed that an aqueous solution of cupric chloride could conceivably remove all amine interferences. Since the solubility of methyl isocyanate is only 6.7% by weight in water, it was thought that the organic isocyanate would possibly pass through aqueous media unmodified; and thus allow the quantitative determination of MIC in the presence of interferences which would be removed in aqueous solutions. The effectiveness of the removal of the interference of mono-methylamine was determined by generating known concentrations of MIC and monomethylamine in air and sampling through an impinger containing 0.5% cupric chloride which was followed by

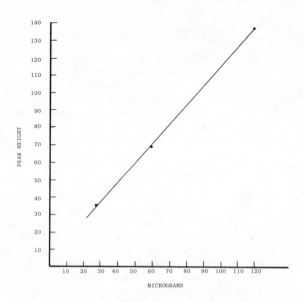

Figure 1.   Typical calibration curve obtained from silica gel

TABLE III

Effects of Humidity Upon Sample
Retention On Silica Gel

Expected ppm	Recovered ppm	% Relative Humidity	Percent Recovery
20.4	20.7	92	101.5
20.4	20.6	92	100.9
20.4	19.2	92	94.1
20.4	20.6	92	100.9
20.4	20.8	92	101.8

$\bar{X}$ = 20.38 ppm   CV =   3.2%
S =   0.66 ppm   A =   0.09%

an adsorption tube containing silica gel. The data that is shown in Table IV lists the amounts of MIC that were recovered in the presence of 100 ppm of monomethylamine. These results indicate that MMA will not interfere with the determination of MIC even at concentrations which approach 100 ppm. To further evaluate the capabilities of the liquid scrubber/solid adsorption technique, a known concentration of MIC was pulled through the sampling system and analyzed by the fluorogenic assay procedure. The results shown in Table V indicate that 98.6% of the expected MIC concentration was recovered through the $CuCl_2$ solution. These experiments indicated that the $CuCl_2$ prefilter is a very effective means of removing the interference of monomethylamine and other amines while allowing the quantitative passage of MIC.

Field Evaluation of the Method

The method was evaluated in the field in order to determine if (a) the adsorption medium functioned properly in the occupational setting, (b) if any sample displacement occurred, and (c) if there might be any additional interferences.

In order to determine if the method functioned properly in the occupational environment, simultaneous samples were taken using impingers containing the cupric chloride prefilter and silica gel tubes without a prefilter. These samples were collected side by side and under the same conditions in industrial environments where MIC was not likely to be present. If there were any ambient interferences, there would be significant differences in the concentrations that were obtained by the collection procedures. Table VI illustrates the results that were obtained and no significant differences in the concentrations could be determined.

Air samples were also collected in industrial atmospheres that contained the organoisocyanate. Table VII contains the results that were obtained and indicate the procedure is capable of measuring MIC in occupational environments.

Amberlite XAD-2 Resin Procedure

Since a 6 hour sampling time was necessary in order to determine the threshold limit value using the silica gel procedure, Amberlite XAD-2 synthetic ion exchange resin was again tested as an adsorption medium, this time using the fluorescamine analytical procedure. Laboratory tests revealed that XAD-2 released the MIC-fluram fluorophor more efficiently at lower concentrations than silica gel. Figures 2 and 3 illustrate the chromatographic response and the linearity of the procedure. Using XAD-2, 238 nanograms of MIC could be

TABLE IV

Recovery of MIC In The Presence
Of Monoethylamine on Silica Gel

Expected Amount, ppm	Recovered Amount, ppm	Percent Recovery
20.4	18.2	89.2
20.4	16.7	82.0
20.4	16.7	82.0
20.4	19.3	94.6
20.4	17.1	83.6

$\bar{X}$ = 88.6   Accuracy = 11.4%
S = 8.2   Precision = 9.25%

TABLE V

Recovery Of MIC Through
0.5% $CuCl_2$ Solution

Expected Amount, ppm	Recovered Amount, ppm	Percent Recovery
20.4	17.4	85.3
20.4	20.0	98.1
20.4	21.1	103.4
20.4	20.2	99.0
20.4	21.9	107.0

$\bar{X}$ = 98.6   Accuracy = 1.4%
S = 8.2%   Precision = 8.32

TABLE VI

Results Of Simultaneous Samples Collected With and
Without $CuCl_2$ Filter In Industrial Environments

Sample No. & Type	Concentration, ppm	Total Volume, liters
1A-Nonfiltered	<0.085	120
1B-Filtered	<0.085	120
2A-Nonfiltered	<0.085	120
2B-Filtered	<0.085	120
3A-Nonfiltered	<0.085	120
3B-Filtered	<0.085	120
T1A-Nonfiltered	<0.11	86.4
T1B-Filtered	<0.11	89.1
T2A-Nonfiltered	<0.11	90.0
T2B-Filtered	<0.11	89.1
Blank	0	0

TABLE VII

MIC Sampling Survey

Sample No.	ppm	Total Volume (L)
I-1	0.09	120
I-2	0.12	120
I-3	0.13	120
I-4	0.09	120
I-5	11.00	123
I-6	0.11	133
I-7	0.21	102
I-8	0.00	129
I-9	0.09	130
I-10	0.12	134
I-11	0.57	37.5
I-12	0.61	37.5
I-13	0.46	37.5
I-14	14.40	37.5
I-15	0.50	37.5

Simultaneous impinger sample using colorimetric
method showed 6.8, 0.2, and 0.3 ppm for I-14,
I-9, and I-10 samples respectively.

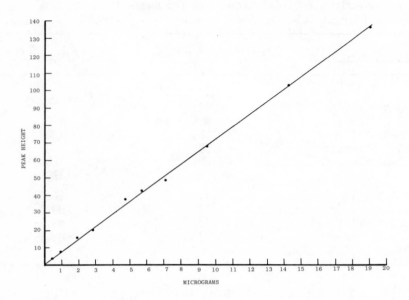

Figure 2.   Typical calibration curve obtained from XAD-2 resin

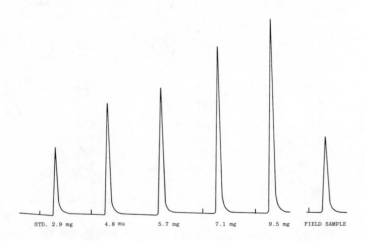

Figure 3.   Typical chromatograms

collected and released for analysis using the HPLC fluorogenic assay procedure. This is equivalent to 0.01 ppm in a 15 liter air sample. The fluorophor produced on the ion exchange resin was the same fluorophor which was produced on the silica gel. Because of the lower limit of detection of the XAD-2 procedure, a significant increase in sensitivity is possible in a shorter sampling time period. In order to determine which collection medium is the better adsorption medium for MIC, known concentrations of the organoisocyanate were generated statically and dynamically in the range of 1.32 ppm to 0.01 ppm, humidity effects were evaluated, removal of monomethylamine interferences, and field tests were conducted.

Collection Efficiency of the Resin

The sorbability of MIC on XAD-2 was tested statically by producing calibration mixture in flexible bags and evaluating the total volume of the bag into adsorption tubes containing the resin. Initial tests at flow rates of 100 cc per minute indicated that sample breakthrough was occurring. However, at a 75 cc per minute flow rate, excellent recoveries were obtained using the resin. Table VIII shows the resin retained 99.6% of the MIC, and that the method has the required precision and accuracy to provide reliable measurements of exposure.

The collection efficiency was evaluated dynamically by using a single chamber dilution system, and a stainless steel cylinder containing a known concentration of MIC. The concentration of the standard cylinder was confirmed by nitrogen-phosphorus flame ionization gas chromatography. Known concentrations were generated at 1.32, 0.65, 0.058, and 0.012 ppm by the addition of diluent air to the calibration mixture from the cylinder. The results are shown in Table IX. Statistical analysis of the results show that the mean recovery was 101.7 percent of expected concentration, while the standard deviation was 0.55 ppm and the accuracy was 1.7%. Linear regression analysis of the results produced a line of best fit with a slope of 1.005, an intercept of 0.006, and a correlation coefficient of 0.997. The regression line is shown in Figure 4. Since the slope of the line is very close to 1 and the intercept is quite small, these results indicate that the method is very accurate and precise at all concentrations.

Humidity Effects

At 60 and 90 percent relative humidities, the effects of moisture laden air upon sample retention were tested by introducing moist diluent air into a known concentration of

TABLE VIII

Recovery Of MIC On Amberlite XAD-2
Ion Exchange Resin From Static System

Expected Concentration, ppm	Recovered Concentration, ppm	Percent Recovery
0.51	0.47	92
0.51	0.50	98
0.51	0.48	94
0.51	0.52	102
0.51	0.49	97
0.51	0.120	94
0.13	0.130	100
0.13	0.126	97
0.13	0.141	109
0.13	0.147	113

$\bar{X}$ Recovery = 99.6   Precision = 6.8%
         S = 6.75   Accuracy = 0.4%

TABLE IX

Recovery Of MIC On XAD-2 From Dynamic System

Expected Amount, ppm	Recovered Amount, ppm	Percent Recovery
0.012	0.011	91.7
0.012	0.011	91.7
0.012	0.015	125.0
0.012	0.013	108.3
0.012	0.011	91.7
0.058	0.063	108.6
0.058	0.057	98.2
0.058	0.058	100.0
0.058	0.055	94.8
0.058	0.051	87.9
0.65	0.67	103.0
0.65	0.61	93.8
0.65	0.61	93.8
0.65	0.66	116.9
0.65	0.67	118.5
1.32	1.28	96.9
1.32	1.30	98.5
1.32	1.31	100.8
1.32	1.35	102.2
1.32	1.36	103.0

$\bar{X}$ = 101.66   Accuracy = 1.7%
S =   0.55   Precision = 10.2%

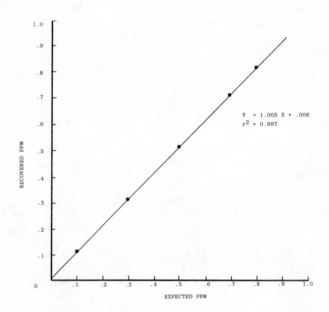

Figure 4. Regression curve for recovered vs. expected ppm using XAD-2 resin

MIC. The resulting concentrations were adsorbed on Amberlite
XAD-2 and analyzed by desorbing and reacting with fluorescamine
and subsequent fluorogenic assay. An average recovery of 101.3
percent was obtained. The excellent recoveries and the small
precision statistic indicate that high relative humidities do
not significantly effect sample collection and retention of MIC
on XAD-2. Table X displays the results.

Storage Stability of Adsorption Tube Samples

In many instances, it is impractical to analyze air samples
immediately after the samples are taken in the field. It is
therefore necessary to know the length of time and under what
conditions samples can be stored without significant loss.
Again, a known concentration of the isocyanate was placed into
glass tubes containing XAD-2 and laboratory air was aspirated
through the tubes. The tubes were placed in a refrigerator and
were analyzed after 1, 3, 5, 7, and 14 days. The data which is
depicted in Table XI indicates that samples can be stored up to
two weeks without appreciable loss of MIC if kept refrigerated.

Removal of Interferences at Low Concentratons

The effectiveness of removal of amine interferences was
evaluated by placing a known quantity of MIC on XAD-2,
attaching the primary section of the tube to the exit port of
micro-impinger, and injecting a known concentration of the
amine while a known volume of air was being pulled through the
system. Figure 5 illustrates the sampling system that was used
during this test. No interference was noted in the presence of
50 ppm of monomethylamine. Table XII shows the recoveries of
MIC that were obtained. Next, a known quantity of MIC was
generated and passed through the $CuCl_2$ solution onto the ion
exchange resin where it was adsorbed. The tubes were analyzed
and an average recovery of 90% was obtained. These results
indicate that MIC can be quantitatively recovered in the
presence of possible amine interferences.

Field Tests of the Method

The ion exchange procedure was evaluated in several
industrial environments by collecting personal, area, and stack
samples. The data shown in Table XIII are the results obtained
from area and personal monitoring. These results indicate that
the method is indeed capable of determining MIC in the
occupational environment.

The ion exchange resin was also used to determine the
emission rate of MIC from a stack at different charge rates.

TABLE X

Retention Of MIC By XAD-2 At High Humidities

Expected Amount, ppm	Recovery Amount, ppm	Percent Recovery	% Relative Humidity
3.4	3.47	102	60
3.4	3.47	102	60
3.4	3.37	99	60
3.4	3.30	96	60
3.4	3.40	100	60
0.08	0.09	112.5	90
0.08	0.08	100	90
0.08	0.08	100	90
0.08	0.081	101	90

$\overline{X}$ = 101.25   Accuracy = 1.3%
S =   4.3   Precision = 4.3%

TABLE XI

Shelf Life Study

Time Period, Days	Percent Recovery
1	97.5
3	97.5
5	104.0
7	89.0
14	95.0

$\overline{X}$ = 96.6
All samples were refrigerated.

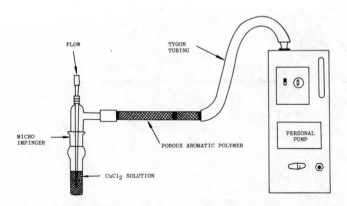

Figure 5.   Sampling method for collecting MIC in the presence of MMA

TABLE XII

RECOVERY OF MIC ON XAD-2 IN THE PRESENCE
OF MONOMETHYLAMINE (50 PPM)

Expected Amount, ppm	Recovered Amount, ppm	Percent Recovery
0.2	0.200	100
0.2	0.194	97
0.2	0.188	94
0.2	0.188	94
0.2	0.188	94
0.2	0.212	106

$\bar{X}$ Recovery = 0.195
S = 0.01

TABLE XIII

RESULTS OF MIC SURVEY USING XAD-2 ION EXCHANGE RESINS

Date	Number	PPM
4-5-78	1A	0.51
"	2A	0.04
"	3A	0.04
"	4A	0.04
"	5A	0.04
"	6A	0.04
"	7A	0.04
"	8A	0.80
5-1-78	1A	0.23
"	2A	0.09
"	3A	0.09
"	4A	0.09
"	5A	0.09
"	6A	0.13
"	7A	0.10
"	8A	0.10
"	9A	0.10
"	10A	0.09
"	11A	0.09
"	12A	0.11
"	13A	0.19
"	14A	1.22
"	15A	0.19
"	16A	0.16
9-5-78	1S	73.96
"	2S	69.08
"	3S	30.22
"	4S	47.28

The effluent stream from the stack contained a high moisture content and even under these conditions the method functioned properly. The results shown in Table XIV show that a proportional increase in concentration was obtained as the charge rate increased. Appendix A describes the analytical method in total using the ion exchange resin as the sampling adsorbent.

TABLE XIV

MIC STACK SAMPLING RESULTS

Charge Rate lb/hr	Total Volume	Total ppm
12	4.16	3.28
12	3.73	5.96
30	2.91	10.39
30	2.58	11.72
360	1.51	25.20
360	1.30	29.47
720	1.30	43.56

ABSTRACT

A novel method for monitoring occupational exposure to methyl isocyanate has been developed. The method involves the collection of methyl isocyanate on an ion exchange resin, reaction with a fluorescent reagent, and analysis by high pressure liquid chromatography. Several parameters such as evaluation of adsorbents and columns, effects of humidity, sampling rates, shelf life, interference from contaminants, desorption technique, limit of detection, and calibration curve were investigated. The procedure is capable of measuring methyl isocyanate at and below the TLV of 0.02 ppm by volume in a 15 liter air sample. The method was evaluated statistically and field tested in the industrial environment.

REFERENCES

1. "Threshold Limit Values for Chemical Substances and Physical Agents in the Workroom Environment with Intended Changes for 1977", Adopted by the American Conference of Governmental Industrial Hygienist.

2. Unpublished work of Union Carbide Corporation.

3. Streuli and Averell, "The Analytical Chemistry of Nitrogen and Its Compounds, Part II", p. 469, Wiley-Interscience, New York, 1970.

APPENDIX A

1. PURPOSE AND LIMITATIONS

This paper describes a procedure for measuring the exposure of personnel to methyl isocyanate (MIC) in air in the occupational environment. The ion exchange adsorbent, together with the high-performance liquid chromatographic procedure as written, is capable of detecting 238 ng of MIC per milliliter. This is equivalent to 0.01 parts per million in a 15-liter air sample volume.

The method is dependent upon the production of an intensely fluorescent fluorophor which provides the basis for a rapid and sensitive assay of methyl isocyanate after collection on the adsorbent. Monomethylamine, which is the only known interference, can be eliminated by absorption in aqueous solution of cupric chloride.

2. PRINCIPLE

The sample is collected by passing air through a glass tube containing ion exchange resin XAD-2 where airborne methyl isocyanate is adsorbed. The concentration of MIC is determined after desorption with a solution of fluorescamine (Fluram) in tetrahydrofuran and analysis by high-performance liquid chromatography using a multiwavelength fluorescent detector.

3. INSTRUMENT PARAMETERS

Chromatograph	Varian 8500 liquid chromatograph equipped with a Dupont 836 fluorescence detector, equipped with an emission filter of 377 nm cut-off and excitation filter of 250-390 nm or equivalent

Column   25 cm x 2 mm x 6.4 mm O.D.
                                    stainless steel packed with
                                    Varian Micropak CH-10 Bonded
                                    Phase
Column Conditions
  Mobile phase   Isocratic: A = Water 25%
                                                B = Methanol 75%

Flow   30 ml per hr

Column pressure   1500 psi (approximately)

Temperature   ambient

Sample size   10 μl sample loop

Retention time   1.0 minutes

4. APPARATUS AND REAGENTS

a) Chroma-Vue Model CC-20 UV Box; Ultra-violet Products,
    Inc., San Gabriel, CA.
b) Fluorescamine (Fluram), Pierce Chemical Company, Box
    117, Rockford, IL 61105.
c) Methyl Isocyanate, 99% minimum
d) Tetrahydrofuran, non spectro-distilled in glass,
    Burdick and Jackson, Muskegan, MI 49442.
e) Screw-cap vials with septums, Pierce Chemical Company.
f) Personal sampling pumps, Sipin Model Sp-2 or equivalent.
g) Purified XAD-2 resin, Applied Science Laboratories,
    Inc., State College, PA 16801.
h) Fire polished glass tubes, 8 mm O.D. x 6 mm I.D. by 15
    cm length.
i) Silane-treated glass wool.
j) End caps, Altech Associates, St. No. 4025.
k) Stop watch.
l) Soap film flowmeter.
m) Syringe, 1 ml solvent flushing syringe; Altech
    Associates, Inc., Arlington Heights, IL.
n) Syringe, 50-microliter Glenco sample syringe, Altech
    Associates, Inc.
o) Syringe, 10-microliter Hamilton.
p) Methanol, C=O-free.
q) Cupric chloride dihydrate.
r) Sodium carbonate.
s) Ethyl ether.
t) Funnel, Buchner, with coarse fritted disc.
u) Vacuum flask, 500-ml.

5. PREPARATION OF ION EXCHANGE XAD-2 RESIN

a)   Weigh 25 g of XAD-2 resin into a Buchner funnel with
     fritted disc.
b)   Wash twice with 50 ml of methanol, using vacuum to pull
     excess methanol from resin.
c)   Wash twice with 50 ml of distilled water, using vacuum
     to pull excess water from resin.
d)   Add 1g of sodium carbonate to 100 ml of distilled water.
e)   Wash resin with sodium carbonate solution and pull
     excess from resin with vacuum.
f)   Rinse twice with 50 ml of ethyl ether and allow to dry
     at room temperature.

6. PREPARATION OF FLUORESCAMINE AND CUPRIC CHLORIDE SOLUTIONS

a)   Fluram   Weigh 0.35 g of fluorescamine to the nearest
     0.1 mg and place in a 100-ml volumetric flask. Add
     tetrahydrofuran and swirl. Dilute to the mark with
     additional tetrahydrofuran.
b)   Pipet 10 ml of this solution into another 100-ml
     volumetric and dilute to the mark with tetrahydrofuran.
     This solution is used for desorption of the MIC from
     the adsorbent.
c)   Store in refrigerator until needed.
d)   CuCl$_2$ Solution   Weigh 5 g of CuCl$_2$ and place into a
     1-liter volumetric flask and dilute to the mark with
     distilled water.
e)   Place 2 ml of this solution into a micro-impinger and
     attach the exit port to the primary section of the
     adsorption tubes by means of a 5.0-cm piece of tubing.
f)   The cupric chloride prefilter is essential to the
     determination if monomethylamine and MIC are known to
     exist in the same environment.

7. PREPARATION OF ADSORPTION TUBES

a)   Cut 8-mm O.D. (6 mm - I.D.) Pyrex glass tubing into
     15.0-cm lengths and fire polish the ends.
b)   Introduce a silane-treated glass wool plug
     approximately 80 mm from the opening.
c)   Add washed XAD-2 resin in lengths of 70 mm for the
     primary section and 30 mm for the backup section.
d)   Add glass wool plugs to the exit and entrance sections
     of the tube and cap with the end caps until ready for
     use.

8. SAMPLING PROCEDURE

a) Immediately before sampling, remove the end caps from
    the adsorption tube and attach the backup section to a
    portable pump.
b) Set the flowrate at 30 to 75 ml per minute.
c) Sample volume should not exceed 15 liters.
d) At the end of the sampling period, cap the ends of the
    tubes and mark for later identification.
e) Return the sample tubes to the appropriate laboratory
    and store in a refrigerator prior to analysis.

9. ANALYTICAL PROCEDURE

a) Uncap the sample tube and remove the glass wool from
    the primary section. Make sure that no particles
    adhere to the glass wool plug.
b) Transfer the XAD-2 resin from the primary section into
    a screw-cap vial.
c) Pipet 2 milliliters of fluorescamine solution into the
    vial and cap the container as tightly as possible.
d) Shake the vials vigorously by hand for 30 seconds and
    with a "rocking" motion wash the XAD-2 resin particles
    to the bottom of the vial in order to achieve good
    contact with the fluorescamine solution.
e) Place the sample in the Brinkman-Chromato-Vue
    Ultraviolet box for 15 minutes at the long wave U.V.
    setting.
f) Remove the vial from the box.
g) Flush the 10-μl loop with 1 ml of CO-free methanol.
    Swirl the sample solution.
h) Dip the needle into the sample solution in the
    desorption vial and withdraw the plunger until the
    volume of the sample in the syringe reaches 40 ul.
    Make sure there are no air bubbles in the injection
    fluid.
i) Inject the entire contents of the syringe into the
    sample injection system.
j) Measure the peak height or area and determine the MIC
    concentration from a previously prepared calibration
    curve.
k) Analyze the backup (small) section of the adsorption
    tube in the same manner as the primary.
l) If the MIC content of the backup section is found to
    exceed 25 percent of the quantity in the primary
    section, the possibility exists that part of the vapors
    have passed through the tube without being adsorbed.
    In the event this occurs, the air sampling will have to
    be repeated, taking a smaller total volume of air
    through the tube.

m) Analyze the blank tube in the same manner as the sample tube.
n) All air samples must be desorbed at the same time as the standards in order to obtain accurate measurements of the actual MIC concentrations collected on the adsorbent.

10. CALIBRATION CURVE

a) Pipet 1 ml of tetrahydrofuran into each of 5 screw-cap vials.
b) Using a 10-ul Hamilton Syringe, inject 0.5, 1, 2, 5, and 7.5 microliters of MIC into respective vials.
c) Swirl each vial. These standards contain 0.476, 0.952, 1.90, 4.76, and 7.14 micrograms of MIC per microliter.
d) Store standards in a refrigerator until needed.
e) With a 10-ul Hamilton Syringe, inject one microliter of each standard into respective previously prepared XAD-2 resin tubes.
f) All standard tubes should be desorbed at the same time as the air samples that were collected in the field. This is to insure that the concentration measurements are accurate and precise.
g) Inject these standards into the chromatograph using the injection technique described in Section 9, Analytical Procedure. Swirl the vial each time prior to withdrawing a sample.
h) Plot peak area or height versus micrograms of MIC per milliliter.

11. CALCULATION

$$\frac{(A-B) \times 24.45 \times 2 \times 760 \times (T + 273)}{V \times MW \times P \times 298} = \text{ppm of MIC}$$

A = micrograms of MIC per ml obtained from calibration curve
B = micrograms of MIC in blank
MW = molecular weight of MIC (57.05)
V = total volume of air sampled in liters
P = pressure (mm Hg) of air sampled
T = temperature ($^{\circ}$C) of air sampled
760 = standard pressure (mm Hg)
273 = standard temperature ($^{\circ}$K)

12. REFERENCE   7-RSC-69

RECEIVED October 22, 1979.

Improved Resolution in High Performance Liquid Chromatography Analysis of Polynuclear Aromatic Hydrocarbons Using Ternary Solvent Systems

BARRY R. BELINKY

National Institute for Occupational Safety and Health,
4676 Columbia Parkway, Cincinnati, OH 45226

Polynuclear aromatic hydrocarbons (PAH's) are produced in most incomplete combustion processes. Examples are internal combustion engines, effluents from coal fired electricity generating plants, tobacco smoke, and from coking operations in steel and aluminum refineries. PAH's are also present in coal tar derived and coal tar containing products such as creosote and roofing pitch. They are found in the water we drink and the air we breathe, and are a ubiquitous component of our environment.

Concern for public health and safety is stimulated by the knowledge that many of these compounds are potent carcinogens. Past analytical efforts to relate chemical composition to carcinogenicity have used quantitation of the cyclohexane or benzene soluble fraction (BSF)(1) and of benzo(a)pyrene (BaP) (2,3,4,5) as indexes of carcinogenicity. However, the BSF is a nonspecific determination, as many nontoxic compounds are found in this fraction. BaP determinations can only give a crude estimate of carcinogenicity because (a) it is only one of many carcinogenic PAH's (b) the carcinogenic activity of different PAH's vary over a wide range and (c) the distribution of individual PAH's can fluctuate greatly from sample to sample. The vast complexity of PAH samples has been shown by Lao (6), who has identified over 120 PAH's in urban airborne particulate matter and Severson (7), who has identified about 900 PAH's in tobacco smoke. It is evident, then, that a need exists to more fully characterize the molecular species found in PAH mixtures.

Chromatographic Separation of PAH's

Both gas chromatography (GC) and high performance liquid chromatography (HPLC) have been extensively utilized in the separation of these complex mixtures. GC, especially when capillary columns are used, has been shown to have better overall resolving power than HPLC. HPLC coupled to a fluorescence detector, on the other hand, can provide sensitivities in the picogram range (8) as opposed to the nanogram range for GC/MS. In addition, stopped flow techniques allow UV or fluorescence spectra to be obtained for individual peaks, thus providing confirmation of structure. Improvement in resolving power of HPLC thus becomes an obvious goal in the effort to identify and quantitate mixtures of PAH's.

One way in which this can be accomplished is through the use of selective monitors. Selective UV detection has been demonstrated by, among others, Krstulovic and Brown (9) at the University of Rhode Island. Wheals (10) utilized selective fluorescence monitoring to differentiate peaks. Neither of these techniques actually improves resolution; they merely simplify the chromatogram either by eliminating peaks or by changing the ratios of overlapping peaks so that they may be determined mathematically. The drawback to such a procedure is that either multiple detectors must be used or multiple runs be made to obtain a complete analysis.

Another method is to optimize those chromatographic parameters which affect resolution. Although this paper is directed at a pragmatic approach to accomplishing this task, a brief detour into the mathematics is needed before we proceed. The fundamental equation describing chromatographic resolution, R_s is

$$R_S = \frac{1}{4} \left[\frac{\alpha}{\alpha - 1} \right] \sqrt{N} \left[\frac{k'}{1 + k'} \right] \qquad \text{Eq. 1}$$

where α, N and k' are, respectively, the separation factor, theoretical plate number and capacity factor.(24)

One can see three routes to an increase in the value of resolution. First, one can increase the plate number N which results in an increase in resolution proportional to the square root of N. The use of microparticulate packings was a major breakthrough in this respect. If we assume, however, that the chromatographer already has at his disposal a high efficiency column, then he must go to great

lengths to obtain any significant increase in
resolution because of the proportionality factor.
Secondly, one can adjust k', the capacity factor.
Figure 1 shows the relationship between k'/(1+k') and
k'. Traditionally this is accomplished by adjusting
the solvent composition so k' falls between 2 and 10,
since resolution falls off rapidly below a k' value of
2, and relatively little increase is obtained for
values of k' greater than 10. Finally the value of α,
the selectivity factor can be adjusted. Obviously,
one technique for changing the selectivity is to
change the stationary phase. Indeed, HPLC analysis of
PAH has been done on silica (11), alumina (12),
cellulose acetate (13,14) and polyamide (13) columns
and even silica columns with specialized bonded phases
such as 3-(2,4,5,7-Tetranitrofluorenimine)propyl-
diethoxysiloxane (15). A change in mobile phase will
also affect α. Therefore, in the present work, the
ternary solvent system acetonitrile/methanol/water was
examined over a wide range of concentrations to
determine optimum mobile phase composition for PAH
analysis. A statistical experimental design strategy
was used for the optimization process.

Development of Optimal Mobile Phase

        Most of the recent literature (16-20) describing
PAH analysis by HPLC has centered on the use of
octadecylsilane bonded stationary phases and either
methanol-water or acetonitrile-water as the mobile
phase. Both isocratic and gradient conditions have
been utilized. The general approach taken to optimize
chromatographic conditions usually is as follows. One
of the two binary solvent systems methanol/water or
acetonitrile/water is selected, and an arbitrary
isocratic composition, say 60/40 or 70/30, is chosen.
A standard mixture is chromatographed and then the
organic/water ratio is adjusted to optimize k'.
Depending upon the nature of the sample, a gradient
may or may not be implemented to reduce analysis time
while maintaining reasonable separation. If the
resolution is insufficient for the analysis at hand,
the other binary system is evaluated in the same
manner. Figure 2 presents a triangular coordinate
system, allowing visualization of all combinations of
the three solvents. Vertex A represents 100%
methanol, vertex B represents 100% acetonitrile, and
vertex C, 100% water. Points X and Y represent the
arbitrary binary solvent systems mentioned previously.

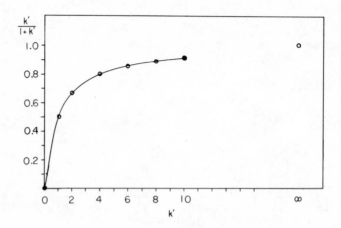

Figure 1.   Plot of $k'/(1 + k')$ *vs.* k'

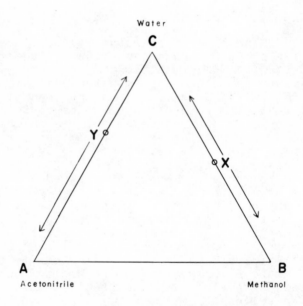

Figure 2.   Representation of binary solvents X *and* Y *as points in the ternary
solvent system* ABC

The arrows along the AC and BC axes are the ranges over which the solvent systems are varied.

Now the question arises: what happens in the center of this triangle where not two but three solvents are present? Are the capacity factors merely averaged? If so, α (which is the ratio of the capacity factors for solute 1 and solute 2) will not be enhanced. Or do more subtle effects occur? Karger (21), Snyder and Kirkland (22), Bakalyar (23) and others have discussed the expanded solubility parameter concept which says that polarity as defined by the Hildebrand solubility parameter is actually a composite of specific intermolecular interactions consisting of dispersive, dipole and hydrogen bonding interactions. No attempt will be made here to develop these subparameters on a theoretical basis. Suffice it to say that much is not yet understood regarding the quantification of these interactions -- especially in aqueous mixtures due to the unique properties of water. At any rate, we cannot yet predict values for resolution in a ternary solvent system based on theoretical considerations. To try to determine optimal solvent ratios in a ternary system by a trial and error approach would involve an inordinate number of experiments -- far more than most analysts would care to make. Nevertheless, a relatively simple way exists to experimentally optimize resolution in the ternary system.

Experimental

Fluoranthene (MC&B), Pyrene and Benzo(a)pyrene (Eastman Organic Chemicals), Benz(a)anthracene and Chrysene (Aldrich Chemical Co.) and Perylene (Pfaultz & Bauer) were used as received to make a standard solution with a concentration of approximately 0.1 mg/ml of each PAH.

Methanol and Acetonitrile (UV grade - Burdick & Jackson Laboratories) and water purified with a Millipore Super Q system were filtered through an 0.5 micron filter and degassed prior to use.

Instrumentation was a Waters Associates HPLC system including two Model 6000A pumps, a Model 440 UV detector fixed at 254 nm, a Model 660 solvent programmer and a Model U6K injector. A Vydac 201 TP reverse phase column (10 micron C-18 packing, 4.6 mm ID x 25 cm) was used throughout.

Discussion

The goal of this investigation was to determine optimum mobile phase composition for PAH analysis using the ternary solvent system acetonitrile/methanol/water. A model PAH standard solution was prepared consisting of three pairs of compounds listed in order of increasing retention: Fluoranthene-Pyrene, Benz(a)anthracene-Chrysene, and Perylene-Benzo(a)pyrene. The basic optimization strategy was as follows: 1) an isocratic ternary solvent system was found which gave maximum resolution of the fluoranthene-pyrene peaks at a k' = 5; 2) two additional isocratic ternary solvent systems were found to optimize the resolution of each of the other two PAH pairs; 3) a solvent gradient was constructed which incorporated all three isocratic compositions. All three optimal isocratic systems were determined simultaneously by means of a Simplex statistical design strategy.

The statisical design employed for the study requires that a bold approach be used: that is, both the upper and lower bounds of the region being investigated should be chosen such that they completely enclose the region of interest. Figure 3 shows this region. In the case of acetonitrile/methanol/water the two vertices where the eluent is strongest for the solutes of interest are pure methanol and pure acetonitrile. The weakest eluent is pure water. However, with pure water the PAH's would never be eluted from the column, so that particular choice is impractical. Therefore, a 65/35 methanol/water composition was chosen as the weakest mobile phase along the AC axis, and a 55/45 acetonitrile/water composition as the lower bound of the BC axis. These points are labeled C' and D' respectively. A Simplex design for a three component mixture requires a triangular coordinate system which obviously has only three vertices. Because of the constraint we have put on the upper bound for water content, not three but four vertices exist. By connecting points B and C', two roughly equal triangular areas are generated, each of which can be thought of as representing an independent ternary solvent system. These two triangular regions ABC' and BC'D' can be represented on an isometric orthogonal plot as seen in Figure 4. Vertex D' is technically a pseudocomponent rather than a component of the system because it is actually a mixture of the components B (acetonitrile) and C (water). Likewise, pseudocom-

ponent C' is a methanol/water mixture. When reading
the orthogonal graph, the line AB represents zero
content of C'. Lines parallel to AB moving closer to
vertex C' represent successively higher C' concentration. Acetonitrile is 100% at point B and
decreases in a linear fashion to zero along the BA and
BC' lines, and to 55% acetonitrile along the BD' line.
    Our objective is to generate response surfaces
which will allow the prediction of resolution at any
point within the regions ABC' and BC'D'. The response
surface is described mathematically by the special
cubic model shown in equation 2.

$$Y = b_1X_1 + b_2X_2 + b_3X_3 + b_{12}X_1X_2 + b_{13}X_1X_3$$
$$+ b_{23}X_2X_3 + b_{123}X_1X_2X_3 \qquad\qquad Eq.\ 2$$

    A measured value Y, which could be the capacity
factor or resolution, is shown as the sum of the
individual contributions of each component or
pseudocomponent in the system. X_1, X_2 and X_3 represent the fraction of each pseudocomponent present.
The b coefficients are determined experimentally.
Note that there are no terms such as $b_{11}X_1X_1$ present
because a solvent's interaction with itself has no
physical meaning in such a system. The responses (Y
values) are measured at each of the concentrations
depicted graphically in Figure 5, which represents one
of the two ternary systems previously described. The
concentration of each of the pseudocomponents is given
around the periphery. The seven closed circles are
the experimentally determined responses at each
vertex, at the midpoint of each binary system, and at
the centroid of the triangle. These seven points will
be used to generate the b coefficients in Equation 2.
The three open circles are also experimentally
determined values, and will be compared with values
calculated from the special cubic model to determine
the degree of fit. All ten values are determined in
duplicate so that an estimate of precision can be
made. The calculation of the "b" values is shown in
Equations 3 through 9, Table I. Substituting the b
values in Equation 2 will allow the prediction of Y
for any given solvent composition within the confines
of the model assuming the model is an accurate
representation of the response surface.

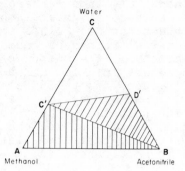

Figure 3. Ternary solvent systems ABC′ and BC′D′

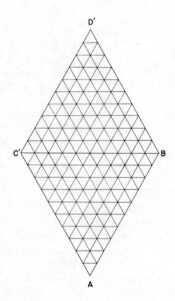

Figure 4. Orthogonal representation of ternary solvent systems ABC′ and BC′D′

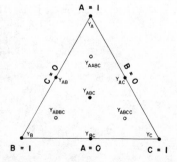

Figure 5. Ternary solvent system design; check points for determination of lack-of-fit indicated by open circles.

Table I

Calculation of Coefficients for Special Cubic Model

$$b_1 = Y_A \qquad\qquad \text{Eq. 3}$$

$$b_2 = Y_B \qquad\qquad \text{Eq. 4}$$

$$b_3 = Y_C \qquad\qquad \text{Eq. 5}$$

$$b_{12} = 4(Y_{AB}) - 2(Y_A + Y_B) \qquad\qquad \text{Eq. 6}$$

$$b_{13} = 4(Y_{AC}) - 2(Y_A + Y_C) \qquad\qquad \text{Eq. 7}$$

$$b_{23} = 4(Y_{BC}) - 2(Y_B + Y_C) \qquad\qquad \text{Eq. 8}$$

$$b_{123} = 27(Y_{ABC}) - 12(Y_{AB} + Y_{AC} + Y_{BC})$$
$$+ 3(Y_A + Y_B + Y_C) \qquad\qquad \text{Eq. 9}$$

The three checkpoints Y_{AABC}, Y_{ABBC} and Y_{ABCC} in Figure 5 are used to verify the validity of the model. This is accomplished by examining the difference between the observed and predicted values of Y at each checkpoint. The lack of fit is given by the expression in Equation 10.

$$S_{LF}^2 = \frac{1}{3} \sum_{i=1}^{3} (\overline{Y}_{oi} - \hat{Y}_i)^2 \qquad\qquad \text{Eq. 10}$$

where

$\overline{Y}_{oi}$ is the observed average response at th checkpoint, and $\hat{Y}_i$ is the predicted response at the ith checkpoint (from equation 2)

Duplicate values of Y for all ten points are used to determine the pooled error variance (Equation 11) and the replication error variance (Equation 12).

$$S_p^2 = \frac{\sum_{j=1}^{10} (Y_{j1} - Y_{j2})^2}{20} \qquad\qquad \text{Eq. 11}$$

$$S_{\overline{Y}}^2 = \frac{S_p^2}{2} \qquad\qquad \text{Eq. 12}$$

where

Y_{j1} and Y_{j2} are the duplicate response determinations at each of the ten solvent compositions.

And finally the lack of fit variance is compared to the replication error variance using an F-test (Eq. 13), which in this case being three components with ten degrees of freedom, is 3.71. If this ratio is less than 3.71, then the fit is good and the equation for the response surface can be considered valid.

$$\text{(F-test)} \quad S_{LF}^2 \div S_{\overline{Y}}^2 < 3.71 \qquad \text{Eq. 13}$$

A total of seventeen different mobile phase compositions are required to generate the response surface for the two Simplex designs as shown in Figure 6. Each run is done in duplicate, and the entire design is randomized to reduce experimental bias. Runs 12 through 17 are the checkpoints used to determine variance and goodness of fit. The overall design is shown in Table II.

Capacity factors, column efficiency in terms of N, and resolution were calculated for each of the six peaks in the chromatograms. Initial attempts to generate response surfaces using either k' or R_s were failures as indicated by the F-test in equation 13. New sets of coefficients for the special cubic model were generated, using log k' and log R_s as the measured responses, which gave acceptable F-tests. Orthogonal plots were then generated for each of the three pairs of test compounds. Although the response surfaces were generated using the log of the response, the isopleths, for clarity, are identified by the actual response, rather than the log of the response. Figure 7 shows the response surface for the capacity factor for fluoranthene as a function of solvent composition. The response surface for resolution of fluoranthene/pyrene is shown in Figure 8. Superimposed is the isopleth for a capacity factor of 5. The solvent composition corresponding to a k' of 5 at which resolution is greatest is shown by the circle. Response surfaces for the other two solute pairs were generated similarly. Figure 9 shows that resolution for benz(a)anthracene and chrysene is at a maximum within the lower triangular region. Again the point of maximum resolution for a capacity factor of 5 is indicated. The perylene/BaP response surface is shown in Figure 10. This Figure demonstrates the

Table II

Simplex Design for Ternary Solvent Optimization

Run	Component				Composition (%)			Response
	A	B	C'	D'	Acetonitrile	Methanol	Water	Y
1	1	0	0	0	0	100	0	YA
2	0	1	0	0	100	0	0	YB
3	0	0	1	0	0	65	35	YC
4	0	0	0	1	55	0	45	YD
5	1/2	1/2	0	0	50	50	0	YAB
6	1/2	0	1/2	0	0	82.5	17.5	YAC
7	0	1/2	1/2	0	50	32.5	17.5	YBC
8	0	1/2	0	1/2	77.5	0	22.5	YBD
9	0	0	1/2	1/2	27.5	32.5	40	YCD
10	1/3	1/3	1/3	0	33.3	55	11.7	YABC
11	0	1/3	1/3	1/3	51.7	21.7	26.7	YBCD
12	2/3	1/6	1/6	0	16.7	77.5	5.8	YAABC
13	1/6	2/3	1/6	0	66.7	27.5	5.8	YABBC
14	1/6	1/6	2/3	0	16.7	60	23.3	YABCC
15	0	2/3	1/6	1/6	75.8	10.8	13.3	YBBCD
16	0	1/6	2/3	1/6	25.8	43.3	30.8	YBCCD
17	0	1/6	1/6	2/3	53.3	10.8	35.8	YBCDD

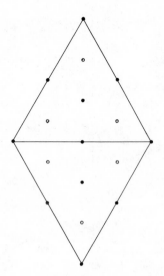

Figure 6. Schematic of two ternary solvent designs containing a common boundary

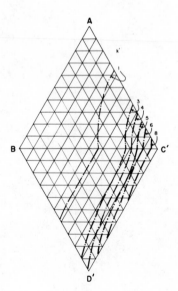

Figure 7.   Response surface for capacity factor, k', *of fluoranthene*

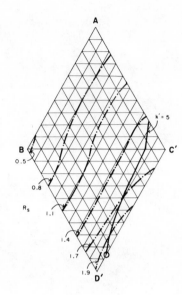

Figure 8. Response surface for resolution, R_s, of fluoranthene and pyrene; (——) is the isopleth for k′ (fluoranthene) = 5.

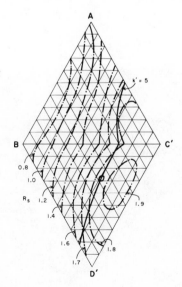

Figure 9. Response surface for resolution of benz(a)anthracene and pyrene; (——) is the isopleth for k′ (benz(a)anthracene) = 5.

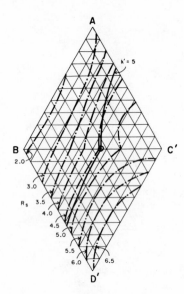

Figure 10.   Response surface for resolution of perylene and benzo(a)pyrene; (———) is the isopleth for k' (perylene) = 5.

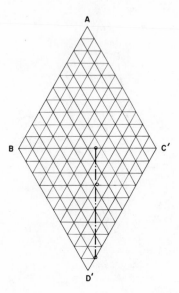

Figure 11.   Optimized solvent gradient for acetonitrile/methanol/water ternary system

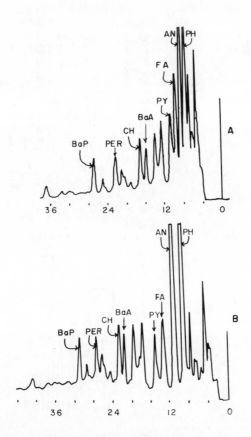

Figure 12.   Comparison of binary and ternary solvent systems for "soft" coal tar pitch: (A) acetonitrile/water, 55:45 to acetonitrile/water, 72:28; linear, 30 min; (B) acetonitrile/methanol/water, 48:8:44 to acetonitrile/methanol/water, 43:37:20; linear, 30 min.

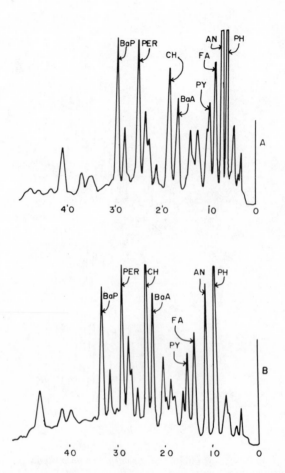

Figure 13.   Comparison of binary and ternary solvent systems for "hard" coal tar
pitch: same solvent ratios as Figure 13; 40-min linear gradient.

flexibility in choosing optimized solvent composition.
The k' = 5 isopleth is roughly parallel to the R_s =
4.5 isopleth over the composition range indicated by
coordinates A = 0.1, B = 0.39, C' = 0.51 to B = 0.62,
D' = 0.38. In practice then, the choice of which
optimal ternary solvent should be used may take other
considerations (such as viscosity or ease of
generating the final gradient) into account. In
Figure 11 a gradient is drawn through the three points
chosen as having maximum resolution at k' = 5 for each
of the pairs studied. The initial mobile phase
composition of this system is 48.4% acetonitrile, 7.8%
methanol and 43.8% water. The final composition is
43% acetonitrile, 37% methanol and 20% water.

The resolution in actual samples for the
optimized ternary mobile phases was compared to that
obtained with the optimized binary mobile phase
(acetonitrile/water) which had been used previously.
Figure 12 shows a comparison of chromatograms obtained
using the binary and ternary solvent systems. The
sample was a soft coal tar pitch which contains a high
proportion of low molecular weight PAH's. The six
test compounds are identified in the figure, along
with the two major components, phenanthrene and
anthracene. Note the near baseline resolution of the
fluoranthene/pyrene pair in the ternary system, and
the resolution of the two large early-eluting
compounds, phenanthrene and anthracene.

Figure 13 shows a similar pair of chromatograms
of a binary sample of a hard coal tar pitch with many
high moleular weight PAH's present. In the upper
chromatogram, the pyrene peak has a shoulder, which is
nearly completely resolved in the ternary system
chromatogram. The two peaks between Pyrene and
Benz(a)anthracene above are seen as four peaks in the
lower chromatogram.

Summary

The use of an acetonitrile/methanol/water eluent
has been shown to improve resolution of PAH
chromatographed on a Vydac reverse phase column. This
improved resolution should result in greater precision
and accuracy in the quantitation of individual PAH.
Determination of optimal solvent concentration is
simplified through application of statistical design
techniques. These techniques can be further utilized
to investigate various ternary mobile phases in
combination with different stationary phases.

Disclaimer

Mention of company names or products does not constitute endorsement by the National Institute for Occupational Safety and Health.

Acknowledgement

The author is indebted to Mr. Dennis Hill of the CDC Parklawn Computer Center who developed the programs to generate the response surface curves, and to Dr. Alexander W. Teass for valuable discussions.

Abstract

The analysis of polynuclear aromatic hydrocarbons (PAH's) presents one of the most challenging tasks to the occupational health chemist. The problems arise from the needs to separate large numbers of structurally similar compounds and simultaneously detect them at extremely low levels. High performance liquid chromatography (HPLC) is a frequently used tool for such analyses. This paper applies statistical experimental design techniques to the improvement of HPLC resolution through optimization of solvent selectivity effects in a ternary solvent system.

Literature Cited

1.   Wallcave, L., Garcia, H., Feldman, R., Lijinsky, W., and Shubik, P. Toxicol. Appl. Pharmacol., (1971) 18, 41-52.

2.   "Scientific and Technical Assessment Report on Particulate Polycyclic Organic Matter". U. S. Environmental Protection Agency (1975) No. PB 241 799.

3.   Sawicki, E., Stanley, T. W., Elbert, W. C., Meeker, J. and McPherson, S. Atmos. Env., (1967) 1, 131.

4.   Sawicki, E., Elbert, W., Stanley, T. W., Hauser, T. R. and Fox, F. T. Int. J. Air Poll., (1960) 2, 273.

5.   Jackson, J. C., Warner, P.O. and Mooney, T. F. Jr. A. I. H. A. J., (174) 35, 276.

6. Lao, R. C., Thomas, R. S., Oja, H. and Dubois,
    L. *Anal. Chem.*, (1973) 45, 908.

7. Severson, R. F., Snook, M. E., Akin, F. J., and
    Chortyk, O. T. In "Carcinogenesis, Vol. 3:
    Polynuclear Aromatic Hydrocarbons"; Jones, P. W.
    and Freudenthal, R. I., Ed.; Raven Press: New
    York, 1978.

8. Christenson, R. G. and May, W. E. *J. Liq. Chrom.*
    (1978) 1 (3)85.

9. Krstulovic, A. M., Rosie, D. M. and Brown, P. R.
    Anal. Chem., (1976) 48, 1383.

10. Wheals, B. B., Vaughan, C. G. and Whitehouse, M.
    J. J. Chromatogr., (1975) 106, 109.

11. Boden, H. *J. Chr. Sci.*, (1976) 14 (8), 391.

12. Golden, C. and Sawicki, E. *Anal. Let.*, (1976) 9
    (10), 957.

13. Klimisch, H. J. *J. Chromatogr.* (1973) 83, 11.

14. Klimisch, H. J. *Anal. Chem.* (1973) 45 (11), 960.

15. Lochmuller, C. H. and Amoss, C. W. *J.
    Chromatogr.* (1975) 108, 85.

16. Eisenberg, W. C. *J. Chr. Sci.*, (1975) 16 (4),
    145.

17. Dong, M., Locke, D. C. and Ferrand, E. *Anal.
    Chem.*, (1976 48 (2), 368.

18. May, W. E., Chesler, S. N., Cram, S. P., Gump,
    B. H., Hertz, H. S., Enagonio, D. P. and Dyszel,
    S. M. *J. Chr. Sci.*, (1975) 13 (11), 535.

19. Oyler, A. R., Bodenner, D. L., Welch, K. J.,
    Liukkonen, R. J., Carlson, R. M., Kopperman, H.
    L. and Caple, R. *Anal. Chem.*, (1978) 50 (7),
    837.

20. Fox, M. A. and Staley, S. W. *Anal. Chem.* (1976)
    48 (7), 992.

21. Karger, B. L. *J. Chromatogr.* (1976) 125, 71.

22.   Snyder, L. R. and Kirkland, J. J. "Introduction
       to Modern Liquid Chromatography" pp 215ff,   John
       Wiley & Sons, Inc., New York (1974).

23.   Bakalyar, S. R., McIlwrick, R. and Roggendorf,
       E. J. Chromatogr. (1977) 142, 353.

24.   Snyder, L. R. and Kirkland, J. J. "Introduction
       to Modern Liquid Chromatography" pp 35-38,   John
       Wiley & Sons, Inc., New York (1974).

25.   "Strategy of Experimentation," Revised Edition, E. I. du
       Pont de Nemours & Co., Wilmington, DE, October, 1975,
       p. 51.

RECEIVED October 30, 1979.

A Sampling and Analytical Method for Vinyl Acetate

DENIS L. FOERST[1] and ALEXANDER W. TEASS

National Institute for Occupational Safety and Health,
4676 Columbia Parkway, Cincinnati, OH 45226

Vinyl acetate is a clear colorless liquid. It has a boiling point of 72 °C and a flash point of -9 °C. In 1977 vinyl acetate production in the United States was 1.60 x 10⁹ pounds (1). This gave vinyl acetate a rank of 45 among the 50 top-volume chemicals produced in the United States during 1977. The major end uses of vinyl acetate were adhesives (30%), paints (20%), textile finishes (15%), and paper coatings (10%). Approximately 15% of the vinyl acetate produced was exported (2).

Exposure to vinyl acetate has caused severe skin irritation and blister formation (3). At levels around 77 mg/m³ (22 ppm) respiratory irritation, evidenced by coughing and hoarseness, was observed in humans. The odor of vinyl acetate at 18 mg/m³ (5 ppm) is detected by almost everyone, although some persons can detect the odor at levels as low as 2 mg/m³ (0.5 ppm). Cognizant of these data, the American Conference of Governmental Industrial Hygienists has recommended an eight-hour time-weighted average exposure limit of 30 mg/m³ (10 ppm) for vinyl acetate in the workplace environment (4). It also recommended that short-term exposures (15 minutes) be held below 60 mg/m³ (20 ppm). While no federal standard for employee exposure toward vinyl acetate exists, the National Institute for Occupational Safety and Health (NIOSH) has recommended that workers be exposed to levels of vinyl acetate in air no higher than 15 mg/m³ (4 ppm) over any 15-minute period (5).

Review of Analytical Methods

Reported procedures for the determination of vinyl acetate in air used bubblers containing a solvent for trapping the vinyl acetate and a spectrometric method, usually following derivatization, for analysis (6-12). Nenasheva presented a procedure for determining vinyl acetate in air also contaminated

---

[1] Current address: Environmental Research Center, Environmental Protection Agency, Cincinnati, Ohio 45268

with dibutyl maleate and 2-ethylhexyl acrylate (6). The samples
were collected using two bubblers in series charged with
ethanol. The three compounds were determined simultaneously by
measuring the absorbance of the solutions at 223 nm, 232 nm, and
245 nm. Concentrations of vinyl acetate as low as 3 µg/mL could
be measured.

Gronsberg reported procedures in which vinyl acetate trapped
from air was oxidized with potassium permanganate to
formaldehyde, which was quantified using chromotropic acid
(4,5-dihydroxy-2,7-naphthalenedisulfonic acid) (7, 8). The
lower analytical limit for vinyl acetate was given at 2.5 µg.
An iron-hydroxamic acid method was used by Andronov and Yudina,
who measured air concentrations of vinyl acetate in the presence
of butyraldehyde, acetaldehyde, and hydrogen chloride (9).
Using two cooled bubblers connected in series and charged with
ethanol, 0.5-1 L of air was sampled at a flow of 0.3 L/min. The
vinyl acetate was converted to N-hydroxyacetamide by the
addition of hydroxylamine hydrochloride and sodium hydroxide.
After 30 minutes, the hydroxamic acid was complexed with iron by
the addition of hydrochloric acid and ferric chloride. The
intensity of the color which developed in 10 minutes was
compared to the intensities of standards. The lower limit of
detection for this method was reported to be 0.3 µg/mL.

Khrustaleva and Osokina (10) determined vinyl acetate in the
presence of 2-ethylhexyl acrylate and dibutyl maleate by forming
the mercurated derivative of vinyl acetate using mercuric
acetate and diethylamine. Separation of the derivatives was
accomplished using paper chromatography. Osokina and Erisman
(11) later reported an optimized procedure for the mercuration
of vinyl acetate. In this study a series of alcohols (C-1 to
C-5) were used as the solvent during mercuration. After paper
chromatography of the mercurated olefin, the spots were
developed with diphenylcarbazide, cut out, and placed in
1-butanol. The amount of complex present was measured
spectrometrically at 565 nm. 1-Butanol and 1-propanol were the
optimum reaction solvents for the mercuration reaction. The
minimum amount of mercurated vinyl acetate detectable on the
chromatographic paper was 0.3 µg. Using a related technique,
Petrova and Boikova (12) sampled air for vinyl acetate using two
cooled impingers connected in series and charged with ethanol.
Sample volumes ranged from 5 to 30 liters; the sampling flow was
0.05 L/min. After sampling, the solutions were treated with
mercuric acetate in solution to mercurate the vinyl acetate
collected. After one hour diphenylcarbazide solution was added
and the absorbance of the resulting solution was measured at
536 nm. The calibration plot was linear from 0.3-10 µg/mL of
vinyl acetate in ethanol.

Impingers and bubblers are not well suited to sampling
workplace air in the breathing zone of the worker. Besides
encumbering the worker, these sampling devices do not protect

the integrity of samples collected, since the contents are subject to spillage and the collection efficiency of the solvent is often not quantitative. Using two bubblers in tandem with cooling, as in the procedures described above (9, 12), precludes taking such personal samples altogether. The analytical procedures reported lack the specificity necessary for unambiguous monitoring for vinyl acetate. However, in some cases the analytical range may be low enough for monitoring in environments where no interferences are present.

Quantitative air sampling with small beds of a sorbent, besides being more convenient for the worker, is more efficient from the standpoint of quantitative sampling of the contaminant and maintaining sample integrity. Gas chromatographic analysis of samples recovered from sorbent beds should eliminate a substantial portion of the interferences giving the method greater specificity. In this report we will describe our research leading to the development of a method based on these techniques.

Experimental

Apparatus. Atmospheres containing vinyl acetate were generated in a dynamic flow vapor generation system. Laboratory compressed air was passed through a membrane filter, then through beds of molecular sieves and activated charcoal, and split into a contaminant and a dilution stream. The contaminant stream, flowing at 0.1-0.2 L/min, passed through a diffusion cell of the design of Miguel and Natusch (13) where it picked up vinyl acetate vapor at ambient temperature. Flowing at 10 L/min, the dilution stream was routed through, or around, a bubbler containing water at ambient temperature and joined the contaminant stream immediately before a mixing chamber. The atmosphere then was passed through the mixing chamber, a six-port manifold, either a Model 15-3008 Hygrodynamics humidity indicator or a Wilks 1A infrared analyzer, and finally out through a laboratory hood. A Model 341 Sage syringe drive was used in the calibration of the infrared analyzer. During breakthrough studies the effluent from the sorbent tubes was monitored with a Model 11-655 Davis flame ionization meter.

Analyses were done with a Perkin Elmer Model 900 gas chromatograph equipped with a flame ionization detector. For evaluation of the charcoal the gas chromatograph was fitted with a 3.0-m x 3.2-mm o.d. stainless steel column packed with 10% TCEP on 80/100 mesh Chromosorb P AW (oven temperature 80 °C, injector temperature 120 °C, detector temperature 150 °C, helium carrier flow 40 mL/min) and was interfaced to a Perkin Elmer PEP-1 GC data system. During the evaluation of Chromosorb 107 an analytical column of 6.1-m x 3.2-mm o.d. silanized stainless steel packed with 10% FFAP on 80/100 mesh Chromosorb W AW was used (oven temperature 60 °C, injector and detector

temperatures 160 °C, helium carrier flow 33 mL/min) and the
gas chromatograph was interfaced to a Hewlett Packard 3352-B
laboratory data system. A Model 132 Century Systems programmed
thermal desorber was interfaced to the gas chromatograph through
polyperfluoroethylene-coated stainless steel transfer lines held
at 160 °C. A Tedlar bag of helium for desorption was attached
to the desorption oven.

MSA organic vapor sampling tubes, containing 150 mg of
activated coconut shell charcoal of lot MSA-8, were used in
breakthrough experiments and for obtaining samples for method
evaluation. Sampling devices containing pre-extracted
Chromosorb 107 (Johns Manville), shown in Figure 1, were
prepared from the sample collector tubes used with the Model 132
Century Systems programmed thermal desorber. Before packing,
the Chromosorb 107 was extracted in a Soxhlet apparatus for 8
hours with water, 8 hours with methanol and 8 hours with
methylene chloride, then dried overnight in a vacuum oven. The
primary desorbing section contained 300 mg of Chromosorb 107
held at either end with porous bronze plugs. The backup section
contained 50 mg of Chromosorb 107 held in place with a porous
bronze plug at one end and a glass wool plug at the other. Each
section was purged with helium at 150 °C for 5 minutes before
use.

Hamilton syringes of 1-, 10-, 25-, or 50-μL capacity were
used. Standards were prepared in 2-mL vials sealed with
Teflon-lined silicon rubber septa and crimped with aluminum
serum caps.

Reagents and Standards. Vinyl acetate, practical grade
inhibited with hydroquinone; hexane, UV grade; cyclohexane,
distilled in glass; and carbon disulfide, spectroquality, were
used. Vinyl acetate was freshly distilled before use. Standard
solutions for calibration curves were made by injecting 1-75 μL
of vinyl acetate into 1.00 mL of hexane.

Measurement with the Infrared Analyzer. The infrared
analyzer was operated in the absorbance mode at 8.02 μm with a
slit width of 1 mm, path length of 5.25 m, and response time of
1 s. A closed recirculating loop containing a metal-bellows
pump, a glass tee, and the infrared analyzer was assembled using
low-volume tubing; the total volume of the system was 5.64 L.
As the motor-driven syringe slowly injected 1 μL of pure vinyl
acetate into the closed recirculating loop at 3.89 nL/s, the
change in absorbance was recorded. This procedure was repeated
five times and the results were averaged. The calculated
concentration plotted against the absorbance gave a straight
line calibration curve.

To protect the sodium chloride optics of the infrared
analyzer, the concentration in the dynamic flow generator was
determined with the atmospheres dry. After the vinyl acetate

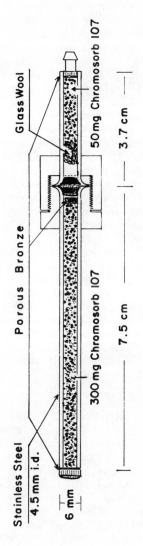

Figure 1. Sampling device

concentration had stabilized, the infrared analyzer was
disconnected and the dilution air routed through the
humidifier. Experiments were performed after the relative
humidity reached the target value. Upon completion of the
experiments, the dilution air was routed away from the
humidifier. When the relative humidity fell below 20%, the
infrared analyzer was again connected into the system. The
vinyl acetate concentration during experiments was determined by
averaging the concentrations measured before and after sampling;
the difference between the two was generally less than 5%.

Breakthrough Experiments. For the breakthrough experiments
the sorbents were packed in 100-mg beds, 4 mm in diameter, and
inserted into the six ports in the manifold. The effluent ends
of the tubes were connected to a common line leading to the
flame ionization detector. While the flame ionization detector,
calibrated with the challenge atmosphere, monitored the
concentration of vinyl acetate in the combined bed effluents,
the pump in the detector drew the challenge atmosphere through
each bed at approximately 0.2 L/min. The output from the
detector, the breakthrough curve, was recorded with a
strip-chart recorder. Most of the porous polymer sorbents
tested were first washed with acetone and dried.

Sampling Procedure. For each sample a clean sampling tube
was connected to a personal sampling pump and the volumetric
stroke factor at 0.1 L/min was determined using a soap-bubble
flow meter. Test atmospheres containing vinyl acetate in
concentrations ranging from 8.2 mg/m^3 to 206 mg/m^3 were then
sampled for 10, 15, or 30 minutes. After sampling, the devices
were disassembled, capped, and labeled. The sample volumes were
determined by multiplying the differences in the initial and
final stroke readings by the volumetric stroke factor. Samples
were sealed with polyethylene caps and stored at room
temperature until analyzed.

Analysis of Samples on Chromosorb 107. Individual
Chromosorb 107 sampling tubes were thermally desorbed at 150 °C
into a 300-mL reservoir using helium at a flow of 75 mL/min.
The desorbed vapors were then transferred to a gas-sampling
valve which injected 2-mL aliquots into the gas chromatograph.
Under the chromatographic conditions given above, the capacity
ratio for vinyl acetate was 4.4. The quantity of vinyl acetate
in the sample was read from a standard curve. After running
samples containing high levels of vinyl acetate, the thermal
desorber was taken through a complete cycle without analysis to
remove traces of vinyl acetate which would interfere with the
analysis of the following sample.

Standards were prepared by loading known amounts of vinyl
acetate onto clean sampling tubes. Apparatus was assembled such

that a sampling tube was preceded by a U-tube and followed by a small pump. With the pump drawing laboratory air through the system at 0.2 L/min, a 2-µL aliquot of a standard solution of vinyl acetate in hexane was injected into the U-tube. In 2-3 minutes the vinyl acetate vapors were swept onto the sorbent tube. The standard sample was subsequently thermally desorbed and analyzed. Calibration curves were obtained by analyzing standard samples at 4-5 different levels and plotting peak area against weight of vinyl acetate per sample.

Analysis of Samples on Charcoal. Each charcoal sampling tube was scored and broken open. The front and backup sections were placed in individual 2-mL serum vials. One milliliter of solvent, carbon disulfide or acetonitrile, was added and the vials were immediately crimped shut. After 30 minutes with occasional agitation, 5 µL of the desorbed solution was injected into the gas chromatograph. The quantity of vinyl acetate in the sample was read from a standard curve.

Standards were prepared by injecting known amounts of freshly distilled vinyl acetate into 1.00 mL of solvent. Calibration curves were obtained by injecting 5.0-µL aliquots of standards and diluted standards into the gas chromatograph and plotting the peak areas versus concentrations. These calibration curves were linear over the range of 5-5000 µg/mL. The precision for replicate injections of a standard at 5 µg/mL was 3% relative standard deviation.

Results and Discussion

Activated Charcoal. The original intent of the research was to develop a sampling technique that used coconut-shell charcoal to collect vinyl acetate vapors from air samples. Therefore, the breakthrough volume and desorption efficiency of vinyl acetate on coconut-shell charcoal were studied.

Breakthrough volume was operationally defined as the volume of air that had passed through the front section of a sampling device when the concentration of analyte in the effluent from that section reached 5% of the concentration in the influent. The results of the breakthrough studies, summarized in Table I, indicate that charcoal has a high affinity for vinyl acetate.

For the study of desorption efficiency, or recovery, of vinyl acetate from the charcoal, known amounts of vinyl acetate, either neat or in solution in cyclohexane, were metered onto 100-mg beds of charcoal. The samples were desorbed with 1 mL of carbon disulfide after 1, 5, or 15 days storage at room temperature. The resulting solutions were analyzed by gas chromatography to determine the amount of vinyl acetate that was desorbed. The desorption efficiencies were then calculated according to the following equation:

Table I
Breakthrough Volumes of Vinyl Acetate on Activated Charcoal[a]

Sampling Rate (L/min)	Concentration[b] (mg/m^3)	Volume Breakthrough (L)
1.0	74.0	167
1.0	66.0	184
0.63	59.1	180
0.15	16.5	188

[a]Beds were 4 mm in diameter and contained 100 mg of charcoal.
[b]Concentration measured by infrared analyzer. Relative
humidity was less than 15%.

$$\text{desorption efficiency} = \frac{\text{amount desorbed}}{\text{amount taken}}$$

Table II and Figure 2 summarize the results of this study. The
desorption efficiency of vinyl acetate was very dependent upon
the loading. For samples stored one day at room temperature,
the desorption efficiency fell below 80% at loadings below
approximately 750 µg. A long-term storage effect was also
apparent. The desorption efficiencies given by the samples
stored for 15 days were an additional 6-22% lower than for day 1.
    The desorbing solvent was changed to acetonitrile, a more
polar solvent, and another desorption-efficiency study
performed. The results are plotted in Figure 2. The desorption
again showed a dependence upon the loading, although at the
lower levels it was higher than when carbon disulfide was used.

Table II
Desorption Efficiencies of Vinyl Acetate
on Coconut-Shell Charcoal

Loading (µg)	Desorption Efficiency (%)		
	Day 1	Day 5	Day 15
4660[b]	100.3 ± 1.6	93.7 ± 1.6	93.9 ± 1.6
1864[b]	95.6 ± 2.5	89.3 ± 2.5	88.1 ± 2.5
932[b]	87.7 ± 5.3	82.0 ± 5.3	81.6 ± 5.3
298[c]	73.0 ± 2.8	62.4 ± 2.8	58.3 ± 2.8
149[c]	68.7 ± 4.4	48.2 ± 4.4	46.7 ± 4.4
75[c]	40.3 ± 5.6	29.1 ± 5.6	24.6 ± 5.6

[a]All samples stored at room temperature and desorbed with
carbon disulfide. Average ± 95% confidence interval given.
[b]Three samples per day. [c]Two samples per day.

However, there was again a reduction in the recovery of the
vinyl acetate after storage of the samples.
The apparent sample instability, also seen in samples taken
of laboratory-generated atmospheres, limits the usefulness of
the method. Additionally, the low desorption efficiencies at
the lower levels of vinyl acetate could be a problem, for other
compounds co-absorbed on the charcoal can alter the desorption
efficiencies of poorly desorbed compounds (14). Thus, a search
for new sorbent was initiated with the goal of minimizing such
problems and developing a better sampling and analytical method.

Chromosorb 107. Nine different solid sorbents, mostly
porous polymers, were screened using breakthrough experiments in
order to select that with the greatest capacity for vinyl
acetate. Initially, challenge atmospheres of low relative
humidity were used to seek those sorbents showing the largest
breakthrough volume for vinyl acetate. Since water vapor is an
important constituent of workplace air, the two most promising
porous polymers were retested using atmospheres of high relative
humidity. The results are summarized in Table III. The effect
of water vapor was substantial, decreasing the capacity of
Chromosorb 107 by 71% and Chromosorb 108 by 83%. Nonetheless,
of the sorbents screened, Chromosorb 107, a porous polymer of
cross-linked acrylic ester, seemed the best for further study.
    Sampling devices containing Chromosorb 107 were prepared
using the sampling tubes designed for the thermal desorption
apparatus. As shown in Figure 1, each contained a 300-mg bed of

Table III
Breakthrough Volumes for Vinyl Acetate
on Various Sorbents[a]

Sorbent	Mesh Size	Relative Humidity (%)	Breakthrough Volume (L)
Durapak OPN	100/120	<15	<0.2
XAD-2	20/40	<15	0.67
Chromosorb 106	20/40	<15	0.80
Porapak Q	50/80	<15	1.96
Chromosorb 106	60/80	<15	2.05
Porapak N	50/80	<15	3.88
Chromosorb 107	60/80	<15	4.31
Chromosorb 108	80/100	<15	4.69
Chromosorb 108	80/100	87	0.81
Silica gel	20/40	84	0.83
Chromosorb 107	60/80	87	1.24
Chromosorb 107[b]	60/80	83	4.0

[a]Challenge concentration 71-146 mg/m^3; flow 0.12-0.28 L/min;
100-mg beds. [b]300-mg bed.

Chromosorb 107 in the front section and a 50-mg bed in the back
section. The breakthrough volume of the 300-mg bed was 4.0 L.
The sampling device had a pressure drop of 12.4 inches of water
(3.1 kPa) at 0.13 L/min and 6.4 inches of water (1.6 kPa) at
0.07 L/min. As the personal sampling pumps were operating near
capacity at 0.13 L/min, 0.1 L/min was selected as an appropriate
sampling flow.

While vinyl acetate could be desorbed from the Chromosorb 107
using either heat or solvent, thermal desorption was
investigated as the technique of choice. This eliminated the
problem of finding a solvent which would not dissolve the
Chromosorb 107, would quantitatively desorb the vinyl acetate,
and contained no impurities which would interfere with the gas
chromatographic analysis. Also, with this technique there was
the possibility of having reusable collection devices.

Thermal desorption was done using a Century Systems Model
132 programmed desorber. This device desorbed the sample at
150 °C into a stream of helium and stored the desorbed vapors
in a 300-mL reservoir. Using the gas sampling valve built into
the programmed thermal desorber, 2-mL samples were injected into
the gas chromatograph, which was equipped with a flame
ionization detector. Thus multiple analyses of each sample were
possible. Helium was used to desorb the sample tubes, because
air at 150 °C was found to degrade the Chromosorb 107 to a
brown powder. After analysis, sorbent tubes suitable for reuse
in the field were prepared by purging the tubes for 2-3 minutes
with helium at 150 °C.

Several calibration procedures were attempted before a
suitable procedure was found. When aliquots of vinyl acetate in
hexane were injected directly into the hot desorbing oven,
erratic results were obtained. This was probably due to
reaction of vinyl acetate on the hot metal surface of the
desorbing oven. Another procedure tested used gas sampling bags
filled with known concentrations of vinyl acetate in helium.
The gas bags were connected directly to the gas sampling valve.
Replicate injections gave good precision. However, this
technique required calculation of the dilution factor between
the reservoir and the gas sampling valve and preparation of
several standard concentrations of vinyl acetate in helium.

In the preferred procedure, samples of vinyl acetate on
Chromosorb 107 were prepared. A glass U-tube was connected to
the inlet end of a clean sampling tube, the outlet of which was
connected to a small pump. As an aliquot of vinyl acetate in
hexane was injected into the U-tube, the pump drew air through
the system at 0.2 L/min such that the vapors were swept onto the
sorbent bed. After 2-3 minutes, or approximately five volume
changes, the pump was turned off and the apparatus was
disassembled. Standard samples prepared in this manner were
thermally desorbed and analyzed. A calibration curve thus

obtained is shown in Figure 3. The analysis of five 1-µg
standards gave a relative standard deviation of 6%. Two
desirable features of this calibration procedure are:
1) standard samples are prepared in the same manner as field
samples; and 2) desorption-efficiency corrections are built into
the calibration curve.
  With the above information the sampling and analytical
procedure was defined. Air would be drawn at 0.1 L/min through
a 300-mg bed of Chromosorb 107 with a 50-mg backup bed used for
checking for overloading of the primary bed. The vinyl acetate
would be thermally desorbed from the Chromosorb 107 and stored
in the vapor state in a 300-mL reservoir, from which 2-mL
aliquots would be taken for analysis by gas chromatography using
flame ionization detection. Since the breakthrough volume for
the primary adsorbing section was 4.0 L, the volume of air to be
sampled should be less, say 3.0 L for safety.

  Method Evaluation. Evaluation of the sampling and
analytical method was accomplished by collecting and analyzing
52 samples of vinyl acetate from atmospheres at greater than 80%
relative humidity according to the scheme in Table IV. Fully
charged personal sampling pumps were used and performed

Table IV
Scheme for Evaluation of the Chromosorb 107-Gas
Chromatography Method for Vinyl Acetate

Concentration Sampled (mg/m^3)	Sample Loading (μg)	Number of Samples	Number Analyzed on		
			Day 1	Day 7	Day 14
blank		6	1	3	2
8.20	12	6	3	2	1
9.04	8	6	2	1	3
8.64[a]	11	6	6	0	0
18.6	54	4	1	1	2
19.8	55	4	2	1	1
19.9	56	4	1	2	1
39.2[a]	67	4	0	2	2
159	223	2	1	1	0
166	249	4	1	3	0
176	264	4	1	1	2
190	266	4	2	1	1
206	309	4	1	0	3

[a]Samples not randomized with respect to storage time.

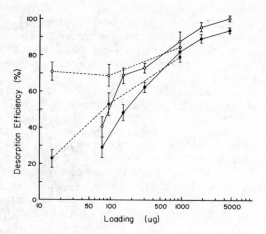

Figure 2. *The relationship between desorption efficiency and loading of vinyl acetate on activated charcoal for different storage periods. The 100-mg beds of charcoal were desorbed with 1.00 mL of (——) carbon disulfide or (– – –) aceto-nitrile after storage at room temperature for (○) 1 day or (●) 5–7 days.*

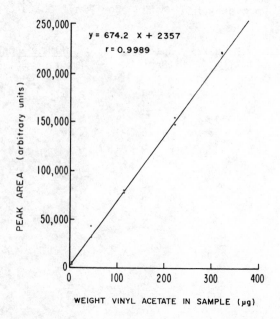

Figure 3. *Calibration curve for the analysis of vinyl acetate-on-Chromosorb 107 samples*

adequately at 0.1 L/min sampling rate. The sampling time was 10 or 15 minutes for the lowest and highest concentrations and 30 minutes for the medium concentration. Except for those collected at 8.64 mg/m^3 and 39.2 mg/m^3, the samples were randomly divided into three groups for analysis at 1, 7, or 14 days after collection. Six blank samples, collected while the contaminant stream of the generation system was stopped, were randomly analyzed. No vinyl acetate was present in these blanks, or in any sample backup sections analyzed.

The analytical results are summarized in Table V. Within a group the sample weight and the concentration varied over a small range. Conversion of the analytical data to percent recovery not only provided a comparison of the method tested with the infrared analyzer, but also normalized the measurements, thus allowing estimation of the precision of the method. The precision, a summary of which is given in Table VI, includes day-to-day variations in the calibration of the infrared analyzer. Assuming the sampling of 1.5 L of air over a 15-minute period, the method appears sufficient for measuring vinyl acetate in air at concentrations as low as 7 mg/m^3 with acceptable precision.

A comparison of the Chromosorb 107-gas chromatography method with the infrared analyzer is given by the recoveries calculated for day 1. It is not obvious which method gives measurements

Table V

Analytical Results for Vinyl Acetate-on-Chromosorb 107 Samples

Storage Time (days)	Average Amount Found (μg)	Range (μg)	Recovery[a] (%)	Number of Samples	Relative Standard Deviation (%)
1	12.1	6.33-15.7	110.4 ± 7.7	9[b]	9.06
1	58.7	52.8-66.9	106.8 ± 6.1	4	3.60
1	269	233-316	105.5 ± 4.7	6	4.26
7	8.63	2.49-15.9	111.9 ± 36	3	13.0
7	58.4	47.3-69.5	95.7 ± 4.5	6	4.45
7	272	228-312	108.8 ± 2.9	6	2.56
14	8.89	6.69-12.7	99.6 ± 11.8	4	7.44
14	51.4	44.2-57.5	90.7 ± 5.2	6	5.44
14	271	239-316	96.6 ± 2.4	6	2.37

[a]Averages ± 95% confidence intervals. Recovery = concentrations measured by Chromosorb 107-gas chromatography method ÷ concentration measured by infrared analyzer. [b]Two of the 11 analyses were excluded as outliers using the t test at the 0.5% significance level.

closer to the true concentrations of vinyl acetate. However, the results are sufficiently close as to suggest that there is no serious problem with the accuracy of either method. Analysis of the randomized samples stored for 14 days at room temperature gave an average recovery of 95.4 ± 6.3%. Theaverage recovery was 105.6 ± 9.4% after 7 days storage and 109.4 ± 8.0 % after 1 day of storage. The storage loss between day 1 and day 14, about 14%, indicates that analysis should be done as soon as possible after sampling for vinyl acetate. The

Table VI
Precision of the Chromosorb 107-Gas Chromatography
Method for Vinyl Acetate

Average Amount Found (μg)	Pooled Relative Standard Deviation (%)
10	9.6
56	4.7
271	3.2

more likely causes of loss were hydrolysis of the ester by water also collected or reaction with the Chromosorb 107 through the vinyl group, although migration of the vinyl acetate to or through the caps was not ruled out. An experiment designed to assess the sample loss with storage under refrigeration was ruined by migration of organic vapors in the refrigerator into the samples, but was not repeated. However, it seems reasonable to expect that storage of the samples at lower temperatures in impermeable containers should retard the loss of vinyl acetate.

Acknowledgement

The assistance of Maria Risholm-Sundman in performing some of the sample-stability studies is gratefully acknowledged.

Disclaimer

Mention of company name or product does not constitute endorsement by NIOSH.

Abstract

A quantitative sampling and analytical method for vinyl acetate in air was developed using sampling tubes packed with 300-mg beds of 60/80 mesh Chromosorb 107. The breakthrough volume was found to be 4.0 liters when 83% relative humidity air at a vinyl acetate concentration of 138 mg/m^3 was sampled at 0.12 L/min. The samples were thermally desorbed and analyzed by gas chromatography with flame-ionization detection. Replicate analyses were possible, because the thermal desorber stored the desorbed vapors in a 300-mL chamber from which aliquots were drawn for analysis.

The sampling and analytical methodology was evaluated by sampling humid test atmospheres containing vinyl acetate at the concentrations 8.2-206 mg/m^3 using personal sampling pumps drawing at 0.1 L/min. At sample loadings of 10 μg the relative standard deviation of the analyses was 9.6% and the concentrations measured were 109% of those given by a reference method. Samples stored at room temperature for 15 days appeared to lose 14% of the vinyl acetate collected.

The use of coconut-shell charcoal as a collection medium was evaluated and found unacceptable.

Literature Cited

1. "Top 50 Chemical Products," Chem. Eng. News (1978) 56(18), 32-37.

2. "Key Chemicals-Vinyl Acetate," Chem. Eng. News (1977) 55(38), 9.

3. "Documentation of the Threshold Limit Values for Substances in Workroom Air," Third Edition, p. 276, American Conference of Governmental Industrial Hygienists, Cincinnati, Ohio, 1971.

4. "Threshold Limit Values for Chemical Substances and Physical Agents in the Workroom Environment with Intended Changes for 1978," p. 30, American Conference of Governmental Industrial Hygienists, Cincinnati, Ohio, 1977.

5. "Criteria for a Recommended Standard ... Occupational Exposure to Vinyl Acetate," DHEW (NIOSH) Publication No. 78-205, p. 1, National Institute for Occupational Safety and Health, Cincinnati, Ohio, 1978.

6. Nenaheva, S. K., Hyg. Sanit. (1969) 34, 372-374; Gig. Sanit. (1969) 34(3), 44-46.

7. Gronsberg, E. Sh., Nov. Obl. Prom.-Sanit. Khim. (1969) 8-14; Chem. Abstr. (1970) 72, 35436k.

8. Gronsberg, E. Sh., Tr. Khim. Khim. Tekhnol. (1970)(1), 186-189; Chem. Abstr. (1971) 75, 88995k.

9. Andronov, B. E. and Yudina, A. K., Nauchn. Raboy, Inst. Okhrany Truda, Vses. Tsentr. Sov. Prof. Soyuzov (1964) 5, 77-81.

10. Khrustaleva, V. A. and Osokina, S. K., Gig. Sanit. (1970)
    35, 80-83; Chem. Abstr. (1970) 73, 38277r.

11. Osokina, S. K. and Erisman, F. F., Gig. Sanit. (1972) 37,
    72-74.

12. Petrova, L. I. and Boikova, Z. K., Gig. Sanit. (1975) 40(6),
    48-49.

13. Miguel, A. H. and Natusch, D. F. S., Anal. Chem. (1975) 47,
    1705-1707.

14. Fracchia, M., Pierce, L., Graul, R., and Stanley, R., Am.
    Ind. Hyg. Assoc. J. (1977) 38, 144-146.

RECEIVED October 10, 1979.

Occupational Health Chemistry

Collection and Analysis of Airborne Contaminants

ROBERT C. VOBORSKY

Sentry Insurance, 1800 North Point Drive, Stevens Point, WI 54481

At no time in modern history has the general
public been more conscious of health and environmental
issues. Therefore, it is somewhat understandable that
we have witnessed, in just a very few years, the enact-
ment of more federal legislation in occupational and
environmental health than has been legislated in the
history of this country, or any other nation. However,
this has been achieved during a period of general
national unrest induced by many social, economic and
political factors.

The state of one's health is determined by hered-
itary factors and the quality of the total environment.
The latter involves the home, community, work place and
recreational pursuits, for the conditions in each can
present health problems. The employee spends only one-
third of his day in the work place and the remaining
time in a home, community and recreational environments.
The great achievement of our modern technology must now
be paralleled by equal progress in our knowledge of the
effects of waste products of this technology upon man's
health and the application of this technology to control
programs. The chemical substances which can characterize
the work environment consist of dust, fumes, vapors,
gases and mists.

The determination of the quality of the work place
requires reliable monitoring programs. Accordingly,
standards are established within which quality determinations must comply. Industry is in the age of compliance.
In environmental or occupational health, regulatory
agencies establish standards by which Industry must
comply. Such health standards have been promulgated by
the Occupational Safety and Health Administration
(OSHA) under the authority granted under the Federal
Occupational Safety and Health Act of 1970. Therefore,
data derived from competent industrial hygiene tests is
the determinant of compliance with health standards
involving chemical agents. Industrial hygiene monitor-

0-8412-0539-6/80/47-120-185$05.00/0

ing programs are also of major significance in determining the effectiveness or efficiency of engineering
measures for controlling hazards or potential exposures
to chemical agents. The most important value of the
data derived from monitoring the work environment is
the correlation of such information with medical and
biological test data obtained through examination of
the worker. Such correlation is the final test of the
safety of the quality within the work environment.

The Occupational Safety and Health Act of 1970
established the National Institute for Occupational
Safety and Health (NIOSH) within the Department of
Health, Education and Welfare. NIOSH is primarily for
the purpose of carrying out the research and educa-
tional functions of the Act. The functions of NIOSH
include the research programs aimed at identifying and
evaluating hazards in the work environment.

In the evaluation of health hazards from toxic and
carcinogenic air contaminants, the sampling and analytical method is a very important tool. NIOSH has researched
the sampling and analysis of over 400 airborne substances
which are categorized as dusts, fumes, vapors, gases and
mists. By adhering to these sampling and analytical
methods, which are established for use by industrial
hygienists in the field and in the laboratory, a reliable and competent assessment of the work environment
will result.

Dust

Dust in the work place is present in varying sizes
and shapes depending on the process. Generally, the
dust which is seen by the human eye is greater than 50
microns. The dust which is capable of entering the
upper respiratory system and eventually the inner most
sections of the lung are less than 10 microns in size.
The respirable fraction of dust is that portion of
airborne particulate matter which is less than 10
microns. Respirable dust generally remains in the work
place atmosphere for long periods of time when ventilation systems are not efficient or are not present at
all. In order for a legitimate assessment of a dust
exposure, the respirable fraction of the dust must be
collected and evaluated. This task is achieved by
using a 10 millimeter nylon cyclone. FIGURE 1 illustrates the cyclone, and TABLE 1 lists the collection
efficiency of the cyclone which is operated at a very
critical flow rate of 1.7 liters of air per minute.
The flow rate is accurately calibrated to within ±5% by
using the calibration train illustrated in FIGURE 2.
The filter holder, containing a 37 mm diameter, 5.0
micron pore size hydrophobic polyvinyl chloride filter,

TABLE 1

COLLECTION EFFICIENCY OF 10MM CYCLONE

Size (Microns)	% Passing Selector (1.70 LPM)
2.0	90
2.5	75
3.5	50
5.0	25
10.0	0

which has been preweighed to the nearest 0.01 milligram
is attached securely to the cyclone prior to calibration.
A minimum sampling period of 60 minutes is recommended
and longer periods of up to eight hours are preferable.
The amount of particulate collected on the filter is
determined by weighing the filter under the same physical
conditions as prior to sampling. The amount of particulate
with respect to total sampling time and flow rate
determines the dust concentration in milligrams per
cubic meter (mg/M^3). The current OSHA Threshold Limit
Value for nuisance or inert respirable dust is 5 mg/M^3.

Monitoring dust atmospheres which are suspected of
containing free silica, the filter containing the
respirable fraction of the dust is analyzed for silica
content. Three analytical methods are currently used
for silica determination. The filter media can be
destroyed and the remaining material re-deposited on a
silver membrane filter and analyzed by X-Ray Diffraction or the remaining material can be pelletized with
potassium bromide and analyzed with a scanning Infrared
Spectrophotometer with a peak resulting at the 800
cm^{-1} line. The third method developed by Talvitie, is
the colorimetric determination of silica as molybdenum
blue at 820 nm's. The silica, or α quartz content is
reported as a percent of the dust collected of the
filter, and a representative threshold limit value is
calculated by the following relationship:

$$Mg/M^3 TLV = \frac{10\ Mg/M^3}{\%SiO_2 + 2}$$

Silica dust can be present in industrial atmospheres in
three forms, α quartz, cristobalite and tridymite,
depending upon the process temperatures. When cristobalite or tridymite are present, one-half the value of
the threshold limit formula is used. The validity of
the results depends on the cyclone and pump system

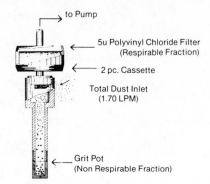

to Pump

5u Polyvinyl Chloride Filter
(Respirable Fraction)

2 pc. Cassette

Total Dust Inlet
(1.70 LPM)

Figure 1. 10-mm nylon cyclone collection system

Grit Pot
(Non Respirable Fraction)

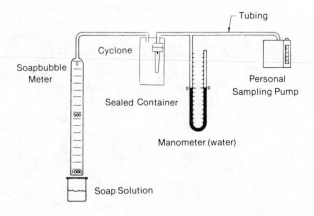

Figure 2. Calibration setup for personal sampling pump with cyclone collection
system

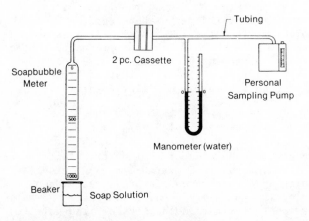

Figure 3. Calibration setup for personal sampling pump with filter cassette

calibration and the precision and accuracy of the
analytical method used for the silica determination.

Metal Fume

Metal fumes in the work place are generated by
heating metal to a high enough temperature to produce
fume which is generally in the oxide state. Exposures
to metal fume are formed during welding, soldering,
smelting, refining, heat treating and finishing operations. The metal of interest is dependant on the
metallurgical composition of the raw ore process materials or alloy being processed.

Collection of metal fume is accomplished by passing
the contaminated air through a filter holder containing
a 37 millimeter, 0.8 micron mixed cellulose ester
membrane filter supported by a cellulose backup pad. A
portable pump and filter system is calibrated for a
flow rate of 1.5 liters of air per minute, using the
calibration train illustrated in FIGURE 3. The accuracy of the calibration must be within ± 5%. A sampling period of one hour is recommended, and longer
periods of time are preferable. Since it is possible
for the filter to become plugged by heavy particulate
loading or by the presence of oil mist or other liquids
in the air, the pump rotameter should be observed
frequently and readjusted accordingly.

The metal fume filter samples are prepared for
analysis by destroying the organic filter media by
heating with redistilled nitric acid on a hot plate.
The resulting metal, in the salt state, is dissolved in
nitric acid and diluted to a known volume with double
distilled water. The solution is analyzed by Atomic
Absorption for the metals of interest. Metals such as
Cadmium, Berylium and Nickel have very low threshold
limit values which are set by OSHA and are frequently
present in the sample in very low quantities. Many
Atomic Absorption units are equipped with a hollow
graphite tube atomizer which increases the sensitivity
dramatically making it easier for the analyst to obtain
reliable results for species present in the sample in
very low concentrations. The validity of the metal
fume data depends on sampling train calibration and the
precision and accuracy of the analytical procedure.
NIOSH has reported a 2% relative standard deviation in
the analytical method which has been collaboratively
tested.

Organic Vapors

Organic vapors are generated in the work place
wherever organic solvents are used. The quantity of

organic vapors present depends on the process temperature, vapor pressure of the solvent and efficiency
of exposure control equipment. Examples of exposures
to organic vapors are evident during painting, cleaning
and degreasing and those operations involving adhesives.
   Organic vapors are easily collected by passing the
contaminated air at a flow rate of 50,100 or 200 cubic
centimeters per minute through a small tube containing
activated charcoal. FIGURE 4 illustrates the components
of a charcoal tube prepared according to NIOSH specifications. The tube is limited to sample volumes of 10
liters of air and can vary depending upon the contaminant's chemical characteristics. Most all organic
vapors are collected on activated charcoal, although
the collection efficiency for aromatic amines and
straight chain amines are greatly increased when tubes
prepared with alumina and silica gel are employed.
   Because of the flow rate involved in sample collection, a portable pump designed for use at low flow
rates is recommended. Many pumps on the market are
equipped with a digital counter which accurately inte-
grates the volume of air sampled. Calibrating the
sampling pump is very important in this monitoring
procedure. FIGURE 5 illustrates a correct method for
accurately determining the flow rate of a typical low
flow collection system.
   The collection tubes are prepared for analysis
using distilled carbon disulfide as a desorbing agent.
The desorption phase is usually complete within thirty
minutes. The carbon disulfide solution is then analyzed
by a Gas Chromatograph equipped with a flame ionization
detector. The separation column specified by NIOSH is
a 20 ft. x 1/8 in. stainless steel column packed with
10% FFAP on Chromosorb W. Alternative columns, such as
10% SE-30 on Chromosorb W or Porapak Q can be used
depending on separation and peak resolving problems.
   The precision and accuracy of the analytical
methods depends strongly on the desorption efficiency
which is the percent removal of contaminent from the
collection media. An Electron Capture detector will
definitely increase the accuracy of chlorinated species.
Precision is increased by using the solvent flush
technique of sample injection.
   Organic Vapors may also be collected in Tedlar,
Mylar, or Saran bags. A drawback to this procedure is
that the sample must be analyzed as soon as possible
because of sample loss through the bag or by absorbing
to the inner walls of the bag. Samples collected on
activated charcoal can be refrigerated for extended
periods of time prior to desorption. Research in the
area of long-term storage has revealed that the organic
species collected tend to drift and equilibrate in both

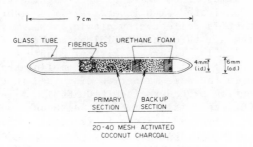

Figure 4.   Charcoal tube sampling device

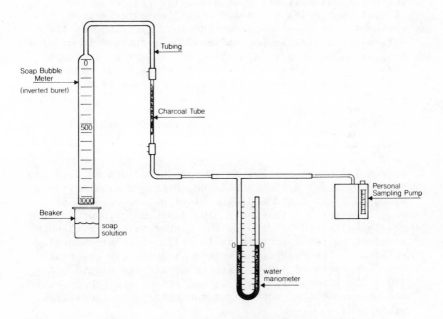

Figure 5.   Calibration setup for personal sampling pump with charcoal tube

the sample section and backup sections of the tube.

Oil Mist

Oil mist is a very common airborne contaminant in
work place atmospheres where process machinery is
cooled or lubricated with industrial grade lubricants.
Oil mist is collected by drawing a known volume of
contaminated air through a cellulose membrane filter at
a flow rate of 1.5 liters of air per minute to trap the
particulate oil mist present. The sampling train is
calibrated in the same manner as discussed in the metal
fume collection procedure (see FIGURE 3). A sample
size of 100 liters is recommended, although longer
samples are preferred. Since it is possible for the
filter to become plugged by heavy particulate oil
loading, the pump rotameter should be observed frequently and readjusted as needed to insure an accurate
sample volume.

The filter is prepared for analysis by extracting
the organic lubricants with distilled reagent grade
chloroform. Prior to analysis by fluorescense spectrophotometry, a bulk sample of the lubricant used in the
work place during sample collection is scanned in order
to select the proper excitation and emission wavelengths.
Standards are prepared from the bulk lubricant, and the
field samples are then analyzed at the predetermined
wavelengths. Samples containing graphite dust or other
inert particulate can be filtered or centrifuged prior
to analysis in order to obtain maximum emission.

Inorganic Gases

Industrial process gases and by-products such as Ammonia,
Sulfur Dioxide, Hydrogen Sulfide, Nitrogen Dioxide,
Hydrogen Cyanide and Hydrogen Fluoride are present in
many industrial situations. The gases described can be
easily collected by drawing the contaminated air through
a midget impinger containing 10 milliliters of absorbing
solution. The collection system is generally calibrated
for flow rates of 1.0-2.0 liters of air per minute. A
100 - 150 liter air sample is sufficient for the detection
and measurement of most gases encountered in industrial
situations.

The absorbing solutions are analyzed either by
specific ion electrode, colorimetry, or titration
depending on the analyte of interest. TABLE 2 presents
a list of absorbing solutions and method of analysis
for a variety of gaseous air contaminants. The overall
precision and accuracy of the method depends on calibration, absorption efficiency, interferences present and
time duration between collection and analysis.

TABLE 2

IMPINGER SAMPLING

GAS	ABSORBING SOLUTION	ANALYSIS
Hydrogen Cyanide	Sodium Hydroxide	Ion Specific Electrode
Sulfur Dioxide	Hydrogen Peroxide	Titration
Hydrogen Sulfide	Cadmium Hydroxide	Colorimetric
Nitrogen Dioxide	Sulfanilic Acid	Colorimetric
Hydrogen Fluoride	Sodium Hydroxide	Ion Specific Electrode
Ammonia	Sulfuric Acid	Ion Specific Electrode

An alternative to the impinger collection method is the use of colorimetric indicating tubes. A specific volume of contaminated air is drawn through a tube containing reactive chemicals which relates the concentration to the length of color stain produced. Originally, the indicating tubes were prepared and calibrated for spot checking which would not give a time indication of the time-weighted average concentration unless multiple samples were taken. Recently, the major tube manufacturers have calibrated a variety of indicating tubes which can be used in conjunction with low flow pumps resulting in a time-weighted average reading for an entire work shift.

Direct-reading field monitors equipped with chart recorders are also available for monitoring many industrial gases over long periods of time in order that an accurate time-weighted average concentration can be produced. Many manufacturing facilities have permanently installed air contaminant monitors equipped with alarms which sound when the threshold limit concentration is exceeded.

Asbestos

Asbestos fibers have been proven to produce lung cancer; and therefore, a strict monitoring requirement has been set forth by OSHA. Monitoring asbestos may tend to be difficult at first, depending on the interference of other particulate in the atmosphere and the volume of air sampled.

Asbestos samples are collected by drawing contaminated air at a flow rate of 1.5 liters of air per minute through an open-face 37mm filter holder containing an 0.8 micron cellulose ester filter. (The filter is housed in a three-piece filter holder or cassette. Prior to sampling, the top part of the cassette is removed in order to expose the total surface area of

the filter in insure uniform particulate and fiber
deposition.) The collection system is calibrated in
the same manner as the metal fume system illustrated in
FIGURE 3. The sampling duration depends on the amount
of dust in the atmosphere to be monitored. Generally,
a 15 minute sample is sufficient for a relatively dust-
free situation. The sample is evaluated by mounting a
small "pie shaped" section of the filter on a slide
using a mounting media prepared by mixing a specified
amount of filter material with equal parts of dimethyl
pthalate and diethyl oxalate. A microscope equipped
with a phase contrast optical accessory, 10 X objectives
and a calibrated portion reticle is used for counting
at 450X. Generally, a count of 100 fibers greater than
5 microns in length is sufficient; and requirements are
that at least 20 fields must be counted. When very low
concentrations are evident, 100 fields or 100 fibers,
whichever occurs is the general rule of thumb. An
ideal count would be 1 to 5 fibers per field. Asbestos
concentrations are reported in fibers per cubic centimeter
which takes into account the fibers counted, area of
the filter, field area of the portion reticle and the
volume of air drawn through the filter.

The primary reason for short-term sampling of
dusty atmospheres is basically that the filter becomes
impregnated with numerous dust particles and fibers and
is very hard to successfully count under the microscope.
Heavy concentration of particulates hinders the sizing
of fibers. Fibers may be partially or entirely obscured
from view. Certain counting rules must be followed in
order to achieve an accurate and statistically significant
count. These rules include recognizing, sizing and
counting of fibers and proper use of the boundaries of
the portion reticle.

NIOSH has collaboratively tested the fiber counting
procedure and has observed a statistical counting error
no greater than 20%.

BIBLIOGRAPHIC REFERENCES

U. S. Department of Health, Education and Welfare, "NIOSH Manual of Analytical Methods," 2nd Edition, Vol. I., II., III., Cincinnati: Public Health Service, 1977.

U. S. Department of Health, Education and Welfare, "NIOSH Manual of Sampling Data Sheets," 1977 Edition, Cincinnatti: Public Health Service, 1977.

Leithe, Wolfgang, "The Analysis of Air Pollutants," Ann Arbor: Ann Arbor Humphrey Science Publishers, 1970.

Leichwitz, K. R., "Detector Tubes and Prolonged Air Sampling," National Safety News, April, 1977.

"Industrial Hygiene Manual," Supplement 109, Occupational Safety and Health Reporter, Bureau of National Affairs, Inc., Washington, D.C., June 16, 1977.

"Environmental Health Monitoring Manual," U.S. Steel Corp., Birmingham, Alabama, 1973.

Orion Research: "Analytical Methods Guide," Sixth Edition, Cambridge, Massachusetts, Orion Research, Inc., 1973.

U. S. Department of Health, Education and Welfare, "The Industrial Environment, Its Evaluation and Control," HSM-99-71-45, Cincinnati: Public Health Service.

Turner, H. C., "Methods for the Determination of Oil Mist," Annals of Occupational Hygiene, Vol. 18, Great Britain, 1975.

Mindruk, R. F., Jr., "Determination of Organic Vapors in the Industrial Atmosphere, Bulletin No. 769, Supelco, Inc., Bellefonte, Pennsylvania, 1977.

"Industrial Hygiene Sampling and Analytical Guide for Airborne Health Hazards," E. I. DuPont de Nemours & Co. (Inc.), 1978.

RECEIVED August 14, 1979.

Evaluation of Organic Solvent Vapors in the Workplace

ROBERT C. VOBORSKY

Sentry Insurance, 1800 North Point Drive, Stevens Point, WI 54481

A potential threat to the health, productivity, and efficiency of man in most occupations and industries, and in his
nonoccupational environments as well, is his exposure to organic
solvents.

Exposures to solvents occur throughout life from conception
to death. Solvent vapors inhaled by the mother often reach the
fetus. The elderly often spend their last days in the hospital
where the odor of the solvents, disinfectants often prevails.
Exposures also occur in the course of daily living. Exposures
may range from the inhalation of vapors from a newspaper freshly
off the news stand, to the intake of the cleaning solvent by all
routes of exposure being used. Effects from the exposure may
range from simple objection to a low concentration odor, to death
at high concentrations. In between, there is a whole spectrum
of effects.

When one considers that there are hundreds of different
solvents, that there are a multitude of exposures to different
concentrations, and that these effects may differ from individual
to individual and may also vary with age, it is apparent that the
number of combinations almost defies imagination and description.

The problem lies in determining what are the effects, which
are harmful and which are not harmful, and at what levels such
effects occur. When the exposure exceeds certain threshold
levels, many of these effects are harmful to ones health and his
ability to function efficiently may be impaired. In some cases,
the effects are irreversible and damage to the body organ can be
permanent.

As in the case of many safety measures, people often do not
utilize the necessary protective measures. Too often there is
more contact with the skin then the user realizes and/or local
ventilation in the breathing zone is not adequate. Concentrations
of organic solvent vapors in air are usually expressed in parts
of vapor per million parts of air (PPM).

The physiological effects of different solvents is far to
complex and variable to be discussed here in depth. However,

0-8412-0539-6/80/47-120-197$05.00/0

certain generalizations can be made. All organic solvents affect
the central nervous system to some extent, acting as depressants
and anesthetics, and causing other effects depending upon the
degree of exposure and the solvent involved. These effects may
range from mild unnoticed effects to narcosis and death from
respiratory arrest. All solvents which contact and wet the skin
will cause dermatitis, an inflammation of the skin. This may be
caused by simple irritation or by systemic damage to the skin.
Even the most inert solvents will dissolve the natural protective
barrier of fats and oils and leave the skin unprotected against
further irritation and harm by the organic solvent.

Organic solvents are usually classified according to their
chemical composition. The aliphatic hydrocarbons, which are
straight or branched chains saturated with hydrogen, act
primarily as depressants to the central nervous system, but
otherwise they are generally as inert biochemically as they are
chemically.

Even as air pollutants, they are among the least reactive
and do not pose a significant problem. The primary problem with
this class of solvents is dermatitis.

The cyclic hydrocarbons, such as cyclohexane, act much in
the same manner as the aliphatic hydrocarbons. A significant
percentage of quantity inhaled may be metabolized to compounds
with a lower order of toxicity. The unsaturated cyclic hydrocarbons generally are more irritating than the saturated forms.
The primary problem is dermatitis.

The aromatic hydrocarbons, such as xylene and toluene,
exhibit their toxic effects on the central nervous system.
Benzene, however, is quite different in that it's toxicity affects
the blood forming organs.

The effects of the halogenated hydrocarbons vary considerably with the number and type of halogen atoms present in the
molecule. Carbon tetrachloride at one end of the scale is highly
toxic, acting acutely by injury to the kidneys, the liver, the
central nervous system and the gastrointestinal tract. Triflu-
orotrichlorethane on the other hand has a very low level of toxicity. Its primary effect of known significance is the depressant
effect on the central nervous system. The chlorinated hydrocarbons in general are more toxic then the common fluorinated
hydrocarbon solvents. Specific effects and toxicities vary
widely, but the most common effects from the chlorinated hydrocarbons of intermediate toxicity are the depressant effect on the
central nervous system, dermatitis, and injury to the liver.

The nitro-hydrocarbons vary in their toxicological
effects depending on whether the hydrocarbon is a pariffin or an
aromatic. The pariffins are known for their irritant effects
accompanied by nausea, and the effects on the central nervous
system and liver becoming significant with acute exposures. The
nitro-aromatics like nitrobezene, are much more hazardous.

The common ketones generally exert a narcotic type action.
All are irritating to the eyes, nose, and the throat, and for
this reason high concentrations are not usually tolerated. (1)(2)
     Personnel concerned with health and safety should recognize
that the use of organic solvents can be a major threat to health,
and that controls are often necessary to prevent detrimental
physiological effects.
     The Occupational Safety and Health Act of 1970 (Public Law
91-596) is one of the most far-reaching federal laws ever enacted.
It applies to all employees of an employer engaged in a business
effecting commerce, except for government employees and employees
and employers at employment sites being regulated under other
federal laws. The Act specifies the employer's obligations to
furnish to each employee a place of employment free from the
recognized hazards that are causing or likely to cause death or
serious physical harm and to comply with standards promulgated
by the Occupational Safety and Health Administration (OSHA). The
responsibility includes the determination of whether a hazardous
condition exists in a workplace, the evaluation of degree of the
hazard and where necessary, the control needed to prevent occupational illness.
     In the field of industrial hygiene, control of the work
environment is based on the assumption that, for each substance,
there exists some safe or tolerable level of exposure below which
no significantly adverse effect occurs. These levels, referred
to in the generic sense as threshold limit values (TLV) refer to
airborne concentrations of substances and represent conditions
under which it is believed that nearly all workers may be re-
peatedly exposed day after day without adverse effect. The TLV
is a Time Weighted Average (TWA) concentration for an eight hour
workday or forty hour work week. Industry must comply with the
Threshold Limit Values regarded by the regulatory agency as
standards for occupational exposure to chemical substances. The
list of chemical substances which have been assigned a threshold
limit appears in Section 1910.1000 (e) Tables Z-1, Z-2, and Z-3
of the Federal Register.
     To aid industry in a monitoring program designed to comply
with these standards, the National Institute for Occupational
Safety and Health (NIOSH), developed methods for the collection
and analysis of those restricted compounds. Method P&CAM-127 in
the NIOSH Manual of Analytical Methods describes the recommended
method of collection and analysis of organic solvents in air. (4)
     Many of the common solvents used in industry which have been
restricted because of their toxicity are listed in TABLE 1.
     The first step in recognizing potential problem areas in an
occupational environment using organic solvents is to become
familiar with the particular operations and raw materials in the
plant. Knowledge of the process and equipment as well as the raw
materials is vital. Process flow sheets from the plant should be

TABLE 1 - ORGANIC SOLVENT MONITORING DATA

ORGANIC CHEMICAL	MOL. WT. (G/MDE)	DENSITY (G/ML)	OSHA STD. TWA (PPM)	SAMPLE RATE (ML/MIN)	SAMPLE TIME (HRS.)	COLLECTION TUBE	DESORPTION EFFICIENCY (%)	TOTAL COEFFICIENT OF VARIATION CV_T
Acetone	58.1	0.79	1000	20	1.5	Charcoal	86±10	0.08
Allyl Alcohol	58.1	0.85	2	20	8	Charcoal	89±5	0.11
Allyl Chloride	76.5	0.94	1	200	8	Charcoal		0.07
Aniline	93.1	1.02	5	100	8	Silica Gel	96	
Benzene	78.1	0.88	1	20	8	Charcoal		
2-Butanone	72.1	0.81	200	20	8	Charcoal	90±5	0.10
2-Butoxy Ethanol	118.2	0.90	50	20	8	Charcoal	99±5	0.06
Butyl Acetate	116.2	0.88	150	20	8	Charcoal	99±5	0.09
Butyl Alcohol	74.1	0.81	100	20	8	Charcoal	88±5	0.07
Camphor	152.2	0.99	2	20	8	Charcoal	98±5	0.07
Carbon Tetrachloride	153.8	1.59	10	50	5	Charcoal	97±5	0.09
Chlorobenzene	112.6	1.10	75	20	8	Charcoal	90±5	0.06
Chloroform	119.4	1.48		20	8	Charcoal	96±5	0.06
Cumene	120.2	0.86	50	20	8	Charcoal	100	0.06
Cyclohexane	84.2	0.78	300	20	2	Charcoal	100	0.07
Cyclohexanol	100.2	0.96	50	20	8	Charcoal	99±5	0.08
Cyclohexanone	98.1	0.95	50	20	8	Charcoal	78±5	0.06
Diacetone Alc.	116.2	0.93	50	20	8	Charcoal	77±10	0.10
1,1-Dichloroethane	99.0	1.18	100	20	8	Charcoal	100	0.06
1,2-Dichloroethylene	97.0	1.28	200	20	2.5	Charcoal	100	0.05
Diethylamine	73.1	0.71	25	100	8	Silica Gel		0.07
Dimethylamine	45.1	0.68	10	100	8	Silica Gel		0.06
Dioxane	88.1	1.03	100	20	8	Charcoal	91±5	0.05
Epichlorohydrin	92.5	1.18	5	50	8	Charcoal		0.06
2-Ethoxyethyl act.	132.2	0.98	100	20	8	Charcoal	74±10	0.06
Ethyl Acetate	88.1	0.90	400	20	5	Charcoal	89±5	0.06
Ethyl Acrylate	100.1	0.94	25	20	8	Charcoal	95±5	0.05
Ethyl Alcohol	46.1	0.80	1000	50	0.33	Charcoal	77±10	0.06
Ethyl Amine	45.1	0.69	10	100	8	Silica Gel		0.11

Table 1 - (Continued)

ORGANIC CHEMICAL	MOL. WT. (G/MDE)	DENSITY (G/ML)	OSHA STD. TWA (PPM)	SAMPLE RATE (ML/MIN)	SAMPLE TIME (HRS.)	COLLECTION TUBE	DESORPTION EFFICIENCY (%)	TOTAL COEFFICIENT OF VARIATION CV$_T$
Ethyl Benzene	106.2	0.87	100	20	8	Charcoal	100	0.04
Ethyl Bromide	109.0	1.45	200	20	3.3	Charcoal	83±5	0.05
Ethyl Butyl Ketone	114.2	0.82	50	20	8	Charcoal	93±5	0.09
Ethyl Ether	74.1	0.73	400	20	2.5	Charcoal	98±5	0.05
Ethyl Formate	74.1	0.92	100	20	8	Charcoal	80±10	0.08
Heptane	100.2	0.68	500	20	3.3	Charcoal	96±5	0.06
Hexane	86.2	0.66	500	20	3.3	Charcoal	94±5	0.06
Hexone (MIBK)	100.2	0.88	100	20	8	Charcoal		0.06
Isoamyl Acetate	88.2	0.81	100	20	8	Charcoal	99±5	0.06
Isobutyl Acetate	116.2	0.87	150	20	8	Charcoal	92±5	0.07
Isobutyl Alcohol	74.1	0.81	100	20	8	Charcoal	84±10	0.07
Isopropyl Acetate	102.1	0.87	250	20	8	Charcoal	85±5	0.07
Isopropyl Alcohol	60.1	0.79	400	20	2.5	Charcoal	94±5	0.06
Isopropyl Amine	59.1	0.69	5	100	8	Silica Gel		0.07
Methyl Acetate	74.1	0.93	200	20	5.5	Charcoal	88±5	0.06
Methyl Acrylate	86.1	0.96	10	20	4	Charcoal	80±10	0.07
Methyl Alcohol	32.0	0.79	200	20	4	Silica Gel		0.06
Methyl Cellasolve	76.1	0.97	25	20	8	Charcoal	97±5	0.07
Methyl Cell. Acetate	118.1	1.00	25	20	8	Charcoal	76±10	0.07
Methyl Chloroform	133.4	1.35	350	20	5	Charcoal	98±5	0.05
Methyl Cyclohexane	98.2	0.77	500	20	3.3	Charcoal	95±5	0.05
Octane	114.2	0.70	500	20	3.3	Charcoal	93±5	0.06
O-Dichlorobenzene	147.0	1.31	50	20	2.5	Charcoal		0.07
Pentane	72.2	0.63	1000	20	1.5	Charcoal	96±5	0.05
2-Pentanone	86.1	0.81	200	20	8	Charcoal	88±5	0.06
Propyl Alcohol	60.1	0.72	200	20	8	Charcoal	87±5	0.08
Propylene Dichloride	113.0	1.16	75	20	8	Charcoal	97±5	0.06
Sec-Amyl Acetate	130.0	0.88	125	20	8	Charcoal		0.05
Sec-Butyl Acetate	116.2	0.88	200	20	8	Charcoal		
Sec-Butyl Alcohol	74.1	0.81	150	20	8	Charcoal		0.07
Stoddard Solvent	.	.	500	20	2.5	Charcoal	96±5	0.05

Table 1 - (Continued)

ORGANIC CHEMICAL	MOL. WT. (G/MDE)	DENSITY (G/ML)	OSHA STD. TWA (PPM)	SAMPLE RATE (ML/MIN)	SAMPLE TIME (HRS.)	COLLECTION TUBE	DESORPTION EFFICIENCY (%)	TOTAL COEFFICIENT OF VARIATION CV_T
Styrene	104.1	0.91	200	20	8	Charcoal	87±5	0.06
Tert-Butyl Acetate	116.2	0.87	200	20	8	Charcoal		0.09
Tert-Butyl Alcohol	74.1	0.79	100	20	8	Charcoal		0.08
1,1,2,2-Tetrachloro-1,2-difluoroethane	203.8	1.64	500	20	1.6	Charcoal		0.07
1,1,1,2-Tetrachloro-2,2-difluoroethane	203.8	.	500	20	1.6	Charcoal	100	0.05
1,1,2,2-Tetrachloro-ethane	167.9	1.59	5	20	8	Charcoal	85±5	0.06
Tetrahydrofuran	72.1	0.89	200	20	7	Charcoal	92±5	0.06
Toluene	92.1	0.87	200	20	8	Charcoal	96±5	0.06
1,1,2-Trichloro-ethane	133.4	1.44	10	20	8	Charcoal	96±5	0.06
Trichloroethylene	131.4	1.47	200	20	8	Charcoal	96±5	0.08
1,2,3-Trichloro-ethane	147.4	1.39	50	20	8	Charcoal		0.07
Turpentine	256.0	0.85	100	20	8	Charcoal	96±5	0.05
Vinyl Toluene	118.1	0.89	100	20	8	Charcoal	85±10	0.06
Xylene	106.2	0.86	100	20	8	Charcoal	95±5	.

obtained and studied. If this is not possible, there are books
describing chemical processes which can provide the information
about the general operations involved and serve as a source for
the terminology used in the particular industry. The early
investigation should cover the toxic materials being used, the
manner of use, the number of workers, exposure potential, and the
control measures being employed at the present time.

Besides information developed in previous surveys, information about the presence and severity of hazards can be obtained
from reported industrial hygiene reviews of similar facilities
and from discussions with workers, medical and management
personnel. Regardless of the extent of information obtained by
this preliminary screening, a survey will be needed to define
the relative concentration of the organic solvent vapors in the
breathing zone of the worker.

It is essential that samples represent the worker's exposure
or the condition to be evaluated. To decide what samples are
representative, the person evaluating the exposure must be able
to decide where to sample, whom to sample, sample duration,
number of samples, and the appropriate sampling period. The
choice of sampling location depends upon the type of information
needed and may necessitate sampling in the breathing zone of the
worker, in the general room air, or directly at the operation. (5)

Evaluation of worker exposure requires samples in the
breathing zone and in general room air or rest area. To define
a potential hazard, check compliance with regulations or obtain
data for control purposes, samples would normally be collected
in the vicinity of the operation itself. In general, samples
are collected in the vicinity of the workers directly exposed
and also workers remote from the exposure who voice complaints.
Sample duration requires that the sample contain sufficient
matter for an accurate analysis and is based on the sensitivity of
the analytical procedure and the estimated air concentration, as
well as the current threshold limit value for the contaminant.
Table 1 contains appropriate sampling duration, sample flow
rates and sample volume.

Thus, the volume of sample needed may vary from a few
liters of air where the estimated concentration is high, to
several cubic meters where low concentrations are expected. The
duration should represent some identifiable period of operating
time, possibly a complete cycle of an operation.

The number and type of samples collected depends to a great
extent upon the operations being studied and whether the threshold limit value is a time weighted average, a ceiling value or
both. For a time weighted average, (TWA), sampling covering
most or all of the work day is preferrable. That is, personal
samplers can be placed on the worker to obtain either one continuous sample covering the work day or consecutive samples covering
the time period for which the threshold limit value is stated,
usually eight hours.

The use of charcoal tubes for the collection of solvent vapors is recommended in the NIOSH method. The charcoal tubes presently used contain 150 milligrams (mg) of coconut charcoal. Figure 1 illustrates the charcoal tube subdivided into two sections of 100 mg and 50 mg of charcoal. The front portion of 100 mg is used to collect the solvent vapors while the 50 mg backup section is intended to determine if solvent breakthrough occurred on the front portion. This is a built-in quality control check. (6)(14)

The charcoal tubes are used in series with the portable personal pump to collect solvent vapors from the air. Calibration must also be conducted on the personal pump to assure the correct flow rate coincides with the pump setting. Using a standard charcoal tube, connect the charcoal tube in between the inlet of the personal pump and the outlet of the 50 mL soap bubble meter. Set the pump at the desired setting and draw air through the charcoal tube. A stopwatch is used to measure the elapsed time between two volume indices. The flow rate is then calculated as cc/min. FIGURE 2 illustrates the calibration train for a low flow personal pump. The battery operated pump is preset at a controlled flow rate and air is drawn through the charcoal tube. The recommended flow rates for many compounds are listed in TABLE 1. To initiate sampling, the sealed ends of the charcoal tube are broken and the tube is placed in the sample holder connected to the inlet of the pump. The arrow marked on the tube indicates the direction of the air flow. The charcoal sampling tube should always be vertical during sampling to prevent channeling of the air in and around the charcoal bed. A convenient clip on the sample holder allows positioning of the holder in the proximity of the breathing zone of the person monitored. The air sampled should not pass through any tubing prior to entering the charcoal tube.

When the desired sample volume is collected, the charcoal tube is removed from the sample holder and both ends are capped with plastic caps provided from the manufacturer. The capped charcoal tubes can be retained for analysis at a later date only if refrigerated below room temperature, otherwise, sample migration may occur between the two sections of the charcoal and void the test. During this sampling procedure, one charcoal tube is opened at the sample side and the ends capped. No air is drawn through this tube, which serves as a blank. The temperature and pressure of the atmosphere being sampled should be measured and recorded during the sampling period in order to correct the sample volume of air to standard temperature (25 degrees Centigrade) and pressure (760 millimeters Mercury). (4)

Removal of the collected sample from the charcoal tube is accomplished by desorption with carbon disulfide or other solvents appropriate for a desirable desorption efficiency. The capped charcoal tube is scored with a file at both ends and the

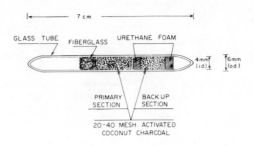

Figure 1.   Charcoal tube sampling device

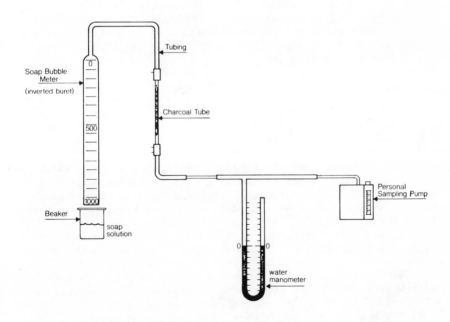

Figure 2.   Calibration setup for personal sampling pump with charcoal tube

ends are broken off. If the charcoal tubes were refrigerated,
they should be warmed to room temperature before the removal
of the charcoal. Each charcoal section is removed and placed
in separate sample vials and sealed. The vial must have a
screwed type top containing a teflon coated septum to permit
sampling with a syringe. The blank charcoal tube is handled
in the same manner as the sample tubes.

To each sealed sample vial, add one milliliter of spectroquality carbon disulfide or freshly redistilled carbon disulfide.
Comparison of various reagent and spectra-grade qualities of
carbon disulfide indicated that spectra-grade carbon disulfide
had the least amount of impurities, which would interfere in the
sample analysis.

All laboratory work with carbon disulfide should be performed in a hood because of its high toxicity. For complete
desorption, the samples should be agitated or periodically shaken
for a period of 30 minutes. If the desorbed sample is not
analyzed immediately, it should be refrigerated, but no longer
than two days. (7)

The sample is analyzed by withdrawing a 5 microliter
aliquot from the sample vial with a 10 microliter syringe and
injected into a gas chromatograph. The solvent flush technique
is recommended to prevent sample blowback or distillation within
the needle of the syringe. The syringe is first flushed with the
carbon disulfide solvent several times to wet the barrel and
plunger of the syringe and approximately one microliter of
carbon disulfide is drawn into the syringe. After the needle
has been removed from the carbon disulfide solvent, the plunger
is pulled back approximately one microliter to separate the solvent flush from the sample with a pocket of air. A suitable
aliquot of the sample is pulled into the syringe and removed
from the sample vial. Immediately pull the plunger back to
minimize evaporation of the sample from the tip of the needle.
At this time, the volume of the sample to be injected is to be
noted for calculation purposes. Injection of the sample is
complete with the sample flushed from the barrel and the needle
of the syringe. The advantage of this method is increased
accuracy and reproducibility of the injected sample volume.
Triplicate injections of the same sample are made and the average
peak area for each compound is then determined.

The separation of most common solvents is possible with a
20 foot by 1/8th inch stainless steel column with 10% Carbowax
20M terephthalic acid derivative (commonly referred to as FFAP)
on 80/100 mesh Chromosorb W AW-DMCS treated. An alternative
column packing is 10% SP-1000 on 80/100 mesh Supelcoport. (7)
The adequate separation of the organic species in the sample is
dependent on the quality of the separating column, temperature
and carrier gas settings on the gas chromatograph. For most
analyses, the Flame Ionization Detector is adequate, although

the Electron Capture Detector is appropriate for chlorinated
species.

Quantification depends on accurate calibration of the gas
chromatograph for each solvent investigated. The method recommended by NIOSH is an absolute calibration using prepared volumetric solutions of each solvent in carbon disulfide. Concentrations equivalent to 0.5, 1.0, 2.0, and 5.0 times the OSHA
limit are prepared using the following equation:

$$\text{ul Solvent} = \frac{F \times L \times V_s \times M}{24450 \times P \times D}$$

F = Fraction or multiple of TLV limit (.5, 1, 2, 5)

L = TLV Limit (PPM)

V_s = Volume of air sampled, (Liters)

M = Molecular Weight

P = Density of Solvent (g/mL)

24450 = Conversion Factor (Molar Volume)

D = Volume of Desorbing Agent, (mL CS_2)

For simplicity, one can desorb the sample charcoal in a vial
containing 0.5 milliliters of carbon disulfide and prepare all
standard mixtures in 0.5 milliliters of carbon disulfide and inject a constant volume of 1 microliter of desorbed sample and
standard into the gas chromatograph. Calibration curves are prepared by plotting concentration of solvent in ul/ml carbon disulfide versus peak area.

Solvent peak areas are compared to the calibration curves to
determine the concentration of each solvent in the sample. The
response of the blank is also converted to concentration and subtracted from the sample concentration. The blank includes the
background of carbon disulfide as well as the background related
to the charcoal tube. With the concentration as ul of solvent/ml
of carbon disulfide, conversion to PPM of solvent/volume of air
sampled is determined by the following equation:

$$\text{PPM} = \frac{\text{ul}}{\text{Liter}} = \frac{\text{ul of Solvent} \times 24450 \times P \times D}{V_s \times M}$$

P = Density of Solvent

D = Volume of Desorbing Liquid (mL CS_2)

M = Molecular Weight of Contaminant

V_s = Volume of Air Sampled

Each solvent investigated is quantified in the same manner using their respective calibration curve and formula. Because an absolute calibration is used, sample analysis and calibration must be performed on the same day. Standards more than one day old should be scrutinized for variations in concentration due to volatilization of solvent from the carbon disulfide into the head space.

Other corrections that must be considered are the collection efficiency of the charcoal tube and the desorption efficiency of carbon disulfide for this specific solvent. TABLE 1 lists the recommended collection tube for each solvent, flow rate to be used in samplings, and desorption efficiency of many organic compounds. (6) The desorption efficiency of carbon disulfide with the charcoal tubes can be determined by injecting a known amount of solvent onto the charcoal. At least five charcoal tubes are sampled and the 100 mg portion removed and placed in a septum sealed vial. A concentration applicable to the threshold limit value of the organic solvent in question is injected onto the 100 mg of charcoal by piercing the septum cap with a microliter syringe. Several concentrations of solvent should be checked to determine the variation in desorption efficiency with solvent concentration. In like manner, standards are prepared by adding the same amount of solvent to the carbon disulfide solution in the vial. The standards are analyzed with the samples. The percent desorption efficiency (D.E.) is determined as:

$$D.E. = \frac{\text{area of sample-area blank}}{\text{area of standard}} \times 100 \%$$

Certain limitations must be considered in the collection of solvent vapors with charcoal tubes. Charcoal tubes have saturation limits for each solvent sampled. When this limit is exceeded, breakthrough occurs. Charcoal is not always the most efficient collection material because of sample stability, adsorption, or desorption properties. Other collection materials (silica gel, alumina) should be considered to improve collection efficiency. Solvent collected could be displaced by another solvent which is more strongly absorbed by the charcoal. High humidity severely decreases the breakthrough volume of the charcoal. Sampling should be restricted during periods of high humidity or the breakthrough efficiencies determined under similar conditions and the sample rate adjusted for the lower collection efficiency. The carbon disulfide does not readily displace all organic solvents from charcoal, and other desorption solvents would be necessary for some compounds to obtain acceptable desorption efficiency. (9)

The Total Coefficient of Variation (CV_T) which includes the Coefficient of Variations for both the sampling and analytical phases of overall procedure are listed in TABLE 1. The following relationship is used for determining CV_T:

$$CV_T = \left[(CV_p)^2 + (CV_A)^2\right]^{\frac{1}{2}}$$

where

CV_P = CV for sample collection (usually 0.05)

CV_A = CV for analytical method

One of the most important objectives of any industrial hygiene monitoring program is to accurately interpret air sampling results. The use of statistics in this assessment process is necessary because all measurements of physical properties contain some unavoidable random measurement error. The variation of occupational exposure measurements is an argument for statistical information; not against it. (10)(15)

The following list details the primary sources of variation that effect estimates of occupational exposure averages:

1. Random sampling device errors (as random fluctuations in pump flowrate),

2. Random analytical method errors (as random fluctuations in a chemical laboratory procedure),

3. Random intraday (within day) environmental fluctuations in a contaminant's concentration,

4. Random interday (between days) environmental fluctuations in a contaminant's concentration,

5. Systematic errors in the measurement process (improper calibration, improper use of equipment, erroneous recording of data, etc.), and

6. Systematic changes in a contaminant's airborne concentration (as due to the employee moving to a different exposure concentration or shutting off an exhaust fan). (11)

Systematic errors can either remain constant through a series of samples (because of improper calibration) or vary abruptly following some change in the process. Systematic errors cannot be accounted for statistically.

Systematic changes in the contaminant exposure concentration for an employee can occur due to:

1. Employee moving to a different work area (as going from a solvent room to a warehouse),

2. Closing plant doors and windows (in cold seasons),

3. Decreases in efficiency or abrupt failure (or plugging) of engineering control equipment such as ventilation systems,

4. Changes in the production process or work habits of the employee.

One of the most important reasons for periodically measuring an employee's exposure every few months is to detect trends or systematic changes in the long-term exposure average. (12)

A single sample or the time weighted average of several consecutive samples taken for the entire time period for which a standard TLV is defined yields the best estimate of the true average concentration of the airborne contaminant. This type of sample is referred to as a "full-period" sample. Typically, a full-period sample would have to be 8 to 36% above the standard in order to demonstrate noncompliance with 95% confidence.

According to Busch and Liedel (13), one can easily calculate an Upper Confidence Limit (UCL) at 95% confidence for a single 8 hour-time weighted average sample by the following equation:

$$UCL = X + 1.645 \ (C.V.)$$

where

X = measurement data divided by the TLV. $\left(\dfrac{Conc.}{TLV} \right)$

C.V. = Coefficient of Variation of sampling/analytical method

1.645 = Critical standard normal deviate for 95% Confidence

If UCL is less than or equal to 1.0, the exposure is classified as being within Compliance limits. If the UCL is greater than 1.0, the exposure is classified as being in Noncompliance with the standard. Refer to TABLE 1 for appropriate C.V. values.

When multiple samples are collected throughout the entire work shift, the Upper Control Limit at 95% confidence may be calculated by the following equation:

$$UCL = \frac{TWA}{TLV} + 1.645 \ (C.V.) \ \frac{\left(T_1^2 + T_2^2 + \ldots T_n^2\right)^{\frac{1}{2}}}{T_1 + T_2 + \ldots T_n}$$

Where

TWA = Time Weighted Average Concentration

$$TWA = \frac{C_1 \ T_1 + C_2 \ T_2 + \ldots C_n \ T_n}{T_1 + T_2 + \ldots T_n}$$

C = Concentration of sample during Time Interval T.

C.V. = Coefficient of Variation of sampling/analytical
method

TLV = Appropriate treshold limit value in OSHA
Standard

If the UCL is less than or equal to 1.0, the exposure is classified as being within compliance limits. If the UCL is greater than 1.0, the exposure is excessive and non-compliance exists.

The effect of the number of samples on requirements for demonstrating compliance can be found by using the equation suggested for multiple samples. The standard exposure average would be $\bar{X}$. Figure 3 illustrates the use of C.V. data when determining compliance using multiple samples throughout the work day.

$$\bar{X} = 1 - \frac{(1.645) \ (C.V.)}{N}$$

Where

$\bar{X}$ = exposure data average

C.V. = Coefficient of Variation of sampling/analytical
method

N = number of samples within an average work shift

Many OSHA standards and those being proposed include monitoring requirements consisting of preliminary surveys to determine whether the exposure is above or below the "Action Level." The Action Level (AL) is one-half the treshold limit value (TLV). If an exposure falls above the AL, it must be monitored at least every two months. If two consecutive exposure measurements taken at least one week apart result in a measurement which is lower than the AL, monitoring may be terminated. A generalized flowchart for exposure determination

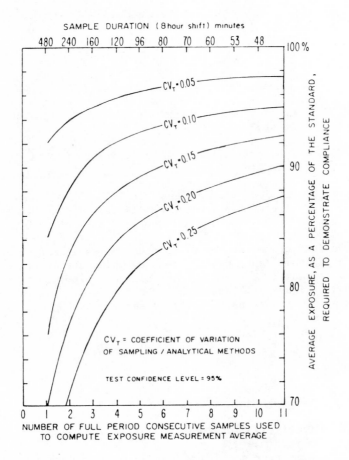

Figure 3.   Effect of full-period consecutive sample size on compliance demonstration (11)

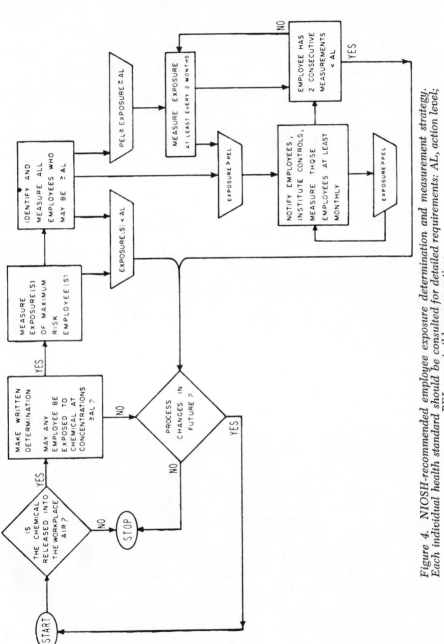

Figure 4. NIOSH-recommended employee exposure determination and measurement strategy. Each individual health standard should be consulted for detailed requirements: AL, action level; PEL, permissible exposure time.

and measurement has been recommended by NIOSH and is illustrated in Figure 4. The flowchart can be used for other airborne contaminants in addition to organic solvent vapors.

LITERATURE CITED

1. Olishifski, J.B., F.E. McElroy: Fundamentals of Industrial Hygiene, Chapter 1, National Safety Council, Chicago, IL (1971).

2. Key, Marcus M, et al: Occupational Diseases - A Guide to Their Recognition, U.S. Dept. of Health, Education and Welfare, NIOSH Publication No. 77-181, Cincinnati, OH (June, 1977).

3. U.S. Department of Health, Education and Welfare, Public Health Service, CDC, NIOSH: The Industrial Environment - It's Evaluation and Control, NIOSH Publication, Cincinnati, OH, Chapter 8 (1973).

4. NIOSH Manual of Analytical Methods, U.S. Dept. of Health, Education and Welfare, NIOSH Publication No. 75-121, Cincinnati, OH (1974).

5. U.S. Dept. of Health, Education and Welfare: An Identification System for Occupational Hazardous Materials, NIOSH Publication, HEW Publication No. 75-126, Cincinnati, OH (1974).

6. McCammon, C.S. Jr.: The NIOSH Charcoal Tube and Other Solid Sorbent Sampling Tube Certification Programs, Amer. Ind. Hyg. Assoc. Journal, 37:489, (1976).

7. Mindrup, R.F., Jr.: Determination of Organic Vapors in the Industrial Atmosphere, Bulletin No. 769, Supelco, Inc., Bellefonte, PA (1977).

8. White, L.D., et al: A Convenient Optimized Method for the Analysis of Selected Solvent Vapors in the Industrial Atmosphere, Amer. Ind. Hyg. Assoc. Journal, 31:225 (1971).

9. U.S. Dept. of Health, Education and Welfare, PHS, NIOSH: NIOSH Manual of Analytical Methods. NIOSH Publication No. 77-157-C. (1977).

10. Armatage, P.: Statistical Methods in Medical Research, John Wiley and Sons, New York, NY (1971).

11. U.S. Dept. of Health, Education and Welfare, PHS., NIOSH: Occupational Exposure Sampling Strategy Manual, NIOSH Publication No. 77-173, P. 13 (1977).

12. IBID

13. IBID

14. U.S. Dept. of Health, Education and Welfare, PHS, NIOSH: Collaborative Testing of Activated Charcoal Tubes for Seven Organic Solvents, NIOSH Publication No. 75-184 (1975).

15. Leidel, N.A., K.A. Busch: Statistical Methods for Determination of Noncompliance, Amer. Ind. Hyg. Assoc. Journal, 36:839-840 (1975).

RECEIVED August 14, 1979.

Monitoring Airborne Contaminants in Chemical Laboratories

FRED HERTLEIN III

INALAB, 1523 Kalakua Avenue, Suite 101, Honolulu, HI 96826

The Occupational Safety and Health Act (PL 91-596, OSHA) protects workers against safety and health hazards in the occupational environment, and requires that all employees be provided a safe and healthy work environment. Can students be defined as "workers" or "employees" according to OSHA? University staff and instructors can be defined as employees, however, a student's protection under OSHA is unclear. Recently, students were provided all the "protection" that employees have under OSHA.

A university was questioned by students if they were exposed to toxic gases and vapors during organic chemistry laboratory sessions. University authorities resolved the students' question by conducting a one month program of air monitoring during four summer session laboratory classes. Concentrations of a variety of organic vapors from solvents used in routine laboratory experiments were measured. Samples of air from the student's breathing zone were collected, and the concentrations determined by gas chromatography. These concentrations were compared with current levels allowed for safe worker exposure to the vapors. The levels also permitted assessment of the laboratory hoods and exhaust ventilation system for effective removal of air contaminants.

EXPERIMENTAL   The sampling and analytical method employed in determining the various solvent vapor concentrations in air are described in detail by White etal (1)and NIOSH (2). Four Bendix National Environmental Instruments Model BDX 30 Personal Samplers were used daily (one in each laboratory) with large size charcoal tubes (SKC cat no. 226-09-100) which contained two sections of activated charcoal per tube (a 400 milligram section followed by a 200 mg backup section to indicate when "breakthrough" of the main section has occurred). The sampling pumps were operated at a rate of one liter per minute and were calibrated by means of an Environmental Compliance Corporation Model 302 Universal Pump Calibrator (a device that generates a thin film of soap which is carefully timed as it traverses a very determined because highly polar compounds such as ketones, amines, organic acids, and alcohols, are often replaced on charcoal by less polar hydrocarbons. The NIOSH method of desorption efficiency determination involves direct injection of known quantities of the solvent(s) onto the charcoal in the sampling tube. The open ends of the tube are capped, and the tube remains at room temperature for one day before analysis. During this one day, the solvent(s) redistribute themselves between the front and rear sections of charcoal. Amount recovered/amount injected is termed the desorption efficiency when expressed as a percentage. In these studies CS_2 was used as the desorption solvent. The desorption efficiency changes from compound, to compound, solvent to solvent, and between batches of charcoal.

The affinity that the solvent vapor has for the activated charcoal or the charcoal's adsorptivity is reflected in the "collection" efficiency. Early studies(1, 3) show that for many solvents, collection efficiencies are similar. No generalization is without exception and therefore test atmospheres should be generated where this information is important. The collection efficiency and desorption efficiency, together with the analytical precision and accuracy are incorporated into the total coefficient of variation for the method. Many solvent vapor sampling methods are not this thoroughly documented in the literature because of the difficulty of generating known test atmospheres. In this study both direct injection and flowing of vapor-air mixtures over the charcoal were used for efficiency determinations; these values are reported in table 1 and required much time and effort to obtain.

RESULTS

Sampling for various hydrocarbon vapors in laboratory atmospheres requires coordination and scheduling. Since all the chemistry laboratory experiments are known at the beginning of the semester, a sampling schedule concentrating on key chemicals can be arranged. Compounds that can be expected to become airborne on each particular day can be anticipated. The highly volatile compounds with high vapor pressure are candidates for monitoring either as product, intermediate or reactant in an experiment. Listing the compounds that can be expected for each day of the semester aids in scheduling. Only compounds listed by OSHA(4)as having a time-weighted-average (TWA) threshold limit value (TLV) should be monitored.

The pre-survey described above helps plan sampling, determine the number of charcoal tubes needed, and helps plan laboratory work for desorption studies and sample analyses required. The pumps required for a study will have to be calibrated, recharged, and maintained. The pre-survey helps plan for these activities. Sampling vials and solvents for standards and desorption can be ordered based on the pre-survey.

TABLE I
EFFICIENCY STUDIES

Trial No.	Components	Desorption Efficiency (Direct Spikes) Percent Recovery	Av Pct	Overall Efficiency (Flowed Spikes) Percent Recovery	Av Pct
1.	Acetone	69 76 72 85 78 70	75	71 73 57	67
2.	Benzene	90 94 94 86	91	106 107 100	104
3.	Bromobenzene	87 92 98	92		
4.	Chloroform	98 103 98	100		
5.	Diethyl ether	85 86 71 92 96 83 93	87		
6.	Dioxane	99 82 91 76 83 80	85		
7.	Ethanol	107 105 111	108	30 18 14 25 24 18	22
8.	Hexane	26 0 0	9		
9.	Methanol	82 65 68	72		
10.	Methylcyclohexanol	97 88 96 103	96	73 82 101	85
11.	Methylene chloride	92 89 85	89	102 91 64	86
12.	Petroleum ether	63 91 83	79	76 81 84	80
13.	Bromobenzene	100 100 107	102	141 220 107	156
	Hexane	79 82 136	99	143 57 21	74
	Ether	90 89 93	91	87 93 107	96
14.	Ether	0 0 0	0	0 0 0	0
	Methanol	83 88 86	86	81 82 64	76
	Dioxane	133 137 80	117	99 99 80	93
15.	Chloroform	86 100 103	96	99 139 48	84
	Methylene chloride	94 93 93	93	110 193 47	117
	Ether	94 94 97	95	86 90 87	88
	Benzene	107 119 100	109	101 145 99	111
	Hexane	87 80 100	89	97 105 85	74
	Dioxane			76 84 64	

TABLE I (Con't)
EFFICIENCY STUDIES

Trial No.	Components	Desorption Efficiency (Direct Spikes) Percent Recovery			Av Pct	Overall Efficiency (Flowed Spikes) Percent Recovery			Av Pct
16.	Benzene	103	103	109	105	69	85	83	79
	Ethanol	100	114	97	104	65	57	50	57
17.	Acetone	66	66	72	68	55	63	51	57
	Methylcyclohexanol	88	75	70	78	28	75	58	54

NOTES

1. Charcoal Tube: Large size; charcoal section a = 400 mg.
   charcoal section b = 200 mg.

2. Flow rates through large size tubes (overall efficiency) was 1 LPM for four hours.

accurately known volume). Before sampling, the tube is opened
at each end and clipped vertically on the student's collar near
the breathing zone. The tube is connected to the sampling pump
with Tygon tubing and the pump is attached to the student's belt.
Sampling duration is timed using a wrist watch synchronized to
the chemistry department's large wall clocks.

The charcoal tube samples were capped and labelled upon
completion of sampling. Sampling data sheets were filled out
listing person's name, pump number, flow rate, initial and final
sampling time, and sample number. Additional information on
compounds to be analyzed for and potential interferences are
listed. Samples are returned to the laboratory for analysis
along with a field blank.

The charcoal tube samples were desorbed with 2 ml. of
chromatoquality carbon disulfide (CS_2), dispensed with an
automatic pipette, in vials with Teflon-lined septum caps. Vials
were agitated for 30 minutes on an SKC developing vibrator
equipped with an automatic timer. Standards and spiked charcoal
tubes with known amounts of solvent were prepared with Hamilton
syringes. A Varian Model 1800 Gas Chromatograph equipped with
a flame ionization detector was used to analyze the CS_2-desorbed
samples. Two GC colums were used:

(1) a Porapak Q, 100/120 mesh, 6' x 2 mm i.d. stainless
    steel column, (designated as column A in Table II), and
(2) a 20% SP-2100 and 0.1% Carbowax 1500 on a Supelco-port
    100/120 mesh, 20' x 2 mm i.d. stainless steel column
    (designated as Column B on Table II)

High purity nitrogen carrier gas was used as the carrier gas.
An Autolab Model 6300 Digital Integrator was used with the Varian
GC to provide a direct readout of elution time (seconds) and
relative area under each peak. A Honeywell Electronic 194
recorder displayed elution times and peak height graphically.

Gas sampling tubes with Teflon stoppered valves on each
end and a septum in the center were used to generate airborne
concentrations of various solvents in air for "overall
efficiency" studies.(Figure 1). In this manner, both the degree
of affinity that the carbon has for each vapor and the degree of
CS_2 desorption for each solvent can be determined when they are
treated as normal samples. Amount recovered after CS_2 desorption
divided by amount volatilized is termed the overall efficiency
when expressed as a percentage.Generating known concentrations
in this manner is usually difficult, so an easier method is
employed which allows one to determine only the degree of CS_2
desorption or the "desorption efficiency". (which has been shown
to generally be fairly comparable to the "overall efficiency"
defined as the sum of   "collection efficiency" and "desorption
efficiency")

Either the "desorption" or "overall" efficiency must be

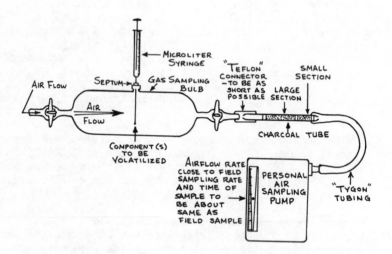

Figure 1.   Determination of overall efficiency

TABLE II ORGANIC VAPOR SAMPLING AND ANALYTICAL RESULTS

Lab/Sample No.	Chemistry Experiment Title	Total Air Sample (Liters)	Components Sought	Total Quantity (mg)	Eff Corr	Correc Tot Qty (mg)	Concen (ppm)	E_m	**Ceil Concen (ppm)
A-1	Steam Distillation of an essential oil	222	methylene chloride	1.7	0.85	2.0	2.6	0.0024	58
A-2	"	124	methylene chloride	2.0	0.85	2.4	5.6	0.0029	69
A-3	Simple and Fractional Distillation of Alcohol	152	acetone ethanol	0.25 0	0.67 0.22	0.37 0	1.0 0	0.00032	16 0
A-4	"	180	acetone ethanol	0.7 0	0.67 0.22	1.0 0	2.3 0	0.00086	42 0
B-1	Nitration of Acetanilide	225	acetone ethanol methylene chloride	0.43 0 2.5	0.67 0.22 0.85	0.64 0 2.9	1.2 0 3.7	0.0040	27 0 83

TABLE II (Continued)

Lab/ Sample No.	Chemistry Experiment Title	Total Air Sample (Liters)	Components Sought	Total Quantity (mg)	Eff Corr	Correc Tot Qty (mg)	Concen (ppm)	E_m	**Ceil Concen (ppm)
B-2	Nitration of Acentanilide	173	acetone	0	0.67	0	0	0	0
			ethanol	0	0.22	0	0	0	0
			methylene chloride	0	0.85	0	0	0	0
B-3	Preparation and separation of o and p - Nitro-phenol	243	acetone	5.48	0.67	8.2	14.2	0.0072	345
B-4	"	180	acetone	2.1	0.67	3.1	7.3	0.0027	131
C-1	Thin layer Chromatography of Dyes & Plant Pigments	100	chloroform	0	0.93	0	0		0
			hexane	0.36	1.00	0.36	1.0		10
			benzene	0.12	0.88	0.14	0.44		4.4
			acetone	0	0.57	0	0		0
			methylene chloride	1.9	0.84	2.3	6.6	0.012	66
			methanol	0	0.00	0	0		0
C-2	"	135	hexane	0.34	1.00	0.34	0.71		9.6
			benzene	0.16	0.88	0.18	0.42		5.6
			acetone	0	0.57	0	0		0
			methylene chloride	1.0	0.84	1.2	2.6	0.056	35

TABLE II (Continued)

Lab/Sample No.	Chemistry Experiment Title	Total Air Sample (Liters)	Components Sought	Total Quantity (mg)	Eff Corr	Correc Tot Qty (mg)	Concen (ppm)	E_m	**Ceil Concen (ppm)
C-2	(cont.)		chloroform	4.35	0.93	4.7	7.1		96
			methanol	0	0.00	0	0		0
C-3	Solvent extraction of Cholesterol from Gallstones	207	diethylether	3.5	0.96	3.6	0.57	0.0057	119
			acetone	0.32	0.57	0.56	1.1		24
			dioxane	0.54	0.76	0.71	0.95		20
			methanol	0	0.00	0	0		0
C-4	"	197	diethylether	2.7	0.96	2.8	4.7	0.012	92
			acetone	0.43	0.57	0.75	1.6		32
			dioxane	0.8	0.76	1.1	1.5		31
			methanol	0	0.00	0	0		0
D-1	Dehydration of 2-Methylcyclohexanol & Gas Chromatography	142	acetone	0	0.57	0	0	0	0
			methylcyclohexanol	0	0.54	0	0		0
D-2	"	143	acetone	0.2	0.57	0.35	1.0	0.00030	15
			methylcyclohexanol	0	0.54	0	0		0

TABLE II (Continued)

Lab/ Sample No.	Chemistry Experiment Title	Total Air Sample (Liters)	Components Sought	Total Quantity (mg)	Eff Corr	Correc Tot Qty (mg)	Concen (ppm)	E_m	**Ceil Concen (ppm)
D-3	Thin layer Chromatography of Plant Pigments	188	acetone	2.7	0.57	4.7	10.5		198
			ether	0.51	1.00	0.51	0.89		17
			benzene	1.3	0.88	1.5	2.5	0.13	47
			chloroform	2.9	0.93	3.1	3.4		63
			dioxane	0	0.74	0	0		0
			methanol	0	0.00	0	0		0
D-4	"	15	acetone	0.83	0.57	1.5	42.1		63
			benzene	0.67	0.88	0.76	15.9		24
			ether	0.08	1.00	0.08	1.8		2.6
			chloroform	5.2	0.93	5.6	76.5	0.099	115
			methanol	0	0.00	0	0		0
			dioxane	0	0.74	0	0		0
E-1	Dehydration of 2-Methylcyclohexanol & Gas Chromatography	93	acetone	0.22	0.57	0.39	1.8	0.00037	16
			methylcyclo-hexanol	trace (<0.0023)	0.54	<0.0043	<0.01		<0.09
E-2	"	105	acetone	3.4	0.57	6.0	24.1	0.0053	253
			methylcyclo-hexanol	trace (<0.0026)	0.54	<0.0049	<0.01		<0.11

TABLE II (Continued)

Lab/ Sample No.	Chemistry Experiment Title	Total Air Sample (Liters)	Components Sought	Total Quantity (mg)	Eff Corr	Correc Tot Qty (mg)	Concen (ppm)	E_m	**Ceil Concen (ppm)
E-3	Isolation of Cholesterol from Gallstones	210	acetone	0.06	0.52	0.11	0.22		4.6
			diethylether	3.2	0.96	3.3	5.2		109
			dioxane	0.9	0.76	1.2	1.6	0.013	33
			methanol	0	0.00	0	0		0
E-4	"	218	acetone	0.25	0.52	0.44	0.85		19
			diethylether	2.4	0.96	2.5	3.8		82
			dioxane	1.1	0.76	1.4	1.8	0.013	39
			methanol	0	0.00	0	0		0
F-1	Grignard reaction	142	acetone	0	0.57	0	0		0
			diethylether	14.4	0.74	19.5	45.3		643
			hexane	0	1.00	0	0		0
			bromobenzene	0.05	0.80	0.06	0.07	0.066*	0.93
			benzene	0.46	0.88	0.52	1.1		16
F-2	"	211	acetone	0	0.57	0	0		0
			diethylether	4.0	0.74	5.4	8.4		178
			hexane	0.02	1.00	0.02	0.03		0.57
			bromobenzene	0.04	0.80	0.05	0.04	0.014*	0.78
			benzene	0.06	0.88	0.07	0.10		2.2

TABLE II (Continued)

Lab/ Sample No.	Chemistry Experiment Title	Total Air Sample (Liters)	Components Sought	Total Quantity (mg)	Eff Corr	Correc Tot Qty (mg)	Concen (ppm)	E_m	**Ceil Concen (ppm)
F-3	Preparation of Paranitroaniline	200	acetone	1.5	0.57	2.6	5.5		109
			ethanol	0	0.57	0	0	0.0060	0
			benzene	0.05	0.79	0.06	0.09		1.9
F-4	"	207	acetone	0.75	0.57	1.3	2.6		55
			ethanol	0	0.57	0	0	0.0050	0
			benzene	0.05	0.79	0.06	0.09		1.9
G-1	Finish the Grignard reaction	95	diethylether	2.9	0.74	3.9	13.5		129
			hexane	2.9	1.00	2.9	8.7		82
			acetone	0.2	0.57	0.35	1.6	0.014*	15
			bromobenzene	0.024	0.80	0.03	0.05		0.47
			benzene	0.05	0.88	0.06	0.20		1.9
G-2	"	92	diethylether	3.7	0.74	5.0	17.9		165
			hexane	3.9	1.00	3.9	12.0		111
			acetone	0.2	0.57	0.35	1.6	0.0052*	15
			bromobenzene	0.06	0.80	0.08	0.14		1.2
			benzene	0.07	0.88	0.08	0.27		2.5

TABLE II (Continued)

Lab/ Sample No.	Chemistry Experiment Title	Total Air Sample (Liters)	Components Sought	Total Quantity (mg)	Eff Corr	Correc Tot Qty (mg)	Concen (ppm)	E_m	**Ceil Concen (ppm)
G-3	Preparation of acetylsalicylic acid	182	benzene	0.45	0.88	0.51	0.88		16
			diethylether	0.45	0.74	0.61	1.1	0.035	19
			acetone	0.4	0.57	0.70	1.6		29
			hexane	0.1	1.00	0.10	0.16		2.8
			petroleum ether	0	0.86	0	0		0
G-4	"	210	benzene	2.5	0.88	2.8	4.2		88
			diethylether	2.4	0.74	3.2	5.0	0.20	106
			acetone	2.9	0.57	5.1	10.2		215
			petroleum ether	0	0.86	0	0		0
			hexane	2.5	1.00	2.3	3.4		71
H-1	Chemistry of milk	145	benzene	0.04	0.79	0.05	0.11		1.6
			methylene chloride	3.06	0.84	3.6	7.1	0.0084	104
			acetone	0.45	0.57	0.79	2.3		33
			ethanol	0	0.57	0	0		0
			hexane	0.06	1.00	0.06	0.12		1.7

TABLE II (Continued)

Lab/Sample No.	Chemistry Experiment Title	Total Air Sample (Liters)	Components Sought	Total Quantity (mg)	Eff Corr	Correc Tot Qty (mg)	Concen (ppm)	E_m	**Ceil Concen (ppm)
H-2	Chemistry of milk	145	benzene	0.04	0.79	0.05	0.11		1.6
			methylene chloride	9.3	0.84	11.1	22.0		320
			acetone	4.2	0.57	7.4	21.5	0.023	312
			ethanol	0	0.57	0	0		0
H-3	Sodium Borohydride Reduction of Camphor	165	acetone	0.25	0.57	0.44	1.1		14
			ethanol	0	0.57	0	0		0
			petroleum ether	0	0.86	0	0	0.0035	0
			benzene	0.04	0.79	0.05	0.09		1.6
H-4	"	200	acetone	0.29	0.57	0.51	1.1		21
			ethanol	0	0.57	0	0		0
			petroleum ether	0	0.86	0	0	0.0038	0
			benzene	0.04	0.79	0.05	0.08		1.6

NOTES

E_m is the equivalent exposure of an individual to a mixture which is defined as follows:

$$E_m = \frac{C_a T_a}{C_1 T_1} + \frac{C_b T_b}{C_2 T_2} + \frac{C_c T_c}{C_3 T_3} + \cdots \frac{C_z T_z}{C_n T_n}$$

where: C_1 = TLV for one component

T_1 = 8 hours or 480 minutes or time allowed for TLV

C_a = Concentration measured in student's breathing zone for same component

T_a = Time that student is actually exposed to C_a

The value of E_m shall not exceed unity (1).

* Does not reflect bromobenzene exposure since no TLV is available to determine mixed exposure.

** The "ceiling" concentration was not determined in this survey because samples must be taken for a sampling period of only 10 minutes. However, "ceiling" concentrations can be estimated under a "worst" possible instance by assuming that all of the material was collected during a time interval of 10 minutes. By using the relationship ppm = $\frac{24450 \times mg/L}{MW}$

where ppm expresses our estimated peak value, MW represents the molecular weight of the organic compound, mg represents the total amount of substance found (4th column from the end) and L indicates the number of liters of air that would have been sampled in a 10 minute interval, we can obtain an estimate as to this highest possible value. This is the manner in which the last column was calculated.

Results for various laboratory experiments are shown in Table II. The salient features of this Table are the very low vapor concentrations noted in the third column from the end. These values represent about a four hour exposure and should therefore be halved in order to obtain the 8-hour time-weighted average concentration. In comparing these values with OSHA standards, it must be borne in mind that OSHA criteria reflect two levels of protection. First, the eight-hour TWA is a level below which a worker can safely function during an eight-hour day, 40 hour week. The ceiling value is a concentration which can be tolerated for no more than fifteen minutes during an eight-hour work shift. Ceiling concentrations were not actually measured, but were calculated on a "worst" possible case basis. It was assumed that all of the organic vapor(s) trapped on the charcoal were obtained during a 15 min. sampling interval. This highly unlikely assumption can be successfully utilized when it is suspected that the 8-hour TWA concentrations will be low.

One should also be aware that skin absorption may be as serious a problem as inhalation on some occassions.

Some experiments show traces of acetone, methylene chloride, chloroform, benzene, and dioxane in the air. Only in one instance (chloroform) was a TLV exceeded. However, pump error may have caused this result. When many solvents or air contaminants coexist in the environment, a total or equivalent exposure must be calculated. The equivalent exposure reflects the contribution of each contaminant to the total exposure. In these studies this value was very low and can be noted in the next to last column of Table II. Solvents like benzene, chloroform, and dioxane are presently suspected carcinogens (5) and laboratory instructors should replace these compounds with safe substitutes whenever possible.

BIBLIOGRAPHY

1. White, L.D., Taylor, D.G., Mauer, P.A., and Kupel, R.E., "A Convenient Optimized Method for the Analysis of Selected Solvent Vapors in the Industrial Atmosphere," Amer. Ind. Hyg. Assoc. J., March - April, 1970, pp. 225-232.

2. "Manual of NIOSH Analytical Methods," 4 volumes, USDHEW, PHS, CDC, National Institute for Occupational Safety and Health, Cincinnati, Ohio, 1974.

3. NIOSH Contract HSM-99-72-98, Scott Research Laboratories, Inc., Collaborative Testing of Activated Charcoal Sampling Tubes for Seven Organic Solvents, 1973.

4. Federal Register, 39, Number 125, June 27, 1974, Occupational Safety and Health Standards.

5. Suspected Carcinogens, A Subfile of the Registry of Toxic Effects of Chemical Substances, HEW Publication no.(NIOSH) 77-149, USDHEW, PHS, CDC, NIOSH, Cincinnati, Ohio, December 1976.

RECEIVED December 4, 1979.

Sampling for Mercaptans by Absorber Tubes

M. W. NATHANS and A. JEONG

LFE Corporation, Environmental Analysis Laboratories,
2030 Wright Avenue, Richmond, CA 94804

The common method applied to the measurement of mercaptan concentrations in workroom air is to collect the mercaptans in a bubbler or impinger with mercuric acetate in acetic acid and to analyze the solutions colorimetrically (1). The disadvantages of sampling by means of impingers are well known, so it was desired to develop a method by which sampling could be accomplished by means of adsorber tubes. Some attempts were made by SRI International who developed and validated a method of collecting butyl mercaptan on silicagel(2), but who was unsuccessful for the lower-molecular weight mercaptans(3). In this paper, we report on an absorber tube method which we have validated for methyl mercaptan, but which is probably applicable to other mercaptans also. Since colorimetry was used for the analysis, the combined sampling and analysis method is not specific for methyl mercaptan. However, work is currently underway to validate the method with a GC finish, which is expected to make the method specific for individual mercaptans.

Experimental

Following Akito's method for sampling for mercaptans in ambient air by means of mercuric-acetate impregnated filter paper(4), we constructed absorber tubes with mercuric acetate-impregnated firebrick. Having been unsuccessful to achieve reproducibility, we subsequently were successful with glasswool plugs wetted with the absorber solution.

Construction of the Tubes. Two plugs of glasswool, weighing approximately 0.25 g. each, are inserted into a pyrex glass tube, 12.5 cm long x 4.8 mm diameter, as follows. The first plug is inserted such that one end is about 1 inch from the end of the tube. This plug is wetted with a 0.5 ml. solution prepared by dissolving 50 g. of mercuric acetate, free of mercurous salts, in about 400 ml. of water, mixed with 25 ml. glacial acetic acid, and diluted to 1 liter. The solution is added through the long end of the tube. The second plug is inserted 1 inch into the long end of the tube and also wetted with 0.5 ml.

of the absorbing solution. The tubes are capped with parafilm or by
any other suitable means until use. When in use, the direction of flow
is such that the wetted ends of the plugs face the air flow. This direction is marked on the outer surface of the tubes.

Measurement of Pressure Drop. Air was pumped through the
tubes by means of a personal sampling pump at a flow rate of 300 ml./
minute, as measured by a rotameter between the pump and the tube.
A "T" between the rotameter and the tube was connected to an open-
end mercury manometer. Alternatively, the pump could be adjusted
so as to yield the same pressure drop for different tubes and to allow
measurement of the flow rate at constant pressure drop.

Generation and Sampling of Test Atmospheres. Methyl mercaptan
was obtained from Matheson Gas Products in a lecture bottle under
2 atm. pressure at 21°C and at a stated purity of 99.5%. Atmospheres
with known concentrations of methyl mercaptan were generated and
sampled in the apparatus shown in Figure 1. A 56-liter Tedlar bag
was filled with air metered by a calibrated dry-test meter. During
filling, a desired quantity of methyl mercaptan was injected by means
of a gas syringe into the mixing chamber through a rubber septum.
Adequate mixing in the bag was assured by kneading.
    The test atmosphere was sampled by drawing the gas at 0.3 l /min-
ute through a train consisting of rotameter, the absorption tube, a
midget impinger filled with 10 ml. of the wetting solution (see above),
and an empty impinger by means of a personal sampling pump. Later,
a manifold was placed after the three-way stopcock so that three samples could be withdrawn simultaneously. However, the capacity of the
bag was such that given the detection limit and the desired concentrations, no more than four samples could be withdrawn from a single
bag filling.

Analysis. The glasswool plugs are carefully pulled out of the
glass tube and placed in individual 25-ml. beakers. Fifteen ml. of
the $HgAc_2$/HAc solution (absorber solution, see above) are added and
the contents of the beakers are swirled carefully. The liquid is transferred to a 25-ml. volumetric flask. The solution is carefully pressed
out of the glasswool with a glass stirring rod. The glasswool is washed
twice with 2 ml. of the $HgAc_2$/HAc solution which is added to the volumetric flask. From this point, the analysis proceeds essentially by
the method of Moore et al.(1). One-and-one-half ml. of a solution
prepared by dissolution of 0.25 g. N, N-dimethyl-p-phenylene diamine
dihydrochloride in 50 ml. concentrated HCl, and one-half ml. of
Reissner solution is added. The latter is prepared by dissolution of
67.6 g. $FeCl_3 \cdot 6H_2O$ in distilled water, dilution to 500 ml., addition
of 72 ml. boiled concentrated HNO_3, and final dilution to 1 liter. The
solutions in the flasks to be analyzed are diluted to the mark with distilled or deionized water, and mixed.

    The contents of the flasks are transferred to 40-ml. centrifuge

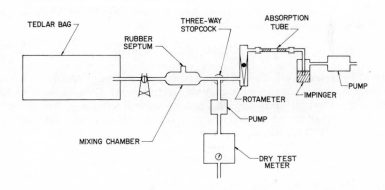

Figure 1.   Apparatus for preparation of gas mixtures and for sampling

cones and centrifuged for 5 - 10 minutes to allow any glass fibers to settle. The absorbance of the supernate is read in a colorimeter at 500 nm between 30 and 45 minutes after the addition of the amine and Reissner solutions.

Standards are prepared from lead methyl mercaptide. A stock standard solution, equivalent to 500 μg CH_3SH/ml., consists of 156.6 mg Pb $(SCH_3)_2$ in 100 ml. of the $HgAc_2$/HAc solution. The working standard solution, equivalent to 10μg CH_3SH/ml., is prepared by a 50-fold dilution of the stock standard solution with $HgAc_2$/HAc. The calibration curve is obtained by applying the analytical procedure to aliquots of 0.5, 1.0, 2.0, 3.0, and 5.0 ml. The lower quantification limit of the method is about o.4 ml., or 4μg CH_3SH.

Validation. The validation followed the Standards Completion Program Statistical Protocol developed by Busch(5). The pooled coefficient of variation of the total procedure, $\overline{CV}_T$, which consists of the composite variations in sampling and analysis, desorption efficiency, and the pump error, is given by:

$$CV_T = \left[(\overline{CV}_2)^2 + 0.1667 \, (\overline{CV}_1)^2 + (0.05)^2 \right]^{1/2}$$

where $\overline{CV}_2$ is the pooled coefficient of variation based on the date for the generated samples at all concentration levels, $\overline{CV}_1$ is the pooled coefficient of variation of the analysis of spiked samples, and the number 0.05 represents the pump error. The coefficient of variation of a set of results generally, is defined as:

$$CV = (\text{standard deviation/mean}).$$

In order to test the feasibility of pooling the coefficients of variation, Bartlett's test for homogeneity of CV's was applied. The CV's may be pooled at the 1% significance level for "n" sets of data, if χ^2 ≤ 2.91, where

$$\chi^2 = \frac{f \ln(CV_2)^2 - \sum_{i=1}^{n} f_i \, \ln(CV_{2,i})^2}{1 + \frac{1}{n\,(n-1)} \frac{1}{f_i} \sum_{i=1}^{n} \frac{1}{f_i}}$$

where $\overline{CV}_2$ is the pooled CV of all generated samples, $\overline{CV}_{2,i}$ is the CV of the samples of the i-th set, f_i is the degrees of freedom associated with $CV_{2,i}$ (= number of data - 1), and

$$f = \sum_{i=1}^{n} f_i.$$

In order to determine $\overline{CV}_1$, spikes at each of two levels were prepared and analyzed: 9.8μg and 29.4μg CH_3SH. For the determination of $\overline{CV}_2$, sets of six samples each were collected from air containing concentrations of CH_3SH of 0.52 mg/m^3, 1.04 mg/m^3 and 1.56 mg/m^3.

Results

Pressure drop. The pressure drop across 24 freshly prepared tubes was determined at a flow rate of 300 ml/minute. The range was 25.0 - 44.0 mm Hg. The mean was 36.7 ± 5.4 (1σ) mm Hg. One outlier was excluded. Conversely, the variation of the flow rate was determined at a constant pump setting, such that the flow rate of one tube used as a reference was 300 ml/minute. The pressure drop was 20.5 mm Hg, the range was 275 - 315 ml/minute. The mean was 292 ± 11 (1σ) ml/minute. Thus, the coefficient of variation was 0.037.

Three tubes prepared about 45 days earlier, capped and stored, were also tested. The pressure drops were 48.5, 47.0 and 60.0 mm Hg respectively. The flow rates at the pump setting which yielded 300 ml/minute through the reference tube were 260, 275 and 275 ml/minute. These results show that unless special precautions are taken, the tubes should probably not be kept for more than 3 or 4 weeks.

Breakthrough: The theoretical capacity of the front section of a tube is about 7.5 mg of CH_3SH. Experimentally, no breakthrough was observed when 58 μg of CH_3SH was absorbed in the front section from air containing CH_3SH at about the 2S level (2 mg/m^3) at a flow rate of 0.2 l/minute. In no test was CH_3SH at about the 2S level (2mg/m^3) at a flow rate of 0.2 l/minute. In no test was CH_3SH found in the backup section. If it is assumed that each tube can be used to up to one-tenth of its theoretical capacity, one could sample for more than 30 hours at 0.3 l/minute at the 1S level. Control over the sample size is, therefore, not necessary over a very wide range.

Precision and Accuracy: In order to determine the precision of the analysis, two sets of 15-ml. solutions of $HgAc_2$ in HAc were spiked with CH_3SH and analyzed: one set with 5 μl. (9.8 μg) and one set with 15 μl. (29.5 μg). The results are shown in Table 1. The results of replicate determinations of CH_3SH collected in absorption tubes are shown in Table 2. Recoveries were calculated from the bag compositions, since it was found that sampling directly by means of impingers yielded results that were consistently about 10% lower than those obtained by sampling by means of the absorber tubes.

Bartlett's test for homogeneity of variances at 0.5, 1 and 1.5 times the OSHA standard showed that the variances may be pooled. Therefore, the coefficient of variation was calculated from the pooled variances:

$$\overline{CV}_1 = 0.092 \qquad \overline{CV}_2 = 0.080 \qquad \overline{CV}_T = 0.010$$

where $\overline{CV}_1$ and $\overline{CV}_2$ are the coefficients of variation of the analysis and of sampling and analysis, respectively, and $\overline{CV}_T$ is the total coefficient of variation of the method including the pump error.

The average recovery was 94.7 ± 8.1%, the same as for the spiked samples.

TABLE 1

Determination of Precision and Accuracy of the Analysis

Spike: $5\,\mu 1$. $CH_3SH(9.8\,\mu g)$		Spike: $15\,\mu 1$. CH_3SH $(29.4\,\mu g)$	
Solution	Recovered (μg)	Solution	Recovered (μg)
1	8.6	1	28.0
2	8.8	2	25.5
3	10.1	3	28.8
4	7.3	4	25.0
		5	26.5
		6	28.2
mean	8.7		27.0
std. dev.	1.15		1.56
CV_1	0.13		0.058
$\overline{CV_1}$	0.0092		

TABLE 2

Determination of Precision and Accuracy of Sampling and Analysis

Conc.	0.52 mg/m^3		1.04 mg/m^3		1.56 mg/m^3
Volume	13.5 l.		13.5 l.		13.5 l.
	Collected (μg)		Collected (μg)		Collected (μg)
1	7.8	1	11.6	1	16.6
2	6.3	2	11.6	2	18.0
3	6.8	3	12.9	3	20.7
4	7.8	4	12.9	4	18.8
5	7.6	5	12.7	5	20.3
		6	13.8		
mean	7.3		12.6		18.9
std. dev.	0.7		0.8		1.5
CV_2	0.091		0.067		0.082
recovery	104%		90%		90%
$\overline{CV_2} = 0.080$					

TABLE 3

STORAGE PROPERTIES

CH_3SH concentration:	1.04 μg/1
Flow rate:	0.30 1/minute
Volume:	13.5 1
Total sampled:	14.0 μg

μg CH_3SH Found

Day	Tube 1	Tube 2	Average
1	13.0	12.8	12.9
2	13.6	12.9	13.2
7	13.1	13.6	13.4
15	12.2	12.0	12.1

Mean:	12.9
Std. Dev.	0.6
CV	0.044

Storage: Samples were collected and analyzed in duplicate after
1, 2, 7, and 14 days' storage at room temperature. The concentrations were about 1 mg/m^3. The results are presented in Table 3.
They show that samples may be stored for at least 7 days. Tubes can
probably be stored for significantly longer periods if they are tightly
capped.

Discussion

The method was validated over the range of 0.54 - 1.62 mg/m^3 at
an atmospheric pressure of 760 mm Hg and a temperature of 22°C.
The probable useful range depends primarily on the sample size. For
a 10-minute sample taken at 300 ml./minute, the lower limit of the
useful range is probably 0.15 mg/m^3, but this limit can be extended
downward by longer sampling times. At the same flow rate and a
sampling time of 60 minutes, the upper limit of the probable useful
range is greater than 2 mg/m^3.

Since the absorbent is an aqueous solution, high humidity is not
expected to interfere with the trapping of the compound. However,
when condensation occurs such as to increase the volume of the absorbent, the air flow may carry some of the absorbent out of the plug,
possibly affecting the recovery of the absorbent adversely.

Interferences are those stated by Moore et al. (4) H$_2$S can produce
both turbidity and color with the analytical method. The turbidity may
be removed by filtration before addition of the color developing reagents. The color interference is insignificant unless appreciably more
than 100 μg of H$_2$S are collected. SO$_2$ up to 10 ppm does not interfere.
NO$_2$ above 6 ppm produces high results. At 14ppm, the NO$_2$ interference is approximately 20%. Dimethyl disulfide interferes on a
mole-for-mole basis. (6)

The method is not specific for individual mercaptans. Specificity
as well as a lower detection limit can be achieved by analysis by gas
chromatography after reconstitution of the mercaptans and collection
in an organic solvent. (4)

Acknowledgment

The major part of this work was supported by a contract with
Shell Development Co., of Houston, Texas, with Mr. D. Morman as
Project Monitor, whose suggestions are greatfully acknowledged. We
also acknowledge the help and suggestion of Mr. H. Y. Gee, Gas Laboratory Supervisor, and Mr. J. Corso, Senior Laboratory Technician,
both of LFE Corporation.

Abstract

In current industrial hygiene practice, sampling for mercaptans
is done by means of an impinger containing 5% HgAc$_2$ in HAc. In order to circumvent the problems associated with impingers, absorber
tubes containing two sections of glasswool wetted with this solution

were constructed and tested. At a flow rate of 300 ml/minute, the pressure drop was 36.7 mm + 14.7%. At contstant pressure drop of 20.5 mm Hg the flow rate was 292 ml./minute ± 3.7%. The coefficient of variation for combined sampling and analysis was determined with standard atmospheres of CH_3SH containing 0.5, 1.0 and 1.5 mg/m^3 and with a general colorimetric procedure for mercaptans for the analysis. Its value was 0.0010. The average recovery was 95% or better.

Literature Cited

1. Moore, H., Helwig, H. L., and Graul, R. J., Amer. Ind. Hyg. Assoc. J. (1960) 21, 466.

2. Taylor, D. G. (Manual Coordinator), NIOSH Manual of Analytical Methods", 2nd ed. DHEW (NIOSH) Publication No, 77-157-C (Method S-350).

3. Private communication.

4. Okita, T., Atm. Env. (1970) 4, 93.

5. Busch, K. A., in Taylor, D. G., Kupel, R. E., and Bryant, J. M., "Documentation of the NIOSH Validation Tests", DHEW (NIOSH) Publication No. 77-185 (1977).

6. California State Department of Public Health, Method No. CAL/OSHA L-128.

RECEIVED October 23, 1979.

Atomic Absorption Spectroscopy in the Occupational Health Laboratory

ALLEN W. VERSTUYFT

Chevron Research Company, 576 Standard Avenue, Richmond, CA 94802

Metals and metallic compounds are among the toxic substances most often found in workplace environments (1,2). Industrial hygienists and hygiene chemists must accurately determine the presence and amount of toxic metals and their compounds in the industrial environment. Accurate methods for the quantification of metals in biological and atmospheric samples are required for the industrial hygienist to properly evaluate the environment. Atomic absorption spectroscopy (AAS) has been the primary method of analysis for toxic metals because AAS is sensitive, specific, and rapid especially compared to colorimetric analysis.

When the Occupational Safety and Health Act (PL 91-596) was enacted in 1970, colorimetric analyses were among the primary methods for quantifying metallic contaminants. Although some colorimetric techniques are still routinely used in industrial hygiene laboratories, the methods development programs of NIOSH, OSHA, research institutes, industrial laboratories, and universities have developed and improved the routine use of AAS for industrial hygiene laboratories. Rapid improvements in AAS instrumentation have allowed determination of microgram quantities of toxic metals collected on filters or in impingers and found in bodily fluids and tissues.

Atomic absorption has become the primary method for determining metal concentrations in industrial hygiene samples. The types of samples that can be analyzed in AAS will be discussed along with acid digestion methods and AAS atomization techniques. No attempt will be made to thoroughly review the theory

0-8412-0539-6/80/47-120-241$06.25/0

of AAS, since excellent reviews and texts are available.
Briefly, when ground state atoms of an element are vaporized by
a conventional flame or electrothermal source, absorption of a
resonance line emitted from a reference lamp, hollow cathode or
electrodeless discharge, occurs decreasing the transmitted radiation. The change in the ultraviolet or visible light is
detected and quantified by a photodetector. The concentraation
of the element is measured by the percentage of absorbance of
light by the ground state of the specific element. The reader
unfamiliar with AAS is referred to Slavin (3) and other excellent texts for a thorough explanation of AAS.

Flame methods are the conventional atomization sources used
in AAS for industrial hygiene (Table I). Air/acetylene at
2150–2400°C is used for the easily atomized elements like lead,
cadmium, and zinc. Refractory metals such as tungsten or vanadium require hotter nitrous oxide/acetylene atomization at
2600–2800°C. The need for greater sensitivity and multielement
analysis from a single filter has increased the use of electrothermal atomization for tin, vanadium, nickel, and other difficult elements. Formation of hydrides combined with flame atomization has been used in some cases to increase sensitivity.
These atomization techniques are used in NIOSH, AIHA, and APHA
approved (recommended) methods (5–7). Although the purpose of
this discussion is AAS techniques, one must briefly consider
collection of samples. The primary method of collecting metal
dust samples and fume samples are 0.8 um and 0.45 um mixed cellulose ester filters. The filter is dissolved in acid or
leached with dilute base, acid, or distilled water to give an
analyte for AAS analysis. A general procedure P & CAM 173 (5),
was developed by NIOSH for the analysis of metals. This method
provides a starting point and standard of comparison for the
analysis of metals.

General Flame – AAS Analysis

The general methods, P & CAM 173, uses mixed cellulose
ester filters for collection of the metal sample, a nitric acid
wet ashing, and flame AAS analysis. Nitric acid wet ashing is
the main wet ashing technique used in industrial hygiene analysis. It is sufficiently vigorous for many of the common metals
including lead, cadmium, and zinc. These three metals are routinely analyzed in the Proficiency Aptitude Testing (PAT) program operated by NIOSH (8) for quality assurance in industrial
hygiene laboratories accredited by the American Industrial
Hygiene Association (AIHA) (9). Other wet acid digestions such
as nitric/sulfuric acids for antimony and tin, or
nitric/perchloric acids for nickel, have results in separate AAS
methods that are adaptations of P & CAM 173. The wet acid
digestion is preferred over dry ashing or low temperature ashing

TABLE I

ANTIMONY OSHA STANDARD 0.5 MG/CU M

Colorimetric	Reaction	Wavelength	Detection Limit
Apha 301 Rhodamine-B	Pink	565 nm	1.0 ug
Apha 802, P & C 107	Urine/Air, Urine	565	0.1 ug/ml
Atomic Absorption	Atomization	Matrix	ug/ml

Method No.	Ashing			
173	H_2SO_4/HNO_3	Flame/Air-C_2H_2(O)	Air	0.04
S-2	HNO_3/HCl	Flame/Air-C_2H_2(O)	Air	0.04

Wavelength 217.6 nm

where volatile species may be lost. The merits and limitation
of wet ashing techniques have been adequately detailed else-
where (10), herein, wet acid digestion effects with specific
elements will be discussed.

The elements, absorption lines, flame types, and interferences associated with the analysis by P & CAM 173 will be discussed and contrasted to other methods for these elements.
Thirty-one metals are analyzed by P & CAM 173; five metals, Al,
Be, Co, Cr, and V are listed as potentially only partially
digested by nitric acid; and Ni, Sb, and Sn may need more vigorous oxidation than just nitric acid.

Antimony. Antimony dust has been analyzed colorimetrically
by formation of a Rhodamine-B complex, 565 nm (Table I). Both
P & CAM 173 (5) and S-2 (11) provide AAS methods for antimony.
Whereas the former method recommends 5:1 nitric:sulfuric acid
digestion, the latter uses only 2-ml nitric acid at 140°C followed by 2 ml of 6 N hydrochloric acid. Either the
nitric/sulfuric acids (10% and 5% v/v) or a 10% tartaric
acid (11) matrix may be used for the analyte solution. Although
the normal analytical wavelength is 217.6 nm, when 10,000 ppm Pb
or 1000 ppm Ca are present in the final solution, then the
231.2 nm analtyical line should be used. A new method for antimony has been developed by NIOSH and will be published in volume
four of the methods manual.

Aluminum. Aluminum, as Al_2O_3, is a nuisance dust. There
may be instances where elemental composition of the nuisance
dustis desired; therefore, Al is included in P & CAM 173.
Aluminum is difficult to dissolve in nitric acid and should be
treated as a refractory metal. Since the nitrous
oxide/acetylene flame is subject to many interferences, both
1000 ppm Cs and 1000 ppm La, a releasing agent, should be added
to the final solution.

Arsenic. Arsine generation or graphite furnace atomization
are preferred to the conventional flame for the sensitivity and
precision required in analyzing this element. The west ashing
used in S-309 (12) requires 10 ml nitric acid and 1 ml of 60%
perchloric acid with heating on a 400°c hot plate. The sample
is analyzed at 193.7 nm with deuterium or hydrogen arc background correction. The arsenic electrodeless discharge (EDL)
source is superior to the hollow cathode (HCL) lamp for sensitivity, noise, and long-term stability. The older colorimetric
analysis for arsenic used impinger collection of the analyte in
a pyridine solution of silver diethyldithiocarbamate (7) that
was quantitated for the orange-yellow 540 nm complex (5,7).
This method is still used for the rapid determination of arsenic
in the field (Table II).

TABLE II

ARSENIC OSHA STANDARDS 0.5 AND 0.2 MG/CU M

Colorimetric	Reaction	Wavelength	Detection Limit
Gutzeit	$As(III) + Zn(H^+)$	HgX_2	1 ug
Jacobs – Molyblue	$As + (NH_4)_6Mo_7O_{24} \cdot 4\ H_2O$	830 nm	1 ug
Vasak – AGDDC	$As - AgS_2CN(C_2H_4)_2$	540	1 ug
Apha 302/803, P & C 140		535	0.1 ug

Atomic Absorption		Atomization	Matrix	ug/ml
Method No.	Ashing			
173	Nitric	$Flame/Air-C_2H_2(O)$	Air	0.2
139	$HNO_3/H_2SO_4/HCLO_4$	$Hydride/Argon-H_2$	Urine	0.001
S-309	$HNO_3/HCLO_4$	Furnace	Air	0.002
S-229	Nitric	Furnace	Ash_3/Air	0.002

Wavelength 193.7 nm

Arsenic can be determined in urine and air, P & CAM 139, by filter collection and hydride flame AAS. Samples are analyzed in 5 ml of 3:1:1 nitric:sulfuric:perchloric acids on a hot plate at 130-150°C. The sample may be wet ashed with 5 ml of 3:2 nitric:sulfuric acids when no perchloric acid hood is available. The sodium borohydride is added to the sample and acidified to generate arsine. This operation should be performed cautiously in a well-ventilated area because arsine gas is extremely toxic.

Arsine has been determined colorimetrically or by collection on activated charcoal and flameless AAS analysis by S-229 (12). Nitric acid desorption of the charcoal offers a safe method of handling the arsenic analyte than arsine generation. This method does not specify use of an EDL as does S-309, however, it is advisable if an EDL source is available.

Barium. Before the routine use of AAS, Ba was analyzed by emission spectrograph or a $KMnO_4$ spot test (13). Alkali and alkaline earth metals are analyzed in nitrous oxide/acetylene flames with ionization suppressants such as 1000 ppm Cs. For barium analysis by P & CAM 173, background correction must be used whenever greater than 1000 ppm calcium is in the analyte solution. There are strong $Ca(OH)_2$ absorptions and emission at 553.6 nm, which is the barium analytical line.

Soluble barium may be determined by S-198 (12) using a hot water leach, hydrochloric acid dissolution, and nitrous oxide/acetylene flame. In this method, 1000-2000 ppm sodium as sodium chloride is used to minimize ionization of barium in the flame. Although background correction is not mentioned in this method, it is strongly recommended when calcium is present.

Beryllium. The low exposure limit for Be, 2 ug/cu m (TWA) or 5 ug/cu m (celing), make the detection of this analyte in small samples very difficult. Beryllium has been analyzed by zenia complexation at 500 nm, and DC or spark spectrograph at 313.1 or 234.9 nm (6,7). Not all Be compounds are dissolved by nitric acid wet ashing described in P & CAM 173; therefore, more oxidizing 10:1:1 nitric:sulfuric:perchloric acid (12 ml total) is necessary. The flameless AAS, S-309, method suggests use of 10 ml of 3M HCl for a final solution. Recent work shows addition of Na_2SO_4 or $(NH_4)_2 SO_4$ is necessary in standards to balance sulfate extracted from filters. The new method on Be should be forthcoming in Volume Four of the NIOSH manual. The background corrector is necessary to minimize false positive signal from molecular scattering at 234.9 nm.

An older Be method, P & CAM 121, discusses air, dust, ore, and swipe samples. More vigorous digestion procedures such as hydrofluoric:nitric acid for filters or potassium fluoride:sodium pyrosulfate fusion and nitric acid digestion for ores. A nitrous oxide/acetylene flame is suggested for this method rarely used (Table III).

TABLE III

BERYLLIUM OSHA STANDARD 2 UG/CU M

Colorimetric		Reaction	Wavelength	Detection Limit
Zenia		Red-Brown Lake	500 nm	2.5 ug
Apha 303 – Morin		Fluorescence	436	0.01
Spectrographic		DC-Arc	313.1	0.05
			234.9	0.002

Atomic Absorption			Atomization	Matrix	ug/ml
Method No.	Ashing				
121	HF/HNO$_3$		Flame/N$_2$O–C$_2$H$_2$	Dust, Swipe, Ore	0.001
173	Nitric		Flame/N$_2$O–C$_2$H$_2$(R)	Air	0.001
S–339	H$_2$SO$_4$/HNO$_3$/HClO$_4$		Furnace	Air	0.005

Wavelength 234.9 nm

Bismuth. No threshold limit value (TLV) or Federal
Standard time weighted average (TWA) has been established for
Bi; however, it is included in P & CAM 173 should a standard be
developed.

Boron. Boron hydride, di-, penta- and deca-, and the boron
halides, trichloride, trifluoride, are the chief compounds of
interest. No adequately documented collection method exists for
any of these compounds, and most recent work in the area has
been futile. Boron oxide is the only compound that can be
analyzed with certainty by P & CAM 173. This compound is a
nuisance dust like aluminum oxide, and the AAS method provides a
means of identifying the compound.

Cadmium. This toxic element is routinely analyzed by AAS
as part of the NIOSH PAT program. Prior to AAS, Cd was analyzed
by dithiozone complexation at 518 nm, which is subject to interferences from Cu, Fe, and Tl. Cd is readily dissolved by nitric
acid wet digestion, P & CAM 173, or S-312 (12). Background
correction is advised to minimize Cd self-absorption at
228.8 nm; however, this is a minor problem.

Calcium. Calcium like barium is best determined by AAS,
since flame emission suffers from background effects where other
alkali metal are present. P & CAM 173 does not recommend the
use of nitrous oxide/acetylene instead of air/acetylene,
although the former offers greater sensitivity and detection
limit when 1000 ppm potassium is added to the standards and
samples. The nitrous oxide/acetylene flame needs the potassium
to minimize the ionization of Ca.
Calcium oxide analysis is described in S-205 which recommends an oxidizing air-acetylene flame, whereas P & CAM 173
recommends a reducing flame. Interferences from Si, Al, and
PO_4^{3-} are reduced by the addition of 1% La. Lanthanum reduces
formation of CaO molecules in the flame. S-205b uses 2:1
nitric:perchloric acid digestion of the calcium oxide to affect
complete dissociate of the oxide.

Chromium. Chromium is not an easily analyzed element
because three distinct standards are listed by OSHA (Tables IV
and V). One standard exists for hexavalent chromium, chromic
acid and chromates, another standard for soluble chromium compounds and chromous salts, and another standard for insoluble
chromium compounds and chromium metal. The permissible amount
of chromium in air decreases as the oxidation state increases.
The analysis of chromium is further complicated by the multi-
plicity of NIOSH methods for chromium compounds. Hexavalent
chromium shall be collected on PVC filters, although a criteria
document for chromic acid (14) specifies mixed cellulose ester
filters. The analytical method described in the hexavalent

TABLE IV

CHROMIUM

Chromium (VI) OSHA Standard 0.1 mg/cu m

Colorimetric	Reaction	Wavelength	Detection Limit
169 or S-317 S-Diphenyl Carbazide	$CR(VI) + (\emptyset NHNH)_2CO$	540 nm	0.05 ug
182	$CR(VI) + 3,3'(MeO)_2$ Benzidine	450 nm	1.0

Atomic Absorption	Atomization	Matrix	ug/ml
Apha 807 – APDC/MIBK	$Flame/N_2O-C_2H_2(R)$	Air	0.02

Chromium (0), Insoluble Compounds OSHA Standard 1.0 mg/cu m

Atomic Absorption		Atomization	Matrix	ug/ml
Method No.	Ashing			
152	Nitric	$Flame/N_2O-C_2H_2$	Air	0.003
S-352	HCl/HNO_3	$Flame/N_2O-C_2H_2(R)$	Air	0.003

Wavelength 357.9 nm

TABLE V

CHROMIUM

Chromium (III) Soluble Compounds OSHA Standard 0.5 mg/cu m

Atomic Absorption		Atomization	Matrix	Detection Limit
Method No.	Ashing			
152	Nitric	Flame/N_2O-C_2H_2	Air	0.003 ug/ml
173	Nitric	Flame/N_2O-C_2H_2(R)	Air	0.003
S-323	Nitric	Flame/N_2O-C_2H_2(R)	Air	0.003

chromium (VI) criteria document (15) is colorimetric s-diphenyl-carbazide, P & CAM 169 or S-317, whereas the chromic acid method recommends complexation with APDC followed by methyl iso-butyl ketone (MIBK) extraction and AAS analysis. In addition to the s-diphenylcarbazide methods of colorimetric analysis at 540 nm, there is another colorimetric method using o-dianisidine complexation, P & CAM 182. O-dianisidine, 3,3'dimethoxy-benzidine, is more selective to complexation of chromium (VI) than s-diphenylcarbazide; and by usiung an ion exchange, column interferences from Ni, V, and Fe and be eliminated. The problem with o-dianisidine is that it is a suspected carcinogen, and this restricts both its availability and use. Further research into the accuracy of these methods at lower levels may be necessary if OSHA reduces the levels of chromium (VI) to 1 ug/cu m.

Soluble chromium compounds require only nitric acid wet ashing and can be determined by P & CAM 173 or S-323 (12). Air-acetylene flame is used for greater sensitivity; both Fe and Ni are interferences. Collection differences as previously mentioned may confuse analysts doing soluble chromium because P & CAM 152, total particulate chromium, specifies collection with a 0.45-micron HAWP; whereas the larger pore, 0.8 micron, AA filter is used for both P & CAM 173 and S-323. Chromium analyses both colorimetric and AAS are subject to interferences from iron and nickel. Both these elements are commonly enountered with chromium, and the analyst should be aware of adjustments necessary to ensure accurate analysis of chromium. In P & CAM 173, a reducing air-acetylene flame minimizes these interferences; however, all the other chromium AAS methods use a reducing nitrous oxide/acetylene flame. The use of a reducing flame with nickel present is contradictory to conventional approaches (3). The nitrous oxide/acetylene is not as sensitive as air/acetylene for chrome; however, the former minimizes iron interferences. The choice of flame type in chrome analysis may depend upon the type of interference present and the sensitivity required. Hexavalent chromium chelated with s-diphenyl carbazide prior to MIBK extraction at 0.5 pH with sulfuric acid can be analyzed after MIBK extraction by AAS (7). Considering severe interferences in colorimetric methods from iron and nickel and the ability to adjust the flame type to minimize these interferences, AAS analysis may be preferred for chrome (VI).

Insoluble chromium compounds and chromium metal may be analyzed by S-352. This method if similar to S-323; however, more consideration is given to vigorous digestion of the sample and to interferences from iron and nickel. The digestion begins with hydrochloric acid and is followed with nitric acid. The digestion procedure is more exacting than P & CAM 152. Considering the presence of interferences, the reducing nitrous oxide-acetylene flame is more specific than the nitrous oxide-acetylene flame described in P & CAM 152.

Cobalt. Cobalt was determined colorimetrically as the nitroso-R salt (13). The use of any nitroso salt comes under scrutiny as a suspected carcinogen. Cobalt can be analyzed at 240.7 nm with an air-acetylene flame; this analytical line is subject to line broadening and self-absorption necessitating background correction. The analyst should be aware that greater than 2000 ppm nickel and chromium can be interferences. P & CAM 173 is being collaboratively tested, and cobalt is an analyte of study for the test.

Copper. Copper is the most easily detected element by AAS. Although copper has been determined as the dithizone complex or ethyl-xanthate (6,13), air-acetylene AAS analysis by P & CAM 173 or S-186 (12) is superior. Copper lamps are used to test AAS instrumentation because the Cu HCl sensitivity is nearly independent of lamp current, and a large linear range is observed for the analytical curve.

Copper like vanadium has a separate OSHA standard for dust and fumes resulting in some confusion for the industrial hygienist in selecting collection media. The 0.2 mg Cu/cu m fume standard is one-fifth the dust standard. The distinction between fumes and mist is somewhat ambiguous. Both methods for copper use nitric acid wet ashing; however, S-186 uses an analyte matrix of hydrochloric acid for AAS aspiration.

Iron. Industrial hygiene chemists have analyzed iron as the o-phenanthroline or thiocyanate complexes (6,13). In the AAS analysis at 248.3 nm with air-acetylene atomization, nickel and silica are interferences. If iron in ferro-vanadium must be analyzed, a more oxidative solution than the ntiric acid wet ashing of P & CAM 173 is required. Nitric acid-hydrofluoric acid will solubilize refractories containing iron.

Indium. Although refractory metals are mentioned in P & CAM 173, it is doubtful that wet ashing with nitric will solubilize noble metals.

Lithium. Lithium aluminum hydride, $LiAlH_4$, is the only lithium compound of interest for Li analysis in IH work. Little work has been reported, except for standard ionization interferences (3) corrected by addition of 1000 ppm Cs to the final solution.

Magnesium. Magnesium oxide, MgO fume, can be analyzed by P & CAM 173 or S-369 (12). Magnesium is the most sensitive element for AAS analysis. Air-acetylewne atomization is generally recommended for Mg analysis; however, Si, Al, and Cu are serious interferences. These interferences can be minimized using the less sensitive nitrous oxide/acetylene flame with 1000 ppm Cs in the final solution.

Manganese. Manganese, as the antiknock gas additive
pi-methyl-cyclopentadienyl manganese tricarbonyl (MMT), has
aroused considerable public health interest. Manganese has previously been analyzed as the $KMnO_4/KIO_3$ complex at
526 nm (13). The oxidizing air-acetylene flame AAS is sensitive
enough to adapt either P & CAM 173 or S-5 (11) to a new lower
standard. Although S-5 recommends maintaining a pH 1 final
solution, this direction is not clearly stated in the method.
Manganese can be extracted by pH controlled APDC chelation and
extracted with chloroform to analyze bulk gasoline for MMT.
Some Mn is lost in partitioning with water.

Mercury. Mercury is a classic heavy metal occupational
toxicant studied by Paracelsus and popularized in Lewis Carol's
Alice in Wonderland. Both elemental and organomercury compounds
are of great interest to industrial hygienists. Elemental mercury is still routinely determined from acidic $KMnO_4$ collection
by dithizone complexation at 515 nm (6) (Table VI). Surprisingly, Hg is not included in P & CAM 173. Elemental mercury has
been determined by flameless AAS (P & CAM 165) for urine,
(P & CAM 167) for blood, and (P & CAM 175) for air samples.
Particulate mercury and organomercury can also be determined
from the membrane filter and Carbosieve B collection media of
P & CAM 175. Mercury in urine, P & CAM 165, is determined by
oxidation of the organic material in urine with nitric acid,
followed by stannous chloride reduction of divalent mercury to
elemental cold vapor mercury. Cold vapor mercury is bubbled
through a Mercury Analyzer System (MAS-50) absorption cell at
254 nm. Elements that readily form amalgams interfere with the
analysis. The mercury in blood analysis, P & CAM 167, is analogous to the urine analysis, except that blood samples are
digested at 54°C with sulfuric acid followed by oxidation with
6% $KMnO_4$. The digestion is very important to thoroughly destroy
organic matter that mercury forms very stable compounds with.
Three forms of mercury are collected in P & CAM 175. A three-
section solid sampler collects particulate on a membrane filter,
organomercuryon the first-stage Carbosieve B absorbent following
the filter; and metallic mercury vapor is amalgamated with
Silvered-Chromosorb P on the second stage of solid sorbent. The
particulate mercury is nitric acid wet ashed and collected on
Ag-Chromsorb P by stannous chloride reduction. This solid sorbent along with the other two sorbent sections is thermal
desorbed into the MAS-50 using a LASL-designed analytical
train. This train has been substantially improved by NIOSH.
The analysis of the particulate mercury by direct analysis if
the cold vapor instead of collection on Ag-Chromsorb P should be
explored. Although Ag-Chromsorb P can be prepared according to
the experimental procedure, this support is not commercially
available. There may be industrial hygiene laboratories where
as MAS-50 is not available for these laboratories, a method by

TABLE VI

MERCURY OSHA STANDARD 0.1 MG/CU M

Colorimetric

	Reaction	Wavelength	Detection Limit
Dithizone	$Mg(II) + 2\ \emptyset NHNHC(S)NN\emptyset$	515 nm	ug/ml

Atomic Absorption

Method No.	Ashing	Atomization	Matrix	Detection Limit
165	Nitric/SnCl$_2$	Cold Vapor	Urine	0.001
	H$_2$SO$_4$, HNO$_3$/ H$_2$SO$^2_4$, KMNO$_4$, SnCl$_2$	Cold Vapor	Blood	0.005
167	H$_2$SO$_4$, KMNO$_4$, SnCl$_2$	Cold Vapor	Blood	0.005
175	Thermal Des.	Cold Vapor	Air	0.001

Kupel or Rathje, as referenced in P & CAM 175, may be used for mercury AAS analysis.

The 253.7 nm analytical line is routinely used for AAS, although the 184.9 nm line is an estimated 50 times more sensitive. This line is beyond the wavelength where flame and atmospheric absorption are prohibitive. Using the cold vapor technique with a nitrogen-purged monochromator would permit greater sensitivity.

Molybdenum. Molybdenum can be analyzed by P & CAM 173 for total Mo, by S-193 (12) for soluble Mo, or by S-376 for insoluble Mo. The standard nitric wet ashing used in P & CAM 173 does not distinghish between soluble and insoluble Mo which have OSHA standards of 5 mg/cu m and 15 mg/cu m. Nitric acid digestion may not dissolve some insoluble Mo that require nitric/perchloric acid or base/nitric acid depending on the solubility properties. Soluble Mo compounds are hot water leached from the cellulose membrane filter used in all three methods. A fuel-rich air/acetylene flame used in P & CAM 173 is replaced by an oxidizing nitrous oxide/acetylene flame to achieve total atomization of Mo as detected at 313.3 nm. Aluminum and traces of acid enhance the Mo flame response; therefore, 400 ppm Al is added to the final solution of both S-193 and S-376; and 0.1 N nitric acid is added to the water leach-soluble Mo final solution, S-193.

Nickel. As the recommended occupational exposure standard for nickel is reduced from 1 mg/cu m to 15 ug/cu m, the analytical methods for nickel, P & CAM 173 and S-206, are used beyond validated limits. The nitric acid wet ashing recommended in P & CAM 173 is inadequate for dissolving refractory nickel compounds. The nitric acid/perchloric acid digestion in S-206 is sufficient to dissolve nickel compounds; however, this oxidation causes losses of chromium and other volatile elements. Often the hygienist wishes to characterize chromium and nickel in the sample simultaneously. Splitting the sample after initial nitric acid digestion decreases sensitivity. Collaborative studies of nickel and chromium analysis by AAS (16) showed severe analytical problems using standard acid digestion and air-acetylene flame at 232.0 nm with background correction. Surprisingly, S-206 for nickel and soluble nickel compounds does not recommend background correction, which is essential to achieve low detection limits.

These AAS methods replaced colorimetric determinations such as alpha-benzildioxime or dimethylglyoxime (6,13) that are subject to positive interferences from copper and cobalt, as well as iron and aluminum (Table VII).

TABLE VII

NICKEL OSHA STANDARD 1 MG/CU M

	Reaction	Wavelength (nm)	Detection Limit
Colorimetric			
Dimethylglyoxime	Chelate – Red	530	5.0 ug
Atomic Absorption	Atomization	Matrix	ug/ml
Method No.	Ashing		
173	Nitric	Flame/Air–C_2H_2(O)	Air	0.005
S–206	Nitric/ Perchloric	Flame/Air–C_2H_2(O)	Air	0.005

Wavelength 232.0

Lead. Lead poisoning has always been a well recognized problem in industrial hygiene as well as a public health problem. The interest in lead analysis is reflected in the NIOSH PAT program where lead is one of the three metals routinely analyzed from filter samples and in the Center for Disease Control (CDC) quality assurance program for the analysis of lead in biological matrixes.

Prior to AAS, lead was analyzed by complexation with dithizone, 510 nm, to yield a red-colored solution. There are four variations of the basic procedure that involved wet ashing followed by preparation of a pH 8.5 citrate/KCN buffered solution from which the lead-dithiozonate is extracted in chloroform. This method, used for air and biological samples (13) is subject to interferences from other divalent metals readily chelated by dithizone. Addition of other complexing agents, double extractions, and pH control have been used to eliminate metal interferences (Table VIII).

The three methods for lead in air are essentially identical; however, one should use S-341 because this method has been validated unlike P & CAM 155 or P & CAM 173. Although all the methods recommend 2-3 ml of nitric acid for wet ashing, the final solutions differ in that P & CAM 155 recommends 1% nitric, P & CAM 173 recommends 1% HCl, and S-341 recommends 10% nitric with EDTA 0.1 M to suppress phosphate, carbonate, iodide, fluoride, and acetate ion that cause flame suppression. EDTA is suggested in P & CAM 173 where interferences are anticipated. Both S-341 and P & CAM 173 use the 217.0 nm line which is twice as sensitive as the 283.3 nm line. Strong nonatomic absorption found when high concentrations of dissolved solid are present requires use of the background corrector. These two methods differ from P & CAM 155 and those for biological analysis, P & CAM 208, 262, which use the 283.3 nm line. The latter methods are nearly identical in range and sensitivity with P & CAM 262 offering greater range for blood and more sensitivity for urine samples. Method 208 fails to clearly explain how blood is prepared for analysis. Lead in urine is complexed with Triton X-100 (2.5%)/ammonium pyrrolidine dithiocarbamate (APDC, 2%) and is extracted from MIBK. The MIBK-PbAPDC is aspirated directly into the flame. The advantage to this method is no wet ashing with nitric and perchloric acid is required for 99% recovery of Pb from biological materials. Method 262 is a refinement of the old P & CAM 101. The biological materials are slowly overnight wet ashed with nitric acid and then treated like samples were for dithizone complexation/chloroform extraction. In this method as in P & CAM 208, APDC/MIBK are used to recover the Pb from the citrate/KCN-buffered solution. This method is fast and does not require a high degree of technical skill; however, the acid digestion does require more time than a simple complexation extraction. Time spent performing the acid digestion is worthwhile because the method is more reliable.

TABLE VIII

LEAD OSHA STANDARD 0.2 MG/CU M

Colorimetric		Reaction	Wavelength (nm)	Detection Limit
Dithizone		Red Solution	510	0.5 ug
				ug/ml
Atomic Absorption		Atomization	Matrix	
Method No.	Ashing			
155*	Nitric	Flame/Air-C_2H_2	Air	0.1
173	Nitric	Flame/Air-C_2H_2(O)	Air	0.01
S-341	Nitric	Flame/Air-C_2H_2(O)	Air	0.01
208*	APDC/MIBK	Flame/Air-C_2H_2(O)	Blood/Urine	0.05
262*	APDC/MIBK	Flame/Air-C_2H_2(O)	Blood/Urine	0.05, 0.01

Wavelength 217.0 nm

*Wavelength 283.2 nm

Sodium. Only P & CAM 173 discusses industrial hygiene analysis of Ns by AAS as an indicator of NaOH exposure. Many laboratories do not have a microtitrator for NaOH analysis; thus, AAS is the best alternative. Sodium is analyzed with an oxidizing air-acetylene flame at 589.6 nm, although the 588.9 nm line is twice as sensitive. Sodium like other alkali and alkaline earths needs control of ionization interferences by addition of 1000 ppm cesium to samples and standards.

Palladium. Flame AAS analysis of Pd is described in P & CAM 173; however, it would probably be preferred to use graphite furnace atomization as in S-191 Pt, soluble salts. An oxidizing air-acetylene flame is used for Pd AAS to minimize interferences from Al, Co, Ni, Pt, as well as Rh and Ru. These interferences may be minimized by complexation of Pd as the bis-pyridine-dithiocyanate (13) and extraction into hexone (3). Interferences may be minimized by the addition of 1000 ppm La. The 244.8 and 247.6 nm lines have equal sensitivity; however, the 247.6 nm line is generally preferred (3). No Federal standard exists for Pd; however, in analogy to Ni and Pt, Pd should be treated with caution.

Platinum. Platinum, due to the low sensitivity required and high atomization temperatures, is analyzed by graphite furnace AAS, S-191. Filter samples are both nitric acid and 2:1 nitric/perchloric acid wet ashes to a final solution representing soluble platinum. The analytical method is pushed to meet the sensitivity requirements of a 0.002 mg Pt/cu m air TWA by using a large collection volume of 720 liters and using 50-ul sample injection for the furnace. The sensitivity could be improved by using 10-ml volumetrics instead of the recommended 25-ml volumetric flasks. No interferences were reported when using the 265.9 nm line; however, the EDL source is recommended for its superior intensity.

Rhodium. Separate OSHA standards exist for metal fumes and dusts at 0.1 mg/cu m and soluble salts at 1.0 ug/cu m. The analysis of fume and dust samples is done with an air-acetylene flame using the 343.5 nm line, S-188 fumes and dusts, and the 369.5 nm line, S-189 for soluble salts. The fumes and dust are nitric acid wet ashed then redissolved in 6 N HCl, similar to Cu (S-186) or Pb (P & CAM 173). Potassium bisulfate (30%) 2.5 ml is added to eliminate interferences from other noble metals. An oxidizing air-acetylene flame minimizes interferences; however, a 95% recovery or lower may be anticipated with this method. S-189, soluble Rh salts, is analogous to S-191, soluble Pt salts; however, only 370 liters of sample is collected because Rh can be detected at 3 ug/ml compared to 10 ug/ml for Pt. This method uses the 369.5 nm line which is half as sensitive as the 343.5 nm line used in S-188. No cation or anion suppressant,

potassium bisulfate, is used in S-189; and no interferences are
reported.

Rubidium. Like Pd, no standard exists for this alkaline
earth; however, it was included in P & CAM 173 possibly in anti-
cipation of a standard. The 780 nm line seems extremely long.
Decreasing the spectral band pass from 4.0 to 0.4 nm greatly
increases the absorbance of high concentration, 50 ppm,
solutions while exerting little effect on 10-ppm
solutions (3). Although P & CAM 173 recommends an oxidizing
air-acetylene flame and 1000 ppm Cs, a cooler reducing flame
which decreases ionization may be equally effective.

Selenium. Selenium has been determined colorimetrically by
formatrion of a diaminobenzidine complex, 420 nm, after an oxidation and distillation (13). Method S-190 for selenium in air
extracts the analyte from filters by 0.1 N nitric acid leach-
ing. The nitric acid extracts are aspirated into an
argon/hydrogen-air flame, and the absorbance is recorded for the
196 nm analytical line. The method discourages the use of a
carbonaceous flame like air-acetyelene. Many analysts use air
acetylene because it is convenient. Background correction is
required for either flame type.

Silicon. Inclusion of silicon in P & CAM 173 is for the
purpose of identifying the elemental composition of amorphous
silica nuisance dust. Unfortunately, the digestion procedure is
not vigorous enough to digest amorphous silica materials. A
reducing nitrous oxide-acetylene flame with a high brightness-
HCl at 251.6 nm provides adequate sensitivity. Polymethyl
siloxane mist in air, P & CAM 227, uses an extraction of the
filter with CS_2 followed by flameless AAS. There are no known
interferences for either method; however, use of a multielement
lamp is discouraged because iron in these lamps has a resonance
at 250.1 nm and 252.2 nm that may effect resolution of the Si.

Strontium. Strontium like Rb and Pd was included in anti-
cipation of a standard. Strontium may be subject to more ionization and chemical interferences than other alkaline earths.
Thorough studies of interfernces from mineral acids, HCl, HNO_3,
and H_2SO_4 are reported (3) as well as from Al, Si, and other
ionization enhancement elements. Sr is strongly ionized, 84%,
in nitrous oxide/acetylene; the addition of 1000 ppm Cs is very
important in suppressing Al, Si, and other interferences that
cause enhancement. The 460.7 nm line is significant for AAS
analysis of Sr.

Thallium. Tl has been determined as a benzyl methyl violet
complex, 585 nm (13). Two AAS methods, P & CAM 173 and S-306
use oxidizing air-acetylene flame with the 276.8 nm line for

analysis. S-306 addresses the many problems in analyzing Tl.
The presence of insoluble Tl compounds will interfer as a positive with acid-soluble insoluble Tl. The acid digestion of
S-304 is identical to P & CAM 173 except for the final solution
volume.

Tin. The standard method for tin and organotin,
P & CAM 176, is a complexation with pyrocatechol-violet sensi-
tized by cetyl trimethylammonium bromide for detection at
662 nm. Two ASS methods for inorganic tin are P & CAM 173 and
S-183. The former does not provide complete oxidation of
inorganic tin and should not be used. S-183 is both specific in
its directions and inherent limitations. Nitric acid:sulfuric
acid (5:1) wet ashing will oxidize all organo and inorganic tin
except the oxide to tin (IV). Although P & CAM 173 recommends
nitrous oxide-acetylene atomization with the 286.3 nm line,
S-183 recommends air-acetylene with the 224.6 nm line. An EDL
source is recommended; however, the use of background correction
at 224.6 nm was not mentioned in S-183. Air-hydrogen gives 2.8
times better sensitivity than air-acetylene; however, the air-
acetylene is sensitive enough for the analysis. The 224.6 nm is
preferred to the 286.3 nm line because the former is twice as
sensitive; however, it does require the use of background correction. Where greater sensitivity is required as with organo-
tins, the graphite furnace AAS is recommened.

Titanium. Titanium dioxide has been determined as the
yellow peroxidation complex at 410 nm (13). Refractory titanium
requires more vigorous dissolution than is used in S-385. After
a nitric acid wet ashing is performed to oxidize all organic
matter, the titanium solution is heated to 400°C in 8 ml of 40%
ammonium sulfate in sulfuric acid until all remaining solids are
dissolved. The solution is diluted for aspiration into a nitrous oxide-acetylene flame with detection at 364.3 nm. Five ml
of 1 N ammonium fluoride is added to the final solution to sta-
bilize Ti enhancement.

Tungsten. Both water-soluble and insoluble compounds are
determined. Particulate tungsten on a filter is first extracted
with water. One ml of 20% w/v sodium sulfate is added to the
extract which is then dilute for analysis by rich nitrous oxide-
acetylene flame at 255.1 nm. The filter is treated with 1:1 HCl
to remove iron and cobalt interferences before being nitric acid
wet ashed and nitric/hydrofluoric acid wet ashed. The residue
is heated with 0.5 N NaOH and treated as soluble tungsten.
Tungsten carbide is determined at less than 100% recovery when
cobalt is present. The detailed method for tungsten developed
by Hull and Eller is in Volume Four of the NIOSH Manual of
Analytical Methods to be published in Winter 1978.

Vanadium. Vanadium can be detected as the phosphotungstate
complex at 410 nm. Cr (VI), Co, Cu, and Ni interfer with this
complex formation. Three AAS method determine total
V (P & CAM 173), vanadium pentoxide dust (S-388), and with this
complex formation. Three AAS methods determine total vanadium
(P & CAM 173), vanadium pentoxide dust (S-388), and fume
(S-391). P & CAM 173 , the standard nitric acid, wet ashing
followed by nitrous oxide-acetylene flame detection at 318.4 nm
will not dissolve ferrovanadium and will not distinguish the
pentoxide from other compounds. The flame method is not sensitive enough to determine pentoxide. Vanadium pentoxide is base
extracted from the filter with 0.1 N or 0.01 N NaOH to separate
it from acid-soluble vanadium compounds. The pentoxide is
analyzed by graphite furnace using the 318.4 nm line. Three
strong lines at 318.3, 318.4, and 318.5 nm are not easily distinguished and are equated as comparable sensitivity--an extreme
oversimplification. The vanadium absorbance can be improved by
addition of 250 ul of nitric acid per 10 ml of final solution
volume.

Yttrium. After initial nitric acid wet ashing, the Y is
2:1 nitric:perchloric acid digested. The resulting $Y(NO_3/ClO_4)$
are solublized with 5 ml of 0.6 M HCl containing 1000 ppm Na.
This solutionis aspirated into a reducing nitrous oxide-acetylene flame at 410.2 nm. The reducing flame and Na are used in
S-200 to minimize Y ionization in the flame. Al, K, and phosphoric acid depress the Y absorbance in the flame; however, 1000
ppm Na minimizes these interferences.

Zinc. AAS analysis of zinc by P & CAM 173 is a standard
application of the method as seen in NIOSH PAT. Zinc in the
divalent state has been analyzed by dithiozonate (13). This
colorimetric method suffers interferences from many other dithizone complexing metals. Zinc is easily determined after nitric
acid wet ashing with an oxidizing air-acetylene flame using the
213.9 nm analytical line and background correction. The AAS
analysis for Zn is as sensitive as more complex activation or
plasma techniques.

Zirconium. Zirconium has been colorimetrically analyzed
using chloroanilic acid complexation at 340 nm after an extraction with p-bromo-mandelic acid from a mineral acid solution.
S-185 for Zr is analogous to S-385 for TiO_2 where nitric acid
wet ashing is followed by nitric/perchloric wet ashing, addition
of ammonium fluoride to enhance sensitivity of the nitrous
oxide-acetylene flame using the 360.1 nm line. Fluoride
enhances the flame absorbance by formation of volatile zirconyl
fluorides and suppression of oxide formation. Anions such as
sulfate and phosphate and ammonium cation may interfer with
digestion and aspiration. The addition of ammonium fluoride

instead of another fluoride seems contradictory; however, the fluoride dominates the ammonium cation.

Future Trends

Multielement analysis will become more important in industrial hygiene analysis as the number of elements per sample and the numbers of samples increases. Additional requirements that will push development of atomic absorption techniques and may encourage the use of new techniques are lower detction and sample speciation. Sample speciation will probably require the use of a chromatographic technique coupled to the spectroscopic instrumentation as an elemental detector. This type of instrumental marriage will not be seen in routine analysis. The use of Inductively Coupled Plasma-Optical Emission Spectroscopy (ICP-OES) (17), Zeeman-effect atomic absorption spectroscopy (ZAA) (18), and X-ray fluorescence (XRF) (19) will increase in industrial hygiene laboratories because they each offer advantages or detection that AAS does not.

ICP-OES is an analytical system that can do simultaneous or sequential determination of up to 50 elements at all concentration levels with a high degree of accuracy and precision. Excellent vaporization-atomization-excitation-ionization is obtained with an argon-supported ICP operated at atmospheric pressure. The emitted spectra is observed with a polychromator or a scanning spectrometer may be used depending on whether simultaneous or sequential determinations are desired. This atomization-excitation process does not exhibit interelement effects often seen in AAS, and ppb range detection is routine. Effective nebulization of samples needs to be improved on; however, ICP and direct-current (DC) plasmas are extremely effective atomization sources that provide the most effective instrumental technique for simultaneous elemental analysis.

Zeeman-effect AAS simplifies the instrumentation and improves the accuracy of AAS measurement by application of a magnetic field to the sample chamber or light source to split the spectral line into three or more lines. The technique eliminates the need for double-beam optics and decreases the background interference fivefold. The ZAA permits measurement of the change in light intensity from the "true" elemental absorbance from scattering, smoke, and vapors. The measurement is based on polarization of the spectral line components. The ability to minimize background becomes extremely critical in arsenic, nickel, and other analyses where the OSH standards are being lowered to detection limit levels.

X-ray fluorescence has been used extensively in air pollution work; however, it has not been used much in industrial hygiene work. XRF has one immediate advantage that it is nondestructive. The many limitations in XRF has been the particle size matching of samples to standards. Many laboratories are working on potential corrections both physically or mathematically for this size problem. If XRD does not find an immediate quantitative use, it would be a valuable qualitative compliment to AAS for determining potential interferences that could be removed chemically prior to AAS analysis.

References

1. Stokinger, H. A., "Metals," in Industrial Hygiene and Toxicology, Vol II, Patty, F. A. (ed.), Wiley-Interscience, 1963.

2. Gaeffer, A. E., Occupational Diseases: A Guide to Their Recognition, DHEW (NIOSH), Pub. No. 77-181.

3. Slavin, W. A., Atomic Absorption Spectroscopy, Wiley-Interscience, 1968.

4. Robinson, J. W., Theory of Atomic Absorption and Fluorescence Spectroscopy, Academic Press, 1974.

5. Taylor, D. G., NIOSH Manual of Analytical Methods, Vol I, 2nd ed., DHEW (NIOSH), Pub. No. 77-157a, 1977.

6. Analytical Guides, American Industrial Hygiene Association, Akron, Ohio.

7. Katz, M., Methods for Air Sampling and Analysis, 2nd ed., American Public Health Assocition, 1975.

8. Schlecht, P.; Crable, J. V.; Kelly, W.; "Industrial Hygiene," in Quality Assurance Practices in Health and Environmental Laboratories, American Public Health Association, 1977.

9. "Laboratory Accreditation Program," American Industrial Hygiene Association, Akron, Ohio.

10. Gorsuch, T. T., The Destruction of Organic Matter, Pergamon Press, 1970.

11. Taylor, D. G. (ed.), NIOSH Manual of Analytical Methods, Vol II, DHEW (NIOSH), Pub. No. 77-157b, 1977.

12. Ibid., Vol III, DHEW (NIOSH), Pub. No. 77-157c, 1977.

13. Jacobs, M. B., Analytical Toxicology of Industrial Inorganic Compounds, Wiley-Interscience, 1967.

14. "Recommended Occupational Exposure Standard for Chromic Acid," DHEW (NIOSH), Pub. No. 73-11021.

15. "Recommended Occupational Exposure Standard for Hexavalent Chromium (VI)," DHEW (NIOSH), Pub. No. 76-129.

16. International Nickel Company, Environmental Affairs Department, private communication.

17. Fassel, V. A., "Quantitative Elemental Analysis by Plasma Emission Spectroscopy," Science, 202, 183 (1978).

18. Maugh, T. H., "The Zeeman Effect: A Unique Approach to Atomic Absorption Spectroscopy," Science, 202, 39 (1978).

19. Dzubay, T. G., X-ray Fluorescence Applications to Environmental Analysis, Ann Arbor Press, 1976.

RECEIVED October 17, 1979.

Metals in Workplace Environment

Optimization of the Analytical Method by Utilizing Ruggedization Techniques

L. S. SHEPARD, G. R. RICCI, G. COLOVOS, and W. S. EATON

Rockwell International, Environmental Monitoring & Services Center, 2421 West Hillcrest Drive, Newbury Park, CA 91320

The wide application of atomic absorption spectrometry (AAS) in the determination of various metallic elements in diverse media is based primarily on the following factors: (a) in most cases AAS has sufficient sensitivity for precise determination of the metallic elements; (b) AAS is relatively free from interference; (c) the required investment for establishing AAS capabilities is small; and (d) the cost per analysis is usually low in comparison with other techniques. The determination of the concentration of metals in the air of workplace environments is achieved by AAS analysis of particulates that have been collected by filtering the air of workplace environments with the exposed filter dissolved in acid. This method (NIOSH P&CAM #173 (1)), with slight revisions, was used to test for Cd, Co, Cr, Ni, and Pb analysis in an interlaboratory test conducted in 1975 (2). The results of these tests showed poor precision and accuracy and also revealed that the major source of the variability was the laboratory analysis portion of the method. Therefore, the need for optimization of the analytical method became apparent, and the effort described here to "ruggedize" the analytical procedure was undertaken.

The terms "Ruggedness Testing" and "Rugged Method" were first used by W. J. Youden (4) to describe his statistical screening of variables of a procedure. He was able to identify and control the important factors, and thus make the method universally applicable or rugged. These terms, as well as the term "ruggedization", are now used for any statistically designed experiments by which the important variables of a method are screened. This basically requires a detailed study of the analytical procedure so that all the parameters affecting the performance are recognized and controlled. Since the resources were not available to characterize the method for all 28 metals listed in NIOSH P&CAM #173, the method was studied only for Be, Cd, Co, Cr, Cu, Mn, Mo, Ni, Pb, and Pd, and ruggedized for all these metals except Pd. The method was not ruggedized for Pd because it was found that an alternate experimental procedure was preferable.

0-8412-0539-6/80/47-120-267$08.50/0
© 1980 American Chemical Society

The ruggedization of the analytical procedure was performed by applying statistical screening techniques to minimize the effort required and, therefore, reduce the time and the cost substantially. The statistical approaches used in this study were those first introduced by Plackett-Burman (3) and Youden-Steiner (4). Both techniques reduce the required effort since they use balanced incomplete block design experiments which can clearly indicate the non-affecting parameters from those that may have an effect. In this study the important variables of the analytical method were identified by using the Plackett-Burman technique. These variables were further tested and brought under control by using conventional single-factor experiments. After this, the original P&CAM method was revised to include the necessary controls for the important variables and was finally tested for "ruggedness" by the Youden-Steiner technique. This final step of the ruggedization was performed with samples collected from the aerosol generation system built especially for this program. This was a dynamic aerosol generation and sampling system and was completely characterized prior to its utilization for sample preparation. The aerosol size distribution was monitored by continuous aerosol sizing instruments and controlled for each sampling run to ensure that at least 90 per cent of the aerosol mass was within the particle diameter range of 0.1 to 10 micrometers. Four independent measurements using different methodologies were used to determine the size distribution of the generated aerosols. The uniformity of particles collected among all sampling positions within a given sampling run, and the reproducibility of the aerosol generation system were characterized by both atomic absorption analysis and X-ray fluorescence analysis (XRF) of five metals.

A discussion of the Plackett-Burman and Youden-Steiner techniques is given below, along with a discussion of the experimental results from their application.

STATISTICAL SCREENING TECHNIQUES

There are several ways to study the effect of various experimental factors on an analytical method. The classical method of studying one variable at a time while holding others constant is extremely inefficient. Other approaches such as regression analysis and complete factorial designs involve a large number of experiments and are also inefficient. For example, a factorial design of seven factors at two levels requires 2^7 or 128 experiments. Therefore, alternate approaches which reduce the experimental work are very attractive.

One such approach is the Plackett-Burman (3) design in which a large number of variables can be screened efficiently by a small number of experiments. This design is based on balanced incomplete blocks which allow the statistical identification of the nonaffecting variables. The remaining relatively small number of variables that may be important can be examined in further detail. In the method proposed by Plackett and Burman, each variable is examined at two levels (high and low) in a series of multifactor experiments. Basic designs for screening as many as 100 variables have been given (3). The Plackett-Burman design used in this study can screen 27 variables (A-AA) with 28 experiments (Table I). The effect of each variable, defined as the average difference of response at high and low levels, is determined by using equation 1.

$$E_A = \frac{\Sigma R\ (+)_i - R\ (-)_i}{N/2} \tag{1}$$

where

E_A = the effect of variable A,

$\Sigma R\ (+)_i$ = the sum of the response of those experiments in which the variable A occurred at the <u>high</u> levels,

$\Sigma R\ (-)_i$ = the sum of the response of those experiments in which the variable A occurred at the <u>low</u> level, and

N = the number of experiments

The significance of each calculated effect is determined by using the t-test. An estimate of standard error for the t-test is obtained according to equation 2.

$$SE = \sqrt{\frac{\Sigma(E(d)_i)^2}{N_d}} \tag{2}$$

where

SE = the estimate of the standard error,

$E(d)_i$ = the calculated effect for "dummy" variable i, and

N_d = the number of dummy variables.

The estimate of the t-test of variable A, t_A, is calculated by dividing the estimate of the effect (E_A) by the estimate of the standard error (SE) - equation 3.

$$t_A = E_A/S_E \tag{3}$$

From the t-test value, the percentage probability of significance (percent PS) can be calculated using equation 4.

$$\text{Percent}\quad PS_A = 100 \times (1-P_A) \tag{4}$$

where

P_A is determined from the t-table for n degrees of freedom, and is the probability that that particular value of t could occur by chance.

An approach similar to that of Plackett and Burman called "Ruggedization" was introduced by Youden (4) for the screening of only seven variables with eight experiments. The combination of the high and low levels of the variables in Youden's design is

TABLE I. Plackett-Burman matrix for 27 variables

VARI-ABLE	Experiment Number																											
---	1	2	3	4	5	6	7	8	9	10	11	12	13	14	15	16	17	18	19	20	21	22	23	24	25	26	27	28
A	+	+	−	−	−	−	+	+	+	−	−	+	−	+	−	−	+	−	+	−	+	+	+	−	+	+	−	−
B	−	+	+	−	−	−	+	+	+	+	−	−	−	−	+	−	−	+	+	+	−	−	+	+	−	+	+	−
C	+	−	+	−	−	−	+	+	+	−	+	−	+	−	+	+	−	−	−	+	+	+	−	+	+	−	+	−
D	+	−	+	+	+	−	−	−	−	−	+	−	−	−	−	−	−	−	+	+	−	+	−	+	+	+	−	−
E	+	+	+	−	+	+	−	−	−	−	−	+	+	+	−	−	+	+	+	+	+	+	+	−	−	+	+	−
F	+	+	+	+	+	+	+	−	−	+	−	+	−	+	−	+	−	+	−	−	+	−	+	−	+	−	+	−
G	+	+	+	+	−	+	−	+	−	−	+	−	−	−	−	+	−	−	+	+	−	+	+	−	+	−	+	−
H	−	+	−	+	+	+	+	+	+	+	−	+	+	+	+	+	−	+	+	+	+	+	+	+	+	+	−	−
I	−	−	−	+	+	+	−	+	+	+	−	+	+	−	+	+	+	−	−	−	+	−	−	+	−	+	+	−
J	−	−	+	+	+	+	+	+	+	+	+	+	+	−	+	+	+	−	+	+	+	+	−	+	+	+	+	−
K	+	−	+	+	+	+	−	+	+	+	+	+	+	+	+	+	+	+	+	+	+	−	−	−	+	+	+	−
L	−	−	−	+	+	+	+	+	+	+	+	+	+	+	+	−	+	+	+	+	+	+	+	+	+	+	−	−
M	+	−	−	−	−	−	−	−	−	−	−	−	−	−	−	−	−	−	−	−	−	−	−	−	−	−	−	−
N	−	−	−	−	−	+	+	+	+	+	+	+	+	+	−	+	+	+	+	+	+	+	−	−	−	−	−	−
O	−	+	+	+	+	+	+	+	+	+	+	+	+	−	+	+	+	+	+	+	+	+	+	+	+	+	−	−
P	+	+	+	+	+	−	+	+	+	+	+	+	+	+	+	+	+	+	+	+	+	+	+	+	+	+	+	−
Q	−	+	−	−	−	+	−	−	−	−	−	+	−	+	−	+	+	+	−	−	−	−	+	+	−	−	+	−
R	−	+	+	+	+	+	+	+	+	+	+	+	+	+	+	+	+	+	−	−	+	+	+	+	+	+	+	−
S	+	+	+	+	−	−	−	+	−	+	+	+	−	+	+	+	+	+	+	−	+	−	+	+	−	−	−	−
T	+	−	−	−	−	−	−	+	+	+	+	+	+	+	+	+	+	+	+	−	−	−	+	+	+	+	+	−
U	−	+	+	+	+	+	−	+	−	+	+	+	+	+	−	+	+	+	+	−	−	+	−	+	−	−	−	−
V	−	+	+	+	+	+	+	−	+	+	+	+	+	+	+	+	+	+	+	+	+	+	+	+	+	+	+	−
W	+	+	−	−	−	−	−	−	−	+	−	+	+	+	+	−	−	+	−	+	+	+	−	+	+	+	+	−
X	−	−	+	−	+	+	+	+	+	+	−	+	+	+	+	+	+	−	−	−	−	−	+	−	−	−	−	−
Y	+	+	+	+	−	−	+	+	+	+	−	−	+	+	+	+	+	+	+	+	+	+	+	+	+	−	+	−
Z	−	+	+	−	−	+	+	−	+	−	−	−	+	+	+	+	+	+	−	−	−	−	−	−	+	−	−	−
AA	+	−	+	+	−	+	−	+	+	−	−	−	+	+	+	+	−	+	+	−	+	+	−	−	−	+	−	−

different from that of Plackett and Burman. The experimental design is presented in Table II.

TABLE II. Youden-Steiner ruggedization experimental design

Experiment Number	Variables						
	A	B	C	D	E	F	G
1	+	+	+	+	+	+	+
2	+	+	-	+	-	-	-
3	+	-	+	-	+	-	-
4	+	-	-	-	-	+	+
5	-	+	+	-	-	+	-
6	-	+	-	-	+	-	+
7	-	-	+	+	-	-	+
8	-	-	-	+	+	+	-

The effect of each variable in the ruggedness test is determined by the difference between the average high and low levels, as is done in the Plackett-Burman design. However, the Youden technique, as modified by Steiner, differs from the Plackett-Burman technique in that the Youden-Steiner experiment is performed in duplicate, and the standard error is estimated differently. An estimate of the experimental error is calculated by equation 5.

$$s = \sqrt{\frac{\left(E_{A1} - E_{A2}\right)^2 + \left(E_{B1} - E_{B2}\right)^2 + \ldots \left(E_{G1} - E_{G2}\right)^2}{7}} \qquad (5)$$

where

s = the estimated experimental error,

E_{A1}, E_{B1},...E_{G1} are the calculated effects of variables A, B,...G in the first experiment, and
E_{A2}, E_{B2},...,E_{G2} are the calculated effects of variables A, B,...G in the second experiment.

For an effect to be significant at the 95% confidence level, it must exceed $1.18s$:

$$E_A = \frac{E_{A1} + E_{A2}}{2} > 1.18s \qquad (6)$$

This is based on the student's t-test for seven degrees of freedom at the 5 percent significance level. It should be noted that although the matrices of the abovementioned screening method have been designed so that main factor effects are not confounded with each other, each main effect may be confounded with two-factor, three-factor, and higher order interactions, thus introducing uncertainty which leads to misinterpretation. However, in the case of analytical methods or other chemical processes, the interaction between higher orders can be anticipated to some extent before the test, or may be suspected after screening for significant factors. In spite of these disadvantages, ruggedization is a powerful statistical tool by which the effects of variables can be screened efficiently. With additional experimental work, these variables can be isolated from the rest and controlled so that the method can be used in any laboratory for the generation of statistically acceptable results.

APPLICATION OF THE PLACKETT-BURMAN TECHNIQUE TO P&CAM # 173

The Plackett-Burman screening technique was used to identify critical variables. The variables which may have an effect on the P&CAM # 173 AAS analysis can be identified as:

1. Variables associated with sample preparation
2. Variables associated with the physical and chemical characteristics of the samples
3. Variables associated with instrumental characteristics.

Table III lists possible variables and the levels at which they may have an effect on the P&CAM # 173 method. The following criteria were used in their selection:

1. Procedural steps may be deliberately or unconsciously eliminated or altered by the participants
2. Physical-chemical effects may introduce significant errors
3. Changes in instrumental parameters or differences in instrumentation may have an effect.

The choice of the variables listed in Table III was based on the original P&CAM # 173 procedure, as modified by the supplementary instructions (1). The importance of the variables listed was self-evident in some cases, and these were most likely to be critical in the analysis. For example, the temperature for bringing a sample to dryness was anticipated to be an important variable because salts of some of the metals (Cd and Pb) are volatile at elevated temperatures. The duration of heating the residue was expected to be significant and interrelated with the temperature. The completion of ashing with perchloric acid ($HClO_4$) was expected to be another critical variable in the analysis. Other variables listed in the first category of Table III were not as readily identified as being critical in the analysis, but were included as variables which might differ in different laboratories applying the method.

The variables related to the chemical and physical characteristics of the samples were expected to have a significant effect on the accuracy of the method. The existence of a concentration effect was considered important on the precision of the analysis, whereas the use of standards, with or without a filter matrix, was expected to have an effect on the accuracy. Interference from one of the analytes or other cations was anticipated to be a signifi-

TABLE III. Variables which may affect the P&CAM #173 procedure

	1. Sample Preparation	Low (-)	High (+)
A	Initial digestion with concentrated HNO_3 (ml)	1.7	2.3
B	Additions of 1 ml HNO_3 after digestion	0	2
C	Drying temperature of residue (^{O}C)	100	320
D	Final treatment with 1.0 ml concentrated HNO_3	No	Yes
E	Dummy	--	--
F	Completion of ashing with 1.0 ml $HClO_4$	No	Yes
G	Dummy	--	--
H	Nitric acid cleaned glassware	No	Yes
I	Duration of heating of residue (min)	2	30
J	Dummy	--	--
K	Residue before dilution	Small volume	Dryness
L	Dilution to volume	H_2O	5% HNO_3
	2. Physical - Chemical		
M	Dummy	--	--
N	Concentration of analyte	Low	High
0	Dummy	--	--
P	Standard with/without sample matrix (± filter)	Without	With
Q	Flame stoichiometry	Lean (*)	Stoichiometric
R	Type of standards (mixed or single analyte)	Single	Mixed
	3. Instrumental		
S	Aspiration rate (ml/min)	5	7
T	Background D_2 correction	No	Yes
U	Shift of wavelength of 0.3 nm	No	Yes
V	Dummy	--	--
W	Cathode current	Optimum	Maximum
X	Burner head	Short	Long
Y	Direct readout of concentration	No	Yes
Z	Slit width (nm)	0.2	0.7
AA	Dummy	--	--

(*) For Cr analysis only, flame stoichiometry at the low level was stoichiometric and at the high level was rich.

cant variable for some of the analyses (e.g. Fe and Ni in Cr analysis). Finally, change in the stoichiometry of the flame during an analysis may have an effect on the precision of the method.

The significance of deliberate or accidental changes of instrumental variables such as aspiration rate, current of the hollow cathode, wavelength, and slit width during an analysis was self-evident. The importance of background correction, especially for the low concentration levels, was another consideration. The importance of the other variables listed, such as the direct read-out of concentration, was dependent upon the proper utilization of these instrumental features by the analyst.

The low (-) and high (+) levels of each variable were selected in a range corresponding to changes which may take place in an analysis either within or between laboratories. As indicated previously, Tables I and III, 28 experiments were performed for 27 variables, seven of which were dummy variables used to estimate standard error. A dummy variable is a vacant space in the experimental matrix which does not represent any procedural change, but is a measure of the standard error as defined previously. In the present study, two calibration curves, one at the beginning and one at the end, have been used for the estimation of the concentration.

RESULTS AND DISCUSSION OF THE PLACKETT-BURMAN SCREENING

Filters spiked with solutions containing the ten metals were used for the initial screening of the method. The solutions which resulted from the acid digestion of these filters were first analyzed for Cu. The results of the Plackett-Burman test are presented in Table IV, which lists the probability for a parameter to be significant. The probabilities are estimated both in terms of instrumental response and concentration. Two significant observations can be made. First, due to statistical flukes or confounding, dummy variables may appear as significant parameters. Second, instrumental parameters such as shift of wavelength (variable U), triple slot vs single slot burner head (variable X), and slit width (variable Z), show a higher probability of significance when estimated using calculated concentration. This demonstrates that optimization of instrumental conditions for a particular metal and concentration range of analysis is not critical for calculated concentrations when the response of the calibration standards is determined under identical instrumental conditions as the sample. Instrumental conditions do, however, affect instrumental response.

The next metal to be screened was Cd, and Table V presents the results. From these data an additional very significant observation related to the concentration level can be made. Calculation of the probability of significance by using the concentration calculated from the first and second calibration curves produced a standard error of 0.57 and 0.60 µg/ml respectively, and showed the

TABLE IV. Application of the Plackett-Burman screening test
to the AAS analysis of Copper.

Variables with probability of significance greater than 70 per cent	Per cent Probability of significance calculated using:		
		Estimated Concentration	
	Instrumental Response	from first calibration curve	from second calibration curve
Dummy D	--	--	80
G	--	--	70
H	90	--	70
Dummy J	--	80	70
K	90	80	70
L	--	80	--
Dummy M	--	80	--
N	--	--	80
Dummy O	90	--	--
P	--	--	80
S	--	70	--
U	95	80	--
W	90	90	70
X	99	70	70
Z	80	--	--
Standard error	0.018 Abs.	0.142 µg/ml	0.218 µg/ml

TABLE V. Application of the Plackett-Burman screening test
to the AAS analysis of Cadmium.

Variables with probability of significance greater than 70 per cent	Per cent Probability of significance calculated using:		
		Estimated Concentration	
	Instrumental Response	from first calibration curve	from second calibration curve
C	--	--	70
Dummy G	70	--	--
H	--	--	70
K	80	70	--
L	70	--	--
N	70	95	95
Q	--	70	--
T	70	70	--
Dummy V	80	--	--
W	80	70	70
X	95	--	--
Y	--	80	70
Standard error	0.040 Abs.	0.573 µg/ml	0.598 µg/ml

concentration level (variable N) to be significant at the 95 percent level. These standard errors are very high when compared
with the spike levels, being about 60 percent of the low level
and 20 percent of the high level of the standard concentrations.
In fact, using these non-optimized conditions, the spiked levels
were close to the analytical detection limit and only the concentration level itself was a significant variable. Indeed, this
experiment shows that at a standard error of 0.57 μg/ml, the
method for Cd was ruggedized with respect to all variables except
concentration of the analyte, which would be expected since the
lower spike concentration was barely detectable over the instrumental noise. Operating the atomic absorption instrument under
non-optimized conditions also negated one of the original requirements that the low level spike be significantly above the detection limit. Repetition of the Cd ruggedization experiment with
optimal instrumental conditions yielded standard errors of 0.035
and 0.025 μg/ml for concentrations calculated using the first and
the second calibration curve, respectively. This represents an
approximate twenty-fold decrease in the standard error. Comparison
of these values with the conventionally determined precision for
synthetic Cd solutions under optimized instrumental conditions
shows that the estimated standard error is comparable to the
instrumental variation to be expected of any Cd analysis. It also
indicates that no other procedural parameters appreciably influenced the standard error. Therefore, instrumental variables should
be kept optimal for each experiment and for all of the metals
studied because it is recognized that these parameters are critical,
especially close to the analytical detection limit. For this
reason, the analytical method must specify that the instrumental
parameters be carefully optimized.

All subsequent experiments for each of the metals were then
performed by using optimized instrumental conditions. Table VI
presents the results of the ruggedization screening using concentrations calculated from the first and second calibration
curves. It also presents the standard error, the independently
determined instrumental precision, and the percent probability of
significance for each parameter studied. The results presented in
Table VI reveal that effects which were insignificant when concentration was calculated with the first calibration curve, appear
as significant with the second. This can be attributed to small
changes in the slope, intercept, and error of the calibration
curves used for the calculation of the concentrations. However, as
has been discussed, ruggedization indicates variables which are
NOT significant. Those which appear as significant MAY OR MAY NOT,
in reality, be significant. Therefore, if a parameter is important, it should have a high probability of significance with either
calibration curve.

In Table VII, the variables which have 90 percent or higher
probability of significance calculated from both the first and
second calibration curves, are presented. Of the significant

TABLE VI. Plackett-Burman screening of variables for the AAS analysis of ten metals.

% Probability of Significance Calculated from the First and Second Calibration Curves(*) — Concentrations of the First and Second Calibration Curves

Metal	Curve	Standard Error (μg/ml)	Expected Instrumental Error (1-3 μg/ml)	A	B	C	D	F	H	I	K	L	N	P	Q	R	T	Y
Be	1st	0.037	0.035	70	--	--	--	--	--	--	--	--	--	--	--	--	--	--
	2nd	0.034		70	70	--	70	--	--	--	--	--	70	--	--	--	--	--
Cd	1st	0.035	0.035	70	--	70	--	--	--	--	80	--	--	--	80	99	--	99
	2nd	0.025		80	--	90	90	--	--	90	70	80	--	--	--	--	--	80
Co	1st	0.045	0.044	70	--	80	--	80	70	80	--	80	--	--	--	90	--	80
	2nd	0.044		70	70*	70	--	95	70	80	--	80	70	--	--	--	80	--
Cr	1st	0.234	0.010	--	--	--	--	99	--	--	--	--	90	--	--	--	90	--
	2nd	0.226		--	--	--	--	99	70	--	70	--	80	--	--	--	90	--
Cu	1st	0.142	0.040	--	--	--	80	--	--	--	80	80	--	--	--	--	--	--
	2nd	0.218		--	--	--	80	--	70	--	70	--	80	80	--	--	--	--
Mn	1st	0.033	0.020	--	--	70	90	99	--	80	--	--	--	--	--	95	--	--
	2nd	0.035		--	--	70	95	99	--	90	--	--	--	--	--	--	--	--
Mo	1st	0.203	0.050	--	--	80	--	--	--	--	99	--	90	--	99	--	80	--
	2nd	0.191		--	--	90	--	--	--	70	99	--	--	95	99	--	90	--
Ni	1st	0.079	0.060	95	--	--	--	--	90	--	--	70	80	--	98	99	80	90
	2nd	0.079		90	--	90	--	80	80	80	--	--	--	--	--	--	70	--

TABLE VI. (Cont'd.) Plackett-Burman screening of variables for the AAS analysis of ten metals.

Metal	Curve	Standard Error (µg/ml)	Expected Instrumental Error (1-3 µg/ml)	% Probability of Significance Calculated from the Concentrations of the First and Second Calibration Curves(*)														
				A	B	C	D	F	H	I	K	L	N	P	Q	R	T	Y
Pb	1st	0.037	0.049	80	--	99	90	--	--	--	--	--	80	--	--	90	90	--
	2nd	0.042		--	--	95	--	--	--	80	70	--	80	--	--	--	--	--
Pd	1st	0.195	0.060	80	70	90	--	99	--	70	99	--	99	--	--	80	80	80
	2nd	0.170		--	80	95	--	99	--	--	99	--	99	80	--	--	--	80

(*) Percent probabilities of significance lower than 70 are not listed

TABLE VII. Variables appearing as significant for both calibration curves and at a confidence level of at least 90% for one of these calibration curves.

Metal	Average Dummy Error (μg/ml)	Expected Instrumental Error (1-3 μg/ml)	% Probability of Significance Calculated from the Concentrations of the First and Second Calibration Curves														
			A	B	C	D	F	H	I	K	L	N	P	Q	R	T	Y
Be	0.036	0.035	--	--	--	--	--	--	--	--	--	--	--	--	--	--	--
Cd	0.030	0.035	--	--	--	--	--	--	--	--	--	--	--	--	99	--	99
Co	0.044	0.044	--	--	--	--	--	--	--	--	--	--	--	--	90	--	--
Cr	0.230	0.010	--	--	--	--	99	--	--	--	--	--	--	--	--	90	--
Cu	0.180	0.04	--	--	--	--	--	--	--	--	--	--	--	--	--	--	--
Mn	0.034	0.020	--	--	--	--	--	--	--	--	--	--	--	--	95	--	--
Mo	0.197	0.050	--	--	--	95	99	--	--	99	--	--	95	99	--	--	--
Ni	0.079	0.060	95	--	--	--	--	--	--	--	--	--	--	--	99	--	--
Pb	0.040	0.049	--	--	99	--	--	--	--	--	--	--	--	--	98	--	--
Pd	0.182	0.060	--	--	95	--	99	--	--	99	--	99	--	--	--	--	--

effects listed in Table VII, some appear to affect the analysis of single elements while others affect groups of elements. The variables A, D, N, P, Q, T, and Y were significant for the elements Ni, Mo, Pd, Mo, Mo, Cr, and Cd, respectively. Whereas variables C, F, K, and R were significant for the groups of elements Pb-Pd, Cr-Mo-Pd, Cr-Mo-Pd, Mo-Pd, and Cd-Co-Mn-Ni-Pb, respectively. Careful study of these significant variables showed that in some cases the cause for being significant could be explained. For example, variable N, concentration of analyte, was expected to be significant for Pd because one of the original intentions, that the low level spike be significantly above the detection limit, was not realized. Imprecision introduced by the experimental variables made the effective detection limit much higher than that expected from the instrumental imprecision alone. Variable P, calculation of sample concentrations using mixed analyte standards with or without the filter matrix, indicates that the presence of the filter matrix decreases Mo response. This can be shown clearly by comparing the slopes of the calibration curves with or without the filter matrix. Variable Q, flame stoichiometry, was not expected to be significant for calculated concentrations, only for absorbance readings. However, for Mo analyzed with an extremely lean nitrous oxide flame, no instrumental response was obtained. Variable R, calculation of sample concentrations using single analyte calibration curves or mixed analyte calibration curves, was significant for Cd, Co, Mn, Ni, and Pb. For Cd and Ni, this was due to a standardization error of the mixed analyte standard solution prepared from deliquescent cadmium nitrate and nickel nitrate salts. Variable T, the use of deuterium-arc background correction, was significant for chromium because the energy of the deuterium lamp drops significantly above 300 nm. At the chromium line (357.9 nm), the output of the D2 lamp is about 10 per cent of its maximum output and results in imprecise operation of the background corrector. Variable Y, calculation of concentration using a single calibration standard to simulate the direct readout function of some instruments, was significant for Cd. This was probably due to a slight nonlinearity of the calibration curve at this concentration range of 0 to 4.0 µg/ml.

The information which is usually obtained from a ruggedization experiment is limited to the identification of the nonsignificant parameters. However, if the expected experimental precision is independently known, it is possible to determine whether the standard error of the ruggedization experiment is comparable to the expected instrumental precision. The standard error of all the 10 metals except Cr, Mo, and Pd (Table VII) is very close to the expected instrumental deviation at spiked concentration levels of 1.0 to 3.0 µg/ml in solution. This indicated that for Be, Cd, Co, Cu, Mn, Ni, and Pb analysis, the screening experiments did not introduce significant imprecision compared to repetitive analysis of synthetic standard solutions of these metals. One variable uniquely significant (99 per cent) for Cr, Mo, and Pd is the treatment with perchloric acid (variable F). An attempt to explain the

TABLE VIII. Effect of perchloric acid treatment on the analyses of Cr, Mo and Pd

	Average Percent Recovery ± Std. Dev.		
	Cr	Mo	Pd
Without perchloric acid	101± 6	41±19	39±32
With perchloric acid	59±33	124%14	82±28

effect of perchloric acid on these metals by utilizing the data available from the ruggedization revealed that percent recoveries (see Table VIII above), depend critically on the presence or absence of perchloric acid, and it shows that the presence of perchloric acid decreased the recovery of Cr and increased the recovery of Mo and Pd. Furthermore, Table VIII indicates that the relatively high standard error can be attributed to the perchloric acid in the case of Cr, but not in the case of Mo and Pd.

SINGLE FACTOR EXPERIMENTS

The application of the Plackett-Burman screening procedure indicated several variables which may have significant effects on the analytical method (Table IX). In order to verify their significance and to control the effects, the variables should be investigated further. In this study, this was accomplished by using classical single-factor experiments. From the variables listed in Table IX, only variables A and K were not studied because A was later tested in a Youden-Steiner ruggedization and K was procedurally controlled by specifying in the procedure that solutions must be taken to dryness at 100 degrees C.

TABLE IX. Variables found significant in the Plackett-Burman screening

		Metal	Per Cent Probability of significance
A	Initial digestion with concentrated HNO_3 (1.7, 2.3 ml)	Ni	(95%)
C	Drying temperature of residue ($100^{\circ}C$, $320^{\circ}C$)	Pb Pd	(98%) (96%)
F	Completion of ashing with 1.0 ml $HClO_4$ (no, yes)	Cr, Mo, Pd	(99%)
K	Residue before dilution (small vol., dryness)	Mo, Pd	(99%)
P	Filter background in matrix (no, yes)	Mo	(99%)
Q	Flame stoichiometry (lean, stoich.)	Mo	(95%)
R	Mixed vs single analyte standards	Cd, Ni, Pb Co Mn	(99%) (90%) (95%)

THE EFFECT OF PERCHLORIC ACID IN Cr, Mo, and Pd ANALYSIS

Both solution samples and spiked filter samples containing Cr (III) and Cr (VI) as $Cr_2O_7^-$ were prepared. Samples were solubilized using both a nitric acid and a nitric-perchloric acid digestion. The data presented in Table X show that low (64 to 71 percent) recoveries and decreased precision for Cr analysis are obtained when either synthetic solutions or spiked filters are digested using a procedure requiring samples containing $HClO_4$ to be taken to dryness. This is true whether Cr (III) exists in solution along with other analytes (Cd, Co, Ni, Pb) or as a single analyte Cr (VI) $Cr_2O_7^=$ solution.

TABLE X. Effect of perchloric acid on the analysis of chromium

Relative response (a) ± Std. Dev. of chromium solution treated with HNO_3 or with HNO_3-$HClO_4$

Metal	Condition	Relative Response (± Std. Dev.)
Cr III (b)		1.02 ± 0.01
Cr VI (c)	HNO_3	0.98 ± 0.03
Cr III (b)		0.71 ± 0.06
Cr VI (c)	HNO_3-$HClO_4$	0.64 ± 0.13
Cr III (b)	HNO_3-$HClO_4$	0.64 ± 0.14
Cr VI (c)	with filter matrix	0.69 ± 0.10

(a)   Response relative to untreated samples
(b)   Mixed analyte standard containing Cd, Co, etc.
(c)   Single analyte $Cr_2O_7^=$ standard

To determine the instrumental response as a function only of the background matrix of the solution, the effect of perchloric acid on Cr, Mo, and Pd was tested independently of the digestion procedure. The variables were: (1) presence of filter matrix in solution; (2) presence of perchloric acid; (3) presence of lanthanum flame buffer in solution; and (4) concentration. The data are presented in Table XI. Slightly high recoveries (4 to 9 percent) were obtained for Cr when the filter matrix was present in solution. Recoveries of approximately 120 percent were obtained from the 1.0 µg/ml samples containing perchloric acid. This was found to be caused by Cr contamination in the perchloric acid. The corrected analytical results showed that the presence of either perchloric acid or lanthanum in solution has essentially no effect on the instrumental response for Cr in a lean air-acetylene flame.

TABLE XI. Study of the effect of perchloric acid on the determination of Cr, Mo, Pd.

	Relative Response ± Std. Dev.		
	Cr	Mo	Pd
Synthetic Standards			
4 µg/ml w/o HClO$_4$	1.00 ± .003	1.00 ± .02	1.00 ± .04
4 µg/ml + 4% HClO$_4$	1.03 ± .004	1.44 ± .07	1.01 ± .01
4 µg/ml + 4% HClO$_4$, 0.5% La	1.02 ± .004	1.75 ± .06	1.04 ± .02
4 µg/ml + 0.5% La	1.02 ± .005	1.75 ± .06	1.03 ± .02
Solutions Containing Filter Matrix			
4 µg/ml + 4% HClO$_4$	1.09 ± .005	1.46 ± .10	0.96 ± .06
4 µg/ml w/o HClO$_4$	0.97 ± .003	0.31 ± .02	1.01 ± .01
1 µg/ml w/o HClO$_4$	1.09 ± .012	0.91 ± .48	0.52 ± .28
1 µg/ml + 4% HClO$_4$	1.20 ± .080	1.55 ± .48	0.95 ± .08
Solutions Containing Filter Matrix and 0.5% Lanthanum			
4 µg/ml + 4% HClO$_4$	1.04 ± .01	1.87 ± .13	1.03 ± .01
4 µg/ml w/o HClO$_4$	*	1.76 ± .00	1.05 ± .01
1 µg/ml w/o HClO$_4$	1.06 ± .02	1.73 ± .15	0.51 ± .02
1 µg/ml + 4% HClO$_4$	1.23 ± .01	1.60 ± .10	1.08 ± .06

* Sample lost

The instrumental response for Mo was found to be affected by the presence of filter matrix, perchloric acid, and lanthanum. The filter matrix causes low Mo response (31 to 91 percent). The response of synthetic solutions and solutions containing filter matrix is enhanced approximately 50 percent if perchloric acid is present in solution, and approximately 75 percent if lanthanum is present in solution. When both perchloric acid and lanthanum are present in solution, the enhancement of response is equivalent to that which would be obtained with the lanthanum alone. For two samples which did not contain lanthanum flame buffer, precision of triplicate analysis was poor (± 48 percent). Aliquots of two sample types which contained added lanthanum flame buffer gave much better precision (± 12 percent). It appears that both perchloric acid and lanthanum are acting as flame buffers or "releasing agents" for atomic Mo in the flame.

The response of Pd for all samples except the 1 μg/ml without perchloric acid were equivalent within the precision of triplicates, to the mixed standard containing no background. Since both the 1 μg/ml without perchloric acid and lanthanum, and the 1 μg/ml without perchloric acid but including lanthanum, were prepared from the same digested spiked filter, it appears that something occurred during digestion which caused a low Pd recovery for this low-level spiked sample. The precision for this sample is poor since two samples out of three gave the low recoveries. It should be noted that the solutions analyzed for Pd are the same solutions analyzed for Cr and Mo, and that low recoveries for other metals were not obtained for these particular samples.

The data presented in this section show that perchloric acid affects Cr recoveries by causing losses during digestion. It is believed that Cr is lost as the volatile species CrO_2Cl_2 during digestion with perchloric acid. The formation of CrO_2Cl_2 during digestion with chloride and the exploitation of this property for the analysis of Cr (VI) is known (5,6,7).

STUDY OF A "MILD" $HClO_4$-HNO_3 DIGESTION AND COMPARISON TO SINGLE-STEP HNO_3

The effect of a perchloric acid digestion, as discussed above, was studied by evaporating the original extract to dryness, followed by additional treatment with perchloric acid and evaporation to a small volume (approximately 0.5 ml). In an attempt to determine if a less vigorous perchloric acid treatment would be an acceptable digestion procedure, additional experiments were performed. In these experiments, a single-step HNO_3 digestion was compared with a mixed HNO_3-$HClO_4$ digestion. Other variables studied were temperature of digestion (100 degrees C vs 175 degrees C), time at dryness (15 minutes vs 120 minutes), and the effect of centrifuging. Each experiment was done in triplicate. The results are presented in Table XII for a one-step nitric digestion, and in Table XIII for a mild, mixed HNO_3-$HClO_4$ digestion. The effect of each variable is

TABLE XII. Effect of digestion variables on recoveries, using a single step HNO$_3$ digestion.

Element	Average % Recovery* ± Std. Dev.	Effect of Variables**					
		Digestion at 100 or 175°C and 15 min. at dryness	Digestion at 100 or 175°C and 120 min. at dryness	Digestion at 100°C and 15 min. or 120 min. at dryness	Digestion at 175°C and 15 or 120 min. at dryness	Digestion at 100°C with or without centrifuging	Digestion at 175°C with or without centrifuging
Be	104.7 ± 0.0	2.5	---	---	---	No data	No data
Cd	104.2 ± 1.0	---	---	---	---	---	---
Co	111.6 ± 1.0	---	---	---	---	---	No data
Cr Lean	109.4 ± 1.4	---	---	---	---	---	No data
Cr Rich	95.6 ± 1.6	6.3	9.0	-5.1	---	---	---
Cu	103.0 ± 0.7	---	4.7	---	---	---	No data
Mn	104.3 ± 1.0	---	---	---	---	No data	No data
Mo	33.3 ± 7.5	---	---	---	---	No data	No data
Ni	115.0 ± 0.0	---	---	-4.3	---	---	No data
Pb	107.2 ± 2.0	---	---	---	---	---	No data
Pd	00.1 ± 4.6	24.0	20.0	34.0	31.0	---	No data

* Average of three samples digested with HNO$_3$
** The magnitude of the effect is defined here as the difference between the average estimated concentration at the high and low levels of the variables. Two times the standard deviation of the recovery was used as the criterion of significance.

TABLE XIII. Effect of digestion variables on recoveries using a mild HNO3-HClO4 digestion. Comparison of effects for a single step HNO3 with a mixed HNO3-HClO4

| Element | Average % Recovery* ±Std. Dev. | Effect of Variables** | | | | | |
		100 vs 175°C Digestion with HNO3-HClO4	Final Addition (or not) of HNO3 at 100°C	Final Addition (or not) of HNO3 at 175°C	Use of Centrifuge (or not) at 100°C	Digestion with HNO3 or with HNO3-HClO4 at 100°C	Digestion with HNO3 or with HNO3-HClO4 at 175°C
Be	101.6±1.0	2.6	2.4	---	No data	2.4	2.4
Cd	99.1±1.0	---	---	---	---	6.7	4.5
Co	108.9±1.0	3.6	---	-3.3	---	2.2	5.2
Cr Lean	102.3±1.1	6.2	8.4	2.2	---	2.7	11.2
Cr Rich	105.2±1.7	---	4.0	3.0	---	-10.0	-14.0
Cu	98.8±0.9	-6.9	-7.4	---	-4.0	10.6	---
Mn	101.6±1.8	---	---	---	No data	2.2	2.6
Mo	125.2±4.1	13.0	---	---	No data	-99.0	-83.0
Ni	111.4±0.6	-3.4	---	---	---	3.8	---
Pb	108.2±1.2	4.0	---	-3.2	---	---	---
Pd	95.7±3.4	-12.0	---	12.0	11.0	11.0	-85.0

*Average of three samples digested with HNO3-HClO4

**The magnitude of the effect is defined here as the difference between the average estimated concentration at the high and low levels of the variables. Two times the standard deviation of the recovery was used as the criterion of significance.

calculated as the average difference of concentration at the high and low levels. The average per cent recoveries and their associated standard deviations of the triplicates are also indicated. A variable was considered as having an effect when the difference in recoveries between high and low conditions was greater than two times their standard deviation. The higher than 100 percent recovery average obtained for most elements (Tables XII and XIII) was attributed to a micro-pipette with wrong calibration. However, no attempt was made to verify this assumption because it did not affect the conclusions drawn from the data, which were the following:

Excluding the data for Mo, Pd, and Cr analyzed with a lean air-acetylene flame, the data of Table XII show fewer significant effects than the data of Table XIII. This indicates that a single-step nitric digestion is less sensitive to changes in the variables studied than is a mixed nitric-perchloric acid digestion.

The standard deviation of the triplicates for these samples spiked at 75 μg/filter (3 μg/ml in solution) is under 2 per cent for all elements except Mo and Pd. This suggests that the mixed HNO_3-$HClO_4$ digestion could yield precise data, provided that the analytical procedure is kept very consistent for all samples.

The data show that a chloride matrix is essential for the digestion of Pd. Therefore, the more vigorous the HNO_3 digestion or the more HNO_3 present in the nitric-perchloric acid digestion, the less Pd is recovered.

The recovery of Mo using the HNO_3 digestion is very low. This was expected since it has been shown that Mo requires a releasing agent in solution, such as $HClO_4$.

Centrifuging was insignificant for samples digested in one step with nitric acid, but seemed to be significant for Cu and Pd in samples digested with nitric-perchloric acid.

The less vigorous nitric-perchloric acid digestion did not lower the recovery of Cr. This suggests that acceptable Cr recoveries can be obtained using a perchloric acid digestion as long as both perchloric and nitric acids are present in solution. Losses occur when a solution containing only perchloric acid is taken to small volume.

Flame stoichiometry appears to be significant for the analysis of Cr in samples prepared by the one-step HNO_3 digestion. Variables which are significant when data are obtained by using a rich air-acetylene flame are found not to be significant when a lean air-acetylene flame is used for analysis.

In summary, the one-step HNO_3 digestion is the preferred digestion technique because it is less sensitive to the procedural variables of temperature and time than is the HNO_3-$HClO_4$ digestion. Chromium analysis must be performed with a lean flame. Analysis of Mo is not accurate unless a releasing agent is present. Palladium does not appear to be solubilized using the one-step HNO_3 digestion.

FLAME-RELATED EFFECTS

The Plackett-Burman screening of this method gave strong indications of some effects which most probably were the result of some type of phenomena occurring in the flame. It was shown, for example, that significant differences were introduced when single analyte instead of mixed analyte standards were used for the calculation of concentrations of Cd, Co, Mn, Ni, and Pb. An explanation for such an effect can be given if interactions between metallic species in the flame resulted in alteration of the light absorption characteristics of the individual elements. It can also be attributed, however, to possible erroneous estimation of the concentration of some elements in the mixed analyte standards. This was demonstrated in one of the early experiments where deliquescent salts of Cd and Ni were used for the preparation of the mixed analyte standards. When standard addition instead of the conventional standardization techniques was used, their concentrations were changed from 986 to 803 µg/ml and from 1520 to 1260 µg/ml for Cd and Ni, respectively. These changes in the nominal concentration can account for the observed differences; therefore, preparation and standardization of mixed analyte standard solutions is very important for the evaluation of the flame-related phenomena. Comparing the characteristics of the calibration curves obtained under various flame conditions with single and mixed analyte standards is a direct, effective way of determining the magnitude of the effect of the flame-related phenomena on the analytical method.

Since Cd, Co, Cr, Ni, and Pb were the metals to be used for the collaborative test, efforts were concentrated toward understanding possible flame-related phenomena for these metals. The various flame conditions studied were all obtained by varying the acetylene flow against a constant air flow of approximately 28 ℓ/min. The lean flame corresponds to an acetylene flow of approximately 4.6 ℓ/min and produces a very intense, short blue cone. The blue flame is more fuel-rich than the lean flame; yet it is slightly leaner than the white flame, and corresponds to an acetylene flow of approximately 6.0 ℓ/min.

Table XIV presents the results of a series of comparisons of calibration curves obtained with single and mixed analyte standards. Both the sensitivity of a particular analyte and the linearity of its calibration curve depend on whether it is analyzed in a single or a mixed analyte matrix and on which flame condition is selected for that matrix.

Using a fuel-rich flame for Co, the linearity of the calibration curve is very good if the single analyte matrix is used, but is poor if Co is analyzed in a mixed metal matrix. A dramatic

TABLE XIV.   Comparison of single analyte and mixed analyte
             calibration curves at various flame conditions

Metal	Flame Stoichiometry	Scale Exp.	Average Slope*±Std. Dev. $(\mu g) \times (ml)^{-1} \times (Abs) \times (Scale\ Exp)$ Single Analyte	Mixed Analyte	Slope Ratio M/S
Be	Lean**	1	18.15±.27	18.00±.19	0.99
Cd	Lean**	1	12.47±.08	12.48±.08	1.00
Co	Lean	3	17.01±.18	16.42±.23	0.96
	Blue	3	16.53±.34	16.19±.05	0.98
	Rich	3	16.28----***	20.15----***	1.24
Cr	Blue	3	13.84±.16	13.98±.07	1.01
	Rich	1	25.11±.32	27.95±.22	1.11
	Very Rich	1	20.52±.50	31.33±.58**	1.53
Cu	Lean	1	22.74±.25	28.47±.12	1.25
	Rich	1	22.49±.20	28.35±.04	1.26
Ni	Lean	3	12.77±.14	12.76±.17	1.00
	Blue	3	12.33±.15	12.41±.07	1.01
	Rich	3	14.83----***	12.98----***	0.88
Pb	Lean**	5	30.68±.34	30.82±.61	1.00

* The average of three individual experiments

** Be, Cd, and Pb showed no flame stoichiometry effects

*** Linearity of curve less than 0.997

increase in sensitivity is experienced for Cr analyzed in the fuel-rich flame. However, the linearity of the Cr calibration curve is poor if analyzed in a mixed metal matrix. The response of Cr in the mixed metal matrix with a fuel-rich flame is varied. A non-linear standard curve is obtained for single analyte Ni standards analyzed in the fuel-rich flame. The effect of the flame condition on the slope and linearity of the Ni calibration curve is shown in Figure 1.

The comparison of single analyte standard curves with mixed analyte standard curves was repeated, adding La flame buffer to all standard solutions. The standard matrix was 0.5 percent La, 10 percent HNO$_3$. These results are presented in Table XV. The only slope ratios which differ from unity by more than one percent are Pb analyzed in a lean flame and Cu analyzed in a lean or rich flame. Therefore, when the analysis of a sample depends on the choice of calibration standards and flame stoichiometry, a La flame buffer added to both samples and standards alleviates the dependence.

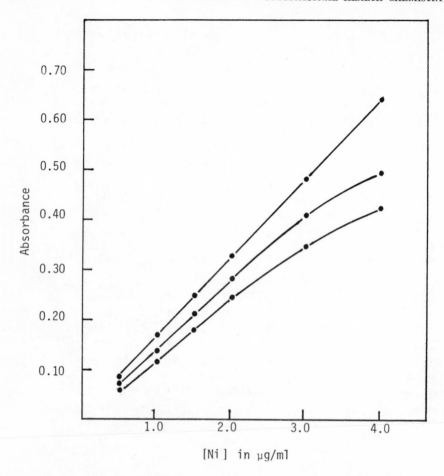

Figure 1. The effect of the acetylene-to-air ratio on the calibration curve of nickel. Curve 1 was obtained with a fuel-rich flame stoichiometry; Curves 2 and 3 were obtained with progressively less fuel-rich flame stoichiometries. All experiments were performed with single analyte solution in 10% HNO₃.

REVISION OF THE METHOD AND RUGGEDNESS TESTING

Screening with the Plackett-Burman technique has shown possible significant effects of some variables on the precision of the analytical method. Further investigation of these variables with single factor experiments verified that the most significant effects were the loss of Cr during digestion with perchloric acid and flame stoichiometry-dependent interelemental effects for Co, Cr, and Ni. This information, along with the experience gained during the characterization of the aerosol generation and sampling system, was utilized for the revision of the analytical procedure. The revised method requires fewer steps and is relatively insensitive to small changes which may occur during an analysis. The new procedure, which basically differs from the original P&CAM #173 only in that

TABLE XV.   Comparison of single analyte and mixed analyte standard
curves obtained with solutions containing 0.5% lanthanum
flame buffer

Metal	Flame Stoichiometry	Scale Exp.	Average Slope* ± Std. Dev. $(\mu g) \times (ml)^{-1} \times (Abs) \times (Scale\ Exp)$		Slope Ratio M/S
			Single Analyte	Mixed Analyte	
Cd	Lean	1	11.66±.13	11.66±.05	1.00
	Rich	1	11.42±.04	11.37±.07	1.00
Co	Lean	3	16.02±.10	15.82±.29	0.99
	Rich	3	14.62±.35	14.60±.20	1.00
Cr	Lean	3	16.71±.04	16.80±.28	1.00
	Rich	1	22.23±.02	22.13±.06	1.00
Cu	Lean	3	8.61±.05	8.79±.009	1.02
	Rich	3	7.58±.02	7.81±.001	1.03
Ni	Lean	3	15.59±.21	15.44±.19	0.99
	Rich	3	14.76±.17	14.77±.11	1.00
Pb	Lean	5	31.54±.09	31.06±.25	0.98
	Rich	5	29.88±.62	30.01±.16	1.00

*The average of three individual experiments

perchloric acid is not used for the digestion and lanthanum flame
buffer is added to the aliquots analyzed for Mo, was tested for
ruggedness with the Youden-Steiner technique. A total of four
tests were performed for final ruggedization. The set of variables
chosen for each of these experiments was very important because if
significant variables were not included, the method would not be
"rugged" with respect to ALL of the significant variables. To avoid
this, variables were selected by carefully examining the written
procedure and then selecting those steps of the procedure most
likely to show variation from one laboratory to another. Digestion
times and temperatures, volume of acid, and single or mixed analyte
calibration standards are examples of such variables. Spiked filters
were used for the first test and the variables studied were the
number of treatments with nitric acid, the temperature of digestion,
temperature to dryness, filtering through Whatman No. 41 paper, and
calculation using single analyte or mixed analyte calibration standards. To aid interpretation, the effect of each analyte was
expressed as percent relative effect (percent RE) by using
equation 7.

$$\%RE_J = 100\ (1 + \bar{E}_J/C_{EST}) \qquad\qquad (7)$$

where
$\bar{E}_J$ = the average effect of variable J in $\mu g/ml$

and

C_{EST} = the estimated concentration of the analyte in µg/ml.

Table XVI presents the results of the first test along with the estimated concentration of each metal, the criterion of significance (1.18s) expressed in µg/ml, and the acceptable range of percent relative effect. The most significant variable in this test was shown to be the filtering through Whatman No. 41 paper. The experimental results indicate that losses of about 25 percent may occur for all metals when the solutions are filtered. This is probably caused by absorption of the cations on the paper. The temperature of digestion and the use of single analyte or mixed analyte standards for the calculation of concentrations also appeared to be significant variables, but due to the main effect of filtering, their real significance is difficult to evaluate. However, the first ruggedness test clearly demonstrated the limitations of both the analytical and the ruggedness testing procedures. The revised analytical procedure neither specified nor excluded filtering of samples. Rather, it was specified that centrifuging should be used when necessary. Filtering was chosen as a variable for this first experiment under the assumption that it would have no effect. This choice could also have been made by any laboratory participating in a collaborative test of the method as written, with predictable consequences. Therefore, a second test excluding filtering as a variable was performed and the results are given in Table XVII. These results show that the only variable which was significant was single analyte vs mixed analyte standards. Single-factor experiments confirmed this variable to have a significant effect on the method, the extent of which depends on the flame stoichiometry. As discussed in the previous section, use of lanthanum flame buffer virtually eliminates this variable and, therefore, the method becomes rugged for all of the variables tested. At this point, the method was revised again to include the use of lanthanum flame buffer, and a step-by-step procedure was written. This procedure was used to conduct a third test using filters loaded with particulates from the generation and sampling system. The results of this test, along with the screened variables, are given in Table XVIII, which shows some of them to be slightly higher than the observed differences. Comparison of the precision of the aerosol generation and sampling system with the analytical precision obtained by using the ruggedized method is shown in Table XIX. On the basis of these results, the new procedure was accepted as rugged for the analysis of Cd, Co, Cr, Ni, and Pb in filter samples containing particulates from the aerosol generation system.

The fourth Youden-Steiner test was performed on filters containing Cd, Co, Cr, Ni, and Pb, and spiked with 12 µg Be, 40 µg Cu, 20 µg Mn, 400 µg Mo, and 160 µg Pd. The results of this test are presented in Table XX, and show that except for Pd, the variables

TABLE XVI. Results of the application of the Youden-Steiner screening test for the evaluation of the effects of the following variables: A - one step vs three step HNO3; c - 100°C vs 175°C digestion; and G - single analyte vs mixed standard. B, D, and f are dummy variables.

Metal	Estimated Concentration µg/ml	Significance Criterion µg/ml	Significance Criterion Percent	Percent Relative Effect						
				A	B	C	D	E	F	G
Be	2.21	0.040	98-102			95.75		75.88		102.67
Cd	2.33	0.055	98-102			96.09		77.51		
Co	2.90	0.049	98-102			94.52		75.24		
Cr	2.90	0.160	94-106			88.28		76.34		96.93
Cu	2.62	0.036	98-102	91.98	96.95	89.31		65.65		
Mn	2.90	0.069	98-102			96.21		76.55		
Mo wo/La	2.90	0.15	94-105	122.76		121.72		117.93		
Mo w/La	2.90	0.11	96-104			91.38		75.52		
Ni	3.66	0.09	98-102			93.44		74.86		93.44*
Pb	2.90	0.04	98-102			93.10		75.86		95.86
Pd	2.89	0.30	90-110			76.12		78.20		

* Both the solution used to spike the filters and the mixed metal calibration standard were prepared from deliquescent $Ni(NO_3)_2 \cdot 6H_2O$ and had to be standardized (standard addition technique) to establish concentration.

TABLE XVII. Results of the application of the Youden-Steiner test for the evaluation of the following variables: A - initial volume HNO3, 2 ml vs 5 ml; B - temperature of digestion, 155°C vs 175°C; C - temperature dry, 100°C vs 115°C; D - time dry, 15 min to 45 min; E - reheat 150°C, 5 min to 15 min; F - dummy; G - calibration standard, single vs mixed.

Metal	Estimated Concentration µg/ml	Significance Criterion µg/ml	Percent	Percent Relative Effect						
				A	B	C	D	E	F	G
Be	2.21	.04	98.2-101.8							97.7
Cd	2.33	.02	99.2-100.8							103.4
Co	2.90	.08	97.2-102.8							96.6
Cr	2.90	.06	97.9-102.1							
Cu	2.90	.04	98.6-101.4							119.6*
Mn	2.90	.03	99.0-101.0							101.4
Mo w/La	2.90	.08	97.2-102.8							
Ni	3.66	.05	98.6-101.4							93.0
Pb	2.90	.06	97.9-102.1							

*Single factor experiments showed that Cu mixed analyte standards give a 25% higher response than single analyte standards for analysis in a lean flame (see Table XIV).

TABLE XVIII. Results of the application of the Youden-Steiner test for the evaluation of the following variables: A - initial volume HNO3 (ml) 2 vs 5; B - temperature of digestion (°C), 1550 vs 1750; C - temperature of dryness (°C), 1000 vs 1150; D - time at dryness (min), 15 vs 45; E - time of reheat at 150°C (min), 5 vs 15; G - calibration standard, single vs mixed. F is a dummy variable.

Metal	Expected μg/ml	Significance Criterion μg/ml	Significance Criterion Percent	Percent Relative Effect A	B	C	D	E	F	G
Cd	0.40	.007	98.2-101.8							
Co	1.62	.021	98.7-101.3		101.9		98.1		101.6	
Cr	2.02	.028	98.6-101.4		101.7			98.1		
Ni	2.24	.017	99.2-100.8		101.4		99.1	98.1	98.6	102.6
Pb	5.24	.048	99.1-100.9	98.9	101.5	101.2		98.3		

TABLE XIX. Comparison of the precision of the aerosol generation and sampling system with the analytical precision obtained by using the ruggedized method.

Element	Aerosol Generation System (a)	Analytical Precision (b)
	Per cent Std. Dev.	
Cd	1.9, 1.8, 3.6, 2.8	2.1
Co	3.4, 2.9, 1.6, 2.8	2.1
Cr	1.7, 1.6, 1.3, 1.2	1.8
Ni	4.2, 2.5, 1.8, 1.8	2.3
Pb	1.7, 1.0, 1.3, 1.2	1.8

(a) Each obtained from 20 samples

TABLE XX. Results of the application of the Youden-Steiner screening test for the evaluation of the following variables: A - initial volume HNO_3 (ml), 2 vs 5; B - temperature of digestion (°C), 155 vs 175; C - temperature dry (°C), 100 vs 115; D - time dry (min), 15 vs 45; E - time of reheat 150°C (min), 5 vs 15. F and G are dummy variables.

| Metal | Expected µg/ml | Significance Criterion | | Percent Relative Effect | | | | | | |
		µg/ml	Percent	A	B	C	D	E	F	G
Be	0.48	.017	96.3-103.7		103.9					
Cu	1.60	.034	98.1-101.9		97.8					

TABLE XXI. Comparison of results of three different analysts applying the ruggedized method to the analysis of aerosol generated filters. All data are expressed as µg/m³ ± % Std. Dev.

Element (loading in µg)	Analyst #1 8 samples analyzed	Analyst #2 8 samples analyzed	Analyst #3 9 samples analyzed	Average of all 25 samples analyzed	Typical analysis of samples from the same generation run
Cd (~ 18)	35.9 ± 2.2	37.3 ± 1.4	38.0 ± 1.9	37.1 ± 2.9	39.1 ± 3.6 40.0 ± 1.6
Co (~ 38)	74.3 ± 1.0	77.8 ± 2.2	76.0 ± 3.8	76.0 ± 3.2	77.0 ± 1.6 79.2 ± 2.8
Cr (~ 60)	117.0 ± 2.6	121.0 ± 2.0	120.4 ± 2.1	119.5 ± 2.6	121.1 ± 1.3 125.8 ± 1.2
Ni (~ 60)	118.1 ± 2.1	116.8 ± 2.1	121.6 ± 2.0	119.0 ± 2.7	119.8 ± 1.8 126.2 ± 1.8
Pb (~ 187)	368.4 ± 1.8	378.7 ± 1.8	375.7 ± 1.7	374.3 ± 2.0	381.6 ± 1.3 389.8 ± 1.2

studied are within 1.2 percent of the significance criterion and, therefore, with respect to the variables studied, the analytical method is "rugged" for the analysis of spiked filters analyzed for Be, Cu, Mn, and Mo in the presence of Cd, Co, Cr, Ni, and Pb. The test also indicates that the method is not rugged for analysis of Pd because analysis of Pd by the proposed method is imprecise and sensitive to the temperature of digestion.

As a final test, three different analysts applied the method to the analysis of Cd, Co, Cr, Ni, and Pb on filter samples from the generation system. The results of this test are presented in Table XXI. Small differences (3 percent) were experienced, but the overall percent standard deviation for each metal compares well with the percent standard deviation obtained in the characterization of the aerosol generation system by analyses performed by a single operator.

ABSTRACT

The optimization of the atomic absorption method of determining metals in particulates found in the air of workplace is described. The Plackett-Burman Youden-Steiner balanced incomplete block designs as well as single-factor experiments were utilized with ten metals: Be, Cd, Co, Cr, Cu, Mn, Mo, Ni, Pb, and Pd. Of the parameters tested, perchloric acid digestion, flame-stoichiometry, and the composition of the calibration standards were the most significant. Perchloric acid affected the recoveries of chromium. This was attributed to the formation of volatile chromylchloride. Flame-related phenomena and interelemental effects were brought under control using lanthanum flame buffer.

The method was studied with both spiked and generated filter samples. The filter samples were generated in a dynamic aerosol generation and sampling system capable of simulating workplace atmospheres. This system was designed, built, and characterized specifically for this study. The particle size of the generated aerosol was in the range of 0.1 to 10 micrometers. The position-to-position variation among the 25 sampling ports was less than ±2.5 percent, and the run-to-run repeatability was better than ±10 percent.

The final evaluation of the analytical procedure with generated filters resulted in a modified procedure which was "rugged" for the analysis of Be, Cd, Co, Cr, Cu, Mn, Mo, Ni, and Pb. The method was not ruggedized for Pd because the absence of perchloric acid from the developed procedure made it incompatible for Pd.

The optimized procedure was ultimately used in a collaborative test between 16 laboratories and consistently yielded excellent recoveries.

ACKNOWLEDGMENT

The authors would like to express their appreciation to the NIOSH Project Officer, Dr. Janet Haartz for the constructive criticism and support during the course of this work. They also gratefully acknowledge the National Institute of Occupational Safety and Health for their financial support of this work through Contract #210-76-0151.

LITERATURE CITED

(1) NIOSH Methods Manual. First edition.
(2) Complete Testing of the NIOSH Method for the Determination of Trace Metals by Atomic Absorption Spectrophotometry. IIT Research Institute. NIOSH Contract CDC-99-74-48. September 1975.
(3) Plackett, R.L. and Burman, J.P. 1946. Biometrika. 33:305.
(4) Youden, W.J. and Steiner, E.H. Statistical Manual for the AOAC. P.O. Box 540, Ben Franklin Station, Washington, D.C. 20044.
(5) Hillebrand, W.F. and Lundell, G.E.F. 1953. Applied Inorganic Analysis. John Wiley and Sons. 526.
(6) Hoffman, J.I. and Lundell, G.E.F. 1939. Research NBF. 22:465.
(7) Smith, F.W. 1938. Ind. Eng. Chem. Anal. Ed. 10:360.

RECEIVED November 30, 1979.

A Field Test of a Procedure for the Identification of Protein-Bearing Particles in Grain Elevator Air

R. M. BUCHAN and G. D. KRAMER

Occupational Health and Safety Section, Colorado State University, Fort Collins, CO 80523

Grain elevators are a major component of an extensive agricultural distribution system. Over 100,000 people are employed at the hundreds of large elevators and the thousands of small country elevators located throughout the United States[1]. These workers are exposed to considerable amounts of grain dust which is generated each time grain is handled.

Although grain dust is considered as a nuisance particulate[2], and as such is supposed to be "biologically inert", there have been numerous studies which have documented that exposure to grain dust resulted in the development of pulmonary disease in a large number of workers. The first report of respiratory difficulty in grain handlers appeared in 1713 when Ramazzini[3] observed that workers in graineries and barns, engaged in sifting and measuring grain, almost all developed shortness of breath and rarely reached old age.

Later epidemiological and clinical investigations of grain handlers have documented a variety of symptoms which resulted from exposure to grain dust. The most commonly reported symptoms in these studies included chronic cough, dyspnea, tightness across the chest and grain fever. In addition, reduced pulmonary function and pulmonary fibrosis were frequently noted[4].

Although the association between the development of pulmonary disease and exposure to grain dust has been recognized for a long period of time the mechanisms by which grain dust exerts its harmful effects remains largely unknown. A number of authors have suggested that the development of pulmonary disease may be primarily the result of a foreign protein reaction. A survey of the literature indicated that the specific reactions involved may be Type 1 and Type III hypersensitivity reactions[3-7].

Since the induction of pulmonary disease may be the result of a foreign protein reaction, rather than measuring a workers total dust exposure as is presently done, it may be more advantageous to examine the component of that exposure that consists of protein bearing particles. The purpose of this study was to demonstrate a method for determining particulate protein concentrations and

0-8412-0539-6/80/47-120-301$05.00/0

size distribution in grain elevator atmospheres and to compare
these parameters with those found under ambient conditions.

Methods and Materials

Sampling Methodology. Air samples were taken at four grain
elevator work sites and one site outside to serve as a control.
The sampling areas were as follows:

    a)   Site 1 was located on the top floor of a country elevator
        where grain was loaded in 24 storage bins;

    b)   Site 2 was located on the main work floor of the county
        elevator where most of the elevator functions were
        directed from;

    c)   Site 3 was located on the bottom floor of the county
        elevator where grain was transported from the bottom of
        the storage bins to the loading area;

    d)   Site 4 was located on the main work floor of the adjacent
        manufacturing elevator, and

    e)   Site 5, which served as the control, was located approxi-
        mately 250 yards upwind of the two grain elevators.

Due to high dust concentrations inside the elevators, samples
were collected with Dupont low flow sampling pumps (model P125)
operated at a flow rate of approximately 120 cc/min. The outside
control samples were collected using a Bendix Sequential Air
Sampler modified for membrane filtration and operated at a flow
rate of approximately 6 lpm due to low particulate concentrations
of the ambient atmosphere. All of the samples were collected on
Millipore Type HA filters which have a pore size of 0.45 μm.

Particle Staining Procedure. As soon as possible after the
samples were collected they were strained for protein according
to a procedure developed by Magill and Lumpkins[8]. The reagents
used in the procedure were as follows:

    Reagent A - 1% by weight aqueous nitric acid
    Reagent B - 1% aqueous solution Ninhydrin in water
    Reagent C - 0.2% Wool Fast Pink RL in 10% acetic acid solution
    Reagent D - 95% undenatured ethyl alcohol

The staining procedure involved placing an absorbent paper
pad into four petri dishes and adding just sufficient amounts of
reagents A, B, C, and D to saturate the pad without immersing it.
A representative section (one fourth wedge) of the Millipore
filter, with dust deposition side up, was placed on each of the
pads for two minutes. Between each treatment the bottom side of
the filter was blotted on a paper towel to remove excess solution.
After the final treatment the filter was dried for one hour at
room temperature. The dry, stained filter was then placed on a
clear microscope slide and made translucent with immersion oil.
Permanent slides were made by sealing the coverslips to the slides
with clear fingernail polish.

The mechanism involved in the staining procedure are not

completely understood. Ninhydrin is frequently used to stain proteinaceous matter but its role in the procedure developed by Magill and Lumpkins[8] remains uncertain. It has been suggested that Ninhydrin may react with some charged groups on the protein molecule and thus enhance dye binding. This is unlikely, however since the pH of the solutions (1.3 - 3.0) should prohibit the Ninhydrin reaction.

Following the field investigation which utilized this staining technique, an attempt was made to determine if Ninhydrin was indeed a necessary reagent. Thus a test was run in which one half of a dust sample was treated according to the procedure described by Magill and Lumpkins[8], while the other half of the filter was treated identically except the Ninhydrin step was omitted. The resultant stain appeared to be of equal intensity on both filter halves. Therefore, it was likely that Ninhydrin has neither a positive nor a negative effect on the staining.

The mechanisms involved in the binding of Wool Fast Pink RL (Figure 1) to the protein molecule is as well not fully understood but probably involves a combination of ionic interactions between the charged groups on the dye and protein molecules, and hydrophobic interactions between the dye and protein molecules.

Particle Analysis. When evaluating a workers exposure by determining size count distribution data for dust collected on membrane filters and analysis by light microscopy, the particles must be sized in a manner which will reflect geometric, aerodynamic, or biological properties to a sufficiently close degree to be an accurate representation of particle properties related to size. In this study sizing was accomplished by determining the projected area of the particle employing the graduated circles of a Porton reticule.

The counting technique was based on the truncated multiple traverse technique as described by Sichel[9]. This is a statistically based method of selecting and counting fields in a stratified manner which improves reliability, minimizes the

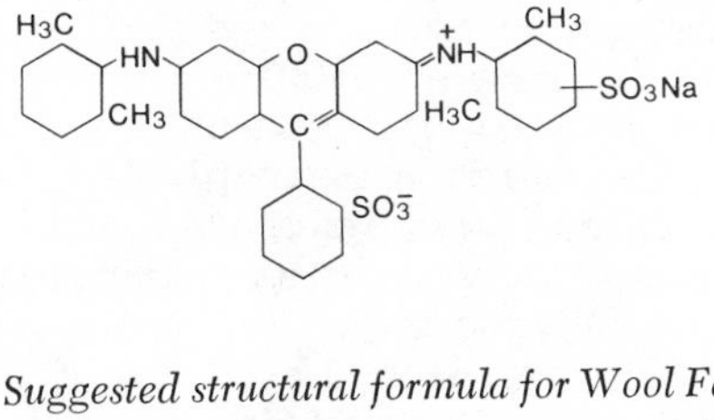

Figure 1. Suggested structural formula for Wool Fast Pink RL

number of individual measurements and is more statistically
unbiased. The first step in the procedure requires a traverse
of the filter beginning at the center and progressing to the
outside edge. A total of ten fields per filter were randomly
chosen per traverse. During this and each subsequent traverse
of the filter, the number of particles in each particle size
interval was recorded. Following the completion of 10 traverses
the number of particles in each size interval was totaled and
weighted by dividing the total number of particles in that size
interval by the number of traverses made to achieve that total.
By this method the number of particles per traverse was calculated. The average number of particles in each size interval was
progressively cumulated and the cumulated percentage of particles
in each size interval was then calculated for making plots, size
versus normalized cumulative percent on log probability graph
paper.

     Data Analysis. When the cumulative percentage of particles
in each size interval was plotted against particle diameter on
log probablity paper the data points approximated a straight line.
The regression line through the experimental data points was then
calculated by the least squares method. Estimates of the geometric median diameter, the geometric standard deviation, and the
percentage of the distribution composed of respirable ($\leq$ 10 μm
diameter) particulates were calculated from the regression
equation. In addition, the concentration, and percentage of
the concentration composed of protein bearing particles, were
calculated. These five parameters were then subjected to an
analysis of variance procedure to determine if they differed
significantly between sites. A difference was considered significant if the p-value was less than or equal to the 0.05 level.

Results and Discussion

     The staining of protein bearing particles by the method
described by Magill and Lumpkins[8], coupled with size-count
analysis by light microscopy, proved to be an excellent means of
measuring the component of a workers exposure composed of
protein bearing particulates. The stained, protein bearing
particles could be easily distinguished from non-protein bearing
particles and were clearly visible in sizes as small as one
micrometer in diameter.
     The five parameters which were analyzed for protein bearing
and total dust distributions at each sampling site were the geometric median diameter, the geometric standard deviation, the
percentage of particles which were respirable ($\leq$ 10 μm diameter),
the concentration, and the percent of the total concentration
composed of protein bearing particles. The results of the
statistical analysis are summarized in Table I. As can be seen
in Table I, the geometric median diameter was not significantly
different for protein bearing particles between the elevator

TABLE I

A Comparison of Mean Values of the
Protein Bearing and Total Dust Distribution
Parameters Between Elevator and Ambient Air

Parameter	Protein Bearing Dust			Total Dust		
	Elevator	Ambient	P≤0.05	Elevator	Ambient	P≤0.05
Geometric Median Diameter	0.47 μm	0.45 μm	No	0.53 μm	0.10 μm	Yes
Geometric Standard Deviation	5.40	6.89	No	4.50	6.12	No
Per Cent Respirable	97.2%	95.4%	Yes	98.5%	99.6%	Yes
Concentration*	44.5	0.31	Yes	123.8	9.2	Yes
Percent of Distribution Containing Protein	-	-	-	38.0%	6.1%	Yes

*Millions of particles per cubic meter of air
μm = micrometers

sites and the control site. If it is the protein bearing dust
which is primarily responsible for the induction of pulmonary
disease, then dust exposures between the elevator sites and the
control sites should not be considered different, in terms of
the geometric mean diameter since partizle size of both
distributions are similar and thus would have like characteristics for pulmonary deposition.

The geometric standard deviation was not significantly
different for the protein bearing or total dusts between the
elevator sites and the control site. Since the geometric
standard deviation and the geometric median diameter for protein
bearing particles did not differ significantly between elevator
sites and the control site, dust exposures at these sites should
not be considered differently in terms of these two parameters.
They may, however, differ significantly in terms of other
parameters such as concentration or percent protein.

The fraction of the dust distribution composed of respirable
particles did differ significantly between the elevator sites
and the control site for both protein bearing and total particles.
However, since the percent of the distribution composed of
respirable particles was so large, and averaged 97.2% for the
protein bearing particles and 98.5% for the total particles, it
is doubtful that these differences would be biologically significant from a health standpoint as total dose in terms of numbers
of inhaled particles would be only slightly different.

The concentration of both protein bearing and total dust
were markedly higher at the elevator sites than at the control
site. It is obvious that the higher concentrations at the
elevator sites would present a greater health hazard than the
concentration at the control site. In addition, the percent of
the concentrations composed of protein bearing particles ranged
from 35.0% to 44.7% at the elevator sites and was only 6.1%
at the control site. Thus, an evaluation of a worker's exposure
based on total dust alone may not reflect all ramifications of
the true hazard potential, since this would not reflect the
relative percentage of protein bearing particles between the
elevator sites and the control sites. It is apparent that
measurement of the protein bearing component of a dust sample may
be a more accurate means of assessing the health potential
associated with dust exposures in grain elevators.

In the future, this method of measuring the component of
a worker's exposure which is made up of protein bearing particles
could be used to investigate the correlation between protein
bearing dust exposures and pulmonary signs and symptoms among
grain handlers. If a good correlation were found, it might
contribute to a clearer understanding of the etiology of grain
dust induced lung disease.

Literature Cited

1. Lehmann, P.: "Grain Elevator Hazards," Job Safety and Health, 3:4-9 (1975).
2. Threshold Limit Values for Chemical Substances and Physical Agents in the Workroom Environment. American Conference of Governmental Industrial Hygienists, Cincinnati, Ohio, 1978.
3. Ramazzini, B.: Diseases of Workers. Translated by W. C. Wright. Hafner Publishing Company, New York (1964).
4. DoPico, G. A., et. al: "Respiratory Abnormalities Among Grain Handlers," American Review of Respiratory Disease, 115:915-927 (1978).
5. Cohen, V. L. and H. Osgood: "Disability Due to Inhalation of Grain Dust," J. Allergy, 24:193-211 (1953).
6. Tse, K. S., P. Warren, M. Janusz, D. S. McCarthey and R. M. Cherniack: "Respiratory Abnormalities in Workers Exposed to Grain Dust," Archives of Environmental Health, 27:74-77 (1973).
7. Warren, P., R. M. Cherniack and K. S. Tse: "Hypersensitivity Reactions to Grain Dust,"J. Allergy and Clinical Immunology, 53:139-149 (1974).
8. Magill, P. L. and E. D. Lumpkins: "Distinguishing Skin Scale Particles," Contamination Control, October, 1966.
9. Sichel, H. S.: "On the Size Distribution of Airborne Mine Dust," J. South African Institute of Mining and Metalurgy, 58:171-225 (1957).

RECEIVED October 17, 1979.

INDEX

INDEX

311

V

W

T